The
Secret
Keepers

Barbara McFarland

authorHOUSE·

AuthorHouse™
1663 Liberty Drive
Bloomington, IN 47403
www.authorhouse.com
Phone: 833-262-8899

Published by AuthorHouse 12/27/2022

ISBN: 978-1-6655-7763-2 (sc)
ISBN: 978-1-6655-7762-5 (e)

Childhood sexual abuse crosses gender lines and is not unique to any ethnic group or religious affiliation.

PREFACE

This is a story of a family affected by childhood sexual abuse. If this issue is too close to home, you may choose not to read it at this point in time. But I ask you to please refer to the resources listed on the last page.

At first I hesitated to write a novel about childhood sexual abuse, uncertain as to how it would be received by readers of women's fiction. It is an incomprehensible act that can be uncomfortable to deal with. As I continued writing, it became clear to me that this story deals with much more than abuse, taking the reader into the lives of mothers and daughters and the complex layers of their relationships as they come face-to-face with the unimaginable. If there is hope for forgiveness and compassion in this horrific situation, then mothers and daughters can transcend any adversities that may befall them.

Although I have never been abused, what inspired me to tackle this issue came from the courageous women who sought therapy from me as a way to heal from their early trauma and live meaningful lives. Their resiliencies never cease to amaze me.

The "Me Too" movement advocates for women who have suffered from sexual violence and sexual harassment. As a result, they are able to step out of the shadows of shame and feel supported: not so for the women who endured childhood sexual abuse. I have tried to explore this very significant difference in *The Secret Keepers*.

As a psychologist, I have published quite a few professional books over the years, one of which, *My Mother Was Right!* was featured on *Oprah*. However, *The Secret Keepers* is my first attempt at writing a novel and it has been much more challenging than I imagined when I first sat before my computer staring at a blank screen. However, with great perseverance and support from my husband, Hal, I managed to painstakingly eke out a first draft.

I thank the women who provided feedback on that initial effort: Susan Crew, Kathleen Fraiz, Michele Fox, Kristen Morgan, Lee Posey, Marion Messerle, Rita Conn, and Lisa Cron. As my editor, Mary Kole always asked the tough questions, challenging me to "show and not tell" and to "stop using those ellipses." I spent two years on the subsequent drafts.

Most of all, I am grateful to the women I've treated over the years who have trusted me with their deepest secrets, sorrows, and sufferings. They are the true heroines of my life.

Barbara McFarland
Cincinnati, Ohio

To
Anna, Kirek and all the animals in the forest
I can see you.

PART I

Sophie

Chicago
The Mid-1960's

ONE

*I didn't know the word fuck back then, but
I sure made up for it years later whenever I thought about that night.*
Addie

If it hadn't been for the gamy odor of fried liver wandering about the kitchen, the evening began like any other at the Gurin house. The circular tiger oak table was covered with platters of kapusta sprinkled with bits of bacon, along with mushrooms of various sizes and shapes which floated in bowls of Irina's garlic and onion marinade. Amidst the rumbles of an oncoming storm, Irina threatened "no dessert" if her granddaughters, Addie and Mary, didn't take a few bites of liver.

"I make few time a month. You eat!" Irina poked her finger at their food while she ladled a thick brown gravy over the meat.

Their faces screwed up in disgust as though they were viewing a dead animal resting before them. They gagged in unison making it clear that ice cream could never justify the horror of eating the corpse that had invaded their plates.

"Adelajda! Marysia! Stop ... H*alas!*" When Irina tried to imitate their contorted faces, her dentures rattled. "Liver good for *krew*! Blood! You no eat, blood go bad."

Both girls peered helplessly at their mother, hoping for an intervention.

Sophie could laugh at her mother's old country quips but not lately. Irina's words felt as if a hornet's nest had landed in her head. "Mother! Stop that nonsense. Speak English and use their American names!"

Not being able to rein in her feelings bothered Sophie. More than bothered, she hated herself when they erupted in front of her girls.

1

Whatever inexplicable barricade she relied on to keep her emotional state in check these past years appeared to be crumbling. In the last few months, she felt a splinter of evil shake loose from within her, but when she reached for it, she was left holding nothing. It was like trying to grasp a dark cloud.

"I tell you. Their names *piękny* ... ah ... beautiful in Polish. Dull in English." Irina untied her flowered apron stained with remnants of the evening's dinner and draped it over a hook near the refrigerator. "At least their papa speak Polish. You not want to learn."

Sophie's in-laws never permitted their son, Frank, to speak English in their home when he was a boy. Being stubborn and oppositional, Sophie would bicker with her mother that as an American she would only speak English.

"Mommy, daddy said our babcia is allowed to use our Polish names. We agreed a long time ago, so please don't be mad." Addie hopped up and wedged herself close to her older sister, Mary, who nodded in agreement.

Sophie approved because her girls would do anything to make their grandmother happy, and she would do anything to make them happy.

Hugging both of them, Sophie marveled at how beautiful they were and yet so dissimilar. Mary's almond-shaped eyes were a few shades darker than Sophie's and her coarse hair was a tawny brown with streaks of copper running through it. The way Mary tilted her head back when she laughed was a sure tip-off that she and Sophie were related. Addie was her father's daughter with stick-straight black hair the color of licorice. They shared lemon-brown eyes that appeared to change color depending on their moods. And like her dad, Addie's oval face held dimples that resembled keyholes.

"*Jestem w domu!* I'm home! Irina! My nose tells me it's liver and onions night!" Frank affectionately patted the top of his mother-in-law's head. "I had a late lunch so I'm not hungry."

"That why you late. Nobody want my liver."

"Daddy! Daddy!" Hefting both of them up with a huff, he winked at Sophie and whispered, "Thanks for the tip-off on tonight's menu!" As soon as he eased his daughters to the floor, Frank folded Sophie into his arms giving her an affectionate squeeze.

"How's my number one girl?" he asked out of earshot from Addie and Mary.

"Better now that you're home."

They kissed.

"Are you Ok?" Frank pulled back and examined her face.

Sophie straightened up, nodded her head and kissed him again. The ten years he had on her were starting to show: flecks of silver at his temples, deepening lines around his mouth and eyes, and the latest portent were the grunts and groans he let loose whenever he asked more of his body than it could handle.

Shooing him off to the living room so she could clean up, Sophie caught a glimpse of Addie traipsing behind him. Her face relaxed into a smile replacing the troubled frown of a few moments ago. Since her own father died when she was seven, between the ages of her own girls, she warmed at the sight of them together.

Sophie scraped the untouched food from their plates and finished up scouring the pans while Mary stacked the dishwasher. Much to Sophie's dismay, Irina caved in and presented her granddaughter with three overflowing scoops of vanilla ice cream speckled with flecks of chocolate chips here and there—her favorite.

"Do dishes later." Irina whispered.

"What about Addie?" Mary asked.

"No worry. She get some."

Sophie choked back her reprimand, aggressively scrubbing the burnt drippings sticking to the pan she was cleaning.

A plate crowded with Irina's home-made *kolaczkis* dusted with powdered sugar rested in the middle of the kitchen table. With creased brows, Irina motioned for Sophie to sit and take one.

Mother and daughter did not share any physical attributes other than the color of their eyes ... like chips of slate. The ladies at church dubbed Irina as the "Polish elf" while Sophie was teased as being the "Polish tower." These monikers were accompanied by laughter and for Sophie, a pinch on her cheek.

When she was able to see her reflection on the bottom of her roasting pan, Sophie joined her mother and nibbled a paper-thin portion of the pastry as she sipped her coffee. She savored the sweetness as it melted on her tongue until a crack of thunder startled her.

"Oh my God!" Sophie shouted dropping her cup to the floor.

"It tunder. Sophie, I worry. What wrong with you?" Using her napkin, Irina dabbed at the puddle of coffee as it crept toward the edge of the table.

"I'm fine, Mother." Empty words. Fearful that if she were to talk about how shaky she had been feeling lately, she'd turn into one of those dandelion spores that blow apart with the slightest disturbance.

"Sophie, you Ok?" Irina pushed her hairnet back leaving a red line on her forehead.

"I'm fine. I haven't been getting much sleep since the teachers have been on strike. Their union leader is insisting that both the superintendent and I attend all of the meetings, which makes no sense to me. They don't need both of us. I have so many other deadlines to meet." Sophie massaged her temples, hoping she had satisfied her mother's curiosity.

"Let's watch TV news to see ..."

"No," Sophie growled, "I don't want to." Sit down and drink your coffee."

The clatter of plates Mary was stacking in the dishwasher made the tension between them more pronounced.

"If you so Ok, why you so skinny? You not eat. I hear you down here at night. And you hair ... needs brush."

Normally, Sophie would twist her wavy tresses into a chignon at the nape of her neck, but in the last few weeks, she let it hang loose like a curtain over her shoulders.

"Babcia's right, Mommy. You've been yelling a lot."

"Nonsense. I have not." She didn't want to hear that her charade was failing.

"Yesterday I hear on TV strike last long time. How long ..." Irina was interrupted by the ruckus coming from the living room.

Addie began shrieking, "Stop! Daddy! Stop!"

Without warning, Sophie clamped her hands over her ears trying to mute the forceful whooshing from rumbling back and forth. She felt a tightening in her chest. Then her legs stiffened, jerking her body up and out of the high back oak chair which toppled over with a bang. Sophie pivoted in circles as if searching for a place to hide. She was drowning in darkness. Her eyebrows crashed into one another. Her lips tightened into a knot.

"Sophie? Sophie?" Irina blurted as she wrestled to reach her daughter.

"Mommy!" Mary cried. "What's wrong with you?"

Sophie couldn't answer. She didn't know. As she tried to fix her attention on Mary, all she could see were shards of her daughter as if she was standing in front of a shattered mirror. When Irina extended her hand, Sophie grabbed a knife and began flailing at the air.

She faltered. She gazed at her hands but they weren't hers. Rage cut into her. She tore into the living room.

Mary nearly toppled her babcia over as she ran after her mother.

"No! You stay here." Irina pushed her back.

For a few seconds Sophie scowled at Frank. Then she tackled him, hollering, "What are you doing? Stop and leave her alone!"

"Sophie! Sophie! Give me that knife! It's me, Frank. What's wrong with you?" When he tried to snatch the weapon, it tumbled to the floor. Kicking it aside, he shoved her away. Sophie's elbow jabbed him on the side of his head.

"What are you doing to that child? Huh?" Sophie dug her nails into Frank's cheek making knife-like lacerations down to his neck.

"You bastard!" She spewed a string of vulgarities into Frank's ear and slammed her head against his forehead. He shrank back.

Stumbling into the room, Irina's attention darted from Addie, who cowered face-down behind the couch bawling into the carpet, to the thrashing bodies wrestling in the middle of the living room.

"Mommy! Don't hurt my daddy!" Addie wailed.

Mary dived on top of her sister. "Babcia! Babcia! Stop them! Please! Mommy! Daddy!"

"Stop, you bastard! Or I'll kill you!" Sophie screamed as spittle sprayed his face.

With a balled fist, she punched Frank splitting the skin over his cheekbone. He bellowed as his knees cracked when they hit the ground. He staggered, and was unable to steady himself when Sophie kneed him in the groin, and then curled her fingers around his neck with such adrenaline infused strength, her face reddened.

Before the girls could witness any more violence, their grandmother hustled them upstairs into their bedroom.

"Blessed Virgin, help us!" Irina implored. The girls bawled as the thumping of fists pounding flesh became audible. Wavering as what to

5

do, Irina started toward the door until she heard the girls' whimpering. She stopped mid-step and then knelt down before them.

"Pray. Stay here. Babcia be back."

As she hurried downstairs, the sour smell of sweat smacked her in the face. Irina saw Sophie sprawled out on the carpet, with an inflamed cut on her face, her dress torn and her hair hanging over her face like greasy strings of unraveled rope. Frank clamped her shoulders down. She kicked him wildly freeing herself from his grip. Lamps and knickknacks crashed to the floor. Frank's pleas were met with vitriol.

"Call the police!" Frank hollered at Irina.

Her knotted fingers made it difficult to dial the operator. "*Wsparcie! Policja! Wsparcie!*"

"I don't understand you, lady. Speak English!"

"Sorry. Help! We need police."

"Hold on. I'll connect you."

"Jefferson Park Precinct. What's the emergency?"

"What? Police? Please." Irina's breathing became jagged.

"Ma'am? What exactly is the emergency?"

"You deaf? Can you hear? We need help!" she pleaded as she ducked when a lamp exploded against the wall.

After relaying their address and phone number, Irina murmured under her breath, "Blessed Mother, what will police do? Will they go to jail?"

For a brief moment, she locked eyes with her daughter. Who was this? As the two women glared at each other, Frank flung Sophie onto her stomach, pinning her down with his entire body; she was hissing and spitting mad ... saliva dripped from the corners of her mouth.

Irina bent low and pushed down on Sophie's legs but was booted backward. Her cries were inaudible among the chorus of rants and cussing. An ear splitting siren along with flashing blue lights bouncing off the walls startled Irina. Wobbling to the door and before she could utter a word, two burly officers barged in on the mayhem.

Making their way through the wreckage, they surrounded the flailing bodies on the floor. Without speaking and in unison, the taller of the two hoisted Sophie to her feet while she continued to flail and curse, and the other lunged for Frank. Twisting his hands behind his back, the officer clamped on handcuffs.

"C'mon, lady. I'm trying to help you!"

Sophie eyes were swollen with rage and then in an instant glazed over looking like two glass marbles. She collapsed. Draping her in his arms, he ordered his partner to get back up since they'd need to keep them separated.

With contusions on his head, a ripped shirt, multiple facial wounds and deep abrasions oozing blood, Frank pleaded. "Wait! My God. Can you hold on? I have two small kids."

"You should have thought of that before, buddy. We cops don't think much of wife beaters," the policeman grumbled as he manhandled Frank out the door.

"Officer. My wife had a complete breakdown. I wasn't beating her ..."

"Ya, sir!" Irina followed them. "My daughter ... she sick. Frank try to help her."

"Ma'am. It won't be long before the other car comes. It's pouring out here. Why don't you go inside and take care of those kids?"

In spite of the storm, porch lights flicked on as curiosity lured the neighbors out of their houses to see what the commotion was about.

"You people go back. We Ok," Irina flapped her hanky into the rain.

"Irina, get to the girls. I'll call you as soon as I can." Frank grunted as he was loaded into the back seat of the squad car.

"The girls!" Irina shouted.

Mary and Addie were cowering with their dolls squished between them. With red-rimmed eyes and wet cheeks, they sprinted toward Irina before she fully opened the door and clutched her legs so tightly, she couldn't move.

"Ok. Everything be Ok." As she petted their heads, her mind dove into a whirlpool of questions. *Where will they take Sophie? Why did she attack Frank? They never fought ... do they hide things from me? We were talking about the strike. And then, boom! Sophie's face twisted into a knot. So unlike her to frighten her girls like that. Maybe what I said upset her? I should keep my mouth shut.*

Clinging to their grandmother, the girls nuzzled into her body as if it was a place to hide. Irina's attention was diverted to their anguish.

"Please! Let go. Babcia no move. Come sit."

The three of them stumbled to the edge of Mary's unmade bed and crowded their bodies so firmly together that their shadows melded into an ominous shape as if they were being guarded by a dark phantom.

Between their convulsive whimpers, the girls began to drill Irina with questions.

"Did the police take them to jail?"

"Why was Mommy so mad at Daddy?"

"Ya. Why was she so mad?"

"When will they be home?"

What could she say? Irina teetered back and forth between trying to explain that their mommy would be Ok, while at the same time running down a laundry list of what could be wrong with her daughter. Exhaustion? Overwork? She didn't want to consider something as deadly as brain cancer but what else could it be? An episode on Dr. Ben Casey planted that seed as a possibility.

Irina could feel their bodies shivering.

"You get sleepies on."

Mary plucked two flannel nightgowns from a hook in the closet and handed the blue striped one to Addie and slid the pink one over her own head. Addie followed suit and then they hopped back to their original places nestling on either side of their grandmother.

Reaching for the multi-colored quilt on Addie's bed, Irina was jerked back by both girls.

"Please stay here!" Addie pleaded.

"I not leave. I get blanket." As she swaddled the coverlet over the three of them, Irina wrestled with myriad explanations for their mother's bizarre actions.

"Ah ... your matka, ah ..." Irina racked her brain for the right English word. How to say confused? "... *zwariowany*."

Irina had been in this country for over fifty years, and yet, she was never able to cast aside her native language with its throaty and harsh cadences which, to her ears, were so robust. The sounds of which swept her back to Warsaw, if for a moment. The English she spoke was a hybrid of both and when under stress she would become unhinged trying to speak "American" properly. However, whenever her son-in-law would speak Polish, she would jiggle her head and say, "English," knowing that would please her daughter.

"Ya, help me ... *zwariowany.*"

When the girls wrinkled up their faces at her Polish, she tried to help with the translation. She made circles with her index finger and pointed to her head.

"Babcia!"

They kicked off the quilt and leapt from the bed.

"No!"

"Our mommy is not!"

"Ya, but she be Ok." The adrenaline that gushed throughout Irina earlier began to ease up. She inhaled, trying to bear up against her exhaustion.

No matter how many times Irina reassured them their mommy was safe and their daddy would be home soon, Mary and Addie would continue to barrage her with questions, many of which she had already answered. As a way to distract them, she decided this was the time for a sanctioned lie. Irina believed the Blessed Virgin gave women the privilege of altering the truth for their children and grandchildren without having to confess it as a sin.

"My matka sick when I was same age as Marysia. She get better and come home."

"What was wrong with her?" Mary pleated her forehead.

"Was she crazy, too?" As a mixture of snot and tears slid down Addie's face, Mary offered her the sleeve of her blouse.

"No! Marysia! That good cotton." Irina retrieved a box of tissues from the nightstand, as she continued with her fabrication. "She fall. Here, wipe."

"How long was she gone?"

"Not long. And see! Babcia Ok. You be Ok, too." Irina imposed a grin on her face, and in doing so, loosened her upper denture, which clattered on the lower one. This would bring giggles from the girls, but not tonight.

As she helped Addie and Mary clean their tear-stained faces, Irina thought back to the day she happened on her matka's dead body.

Her mother's skillfulness as a seamstress was second to none. One afternoon, she needed several strips of hand-made lace from a neighbor down the street to finish a skirt for a customer before dinner time. Irina was out the door as soon as her mother asked her to run the errand.

But on this day, the neighbor lady was baking *kolaczki* and insisted Irina stay and have a few. These cookies were Irina's favorite, particularly those filled with apricot jam. The orange filling and the sweetness of the pastry made her forget the urgent nature of her mission. So, the two of them gabbed until the entire plate was empty.

Carefully holding the lace, Irina skipped home with a full tummy.

Twirling and humming through the door, she hesitated when she saw her mother hunched over her sewing machine with swatches of fabric scattered at her feet. "*Matka?*" She toppled to the floor. Irina screamed.

"Papa! Papa! *Coś jest nie tak z matką! Moja wina!" Something wrong with my matka. My fault."* His reassurances were met with wails of grief and continued admissions of guilt.

The next day, as they knelt before the silver casket in their living room, her papa relentlessly tried to convince her that she was not to blame ... that she couldn't have saved her matka, But Irina did not believe him. Placing her pillow and *pierzyna* before the coffin, Irina enfolded herself in the feather-stuffed cover and refused to leave. Her papa had to drag her away on the day of the burial.

For weeks afterwards, Irina was unable to sleep or eat until she decided to make a seven-day novena to the Blessed Virgin asking for a sign of her innocence. On the eighth day, as she was preparing dinner, she balanced on her tiptoes to get a skillet when an object from above struck her on the head. She shuddered as she cradled a spool of her mother's thread. Falling down on her knees, she thanked the Blessed Virgin for this sign.

Her papa was right! Irina rushed to him, and presented her miracle. When he knelt down in front of her, he held up the spool right before her eyes. Her papa explained how mothers and daughters are connected by a silk thread, and that this was a gift from her matka.

Other than her papa, Irina kept her miracle a secret because she believed revealing it would diminish the Blessed Virgin's trust in her. So she locked it in her heart except for the part about mothers and daughters which she revealed to Sophie on her eighth birthday. And now, she prayed that Sophie would remember the thread, wherever she was tonight.

As she thumped her feet against the bedframe, Mary interrupted this memory. "Did your mommy come home soon?"

"Ya. Your matka home soon, too. We make novena for her. We make altar here like mine. Maybe tomorrow."

"Babcia, will you sleep with us tonight? Please?"

"Ya. Of course."

"All of us in here with me," Addie insisted.

"This bed for one," Irina said.

"Please."

With their bodies entwined, the three of them wriggled until they fit together like a jigsaw puzzle. As she was teetering on the edge of the mattress, Irina prayed for their mommy.

"Prayer for my daddy, too," Addie interjected.

As soon as the girls drifted off, Irina slipped out of bed and contacted the police to find out about Sophie and Frank, but soon hung up without any news.

When she settled into her own bed, she threaded her crystal rosary between her fingers, and at last, was able to release her tears.

It was midnight. *Where was Frank? Where was Sophie? Surely the police wouldn't have kept them locked up.* Irina phoned the station again, and her questions were met with gibbering she didn't understand. Her daughter's bizarre behavior replayed itself in her mind and filled her with a crushing feeling of dread.

As Irina tried to construct a timeline, it occurred to her that Sophie became secretive some months ago on the day Adelajda was like a jackrabbit hopping through the house urging her mother to hurry up so they could get to the store right as it opened.

That Christmas, Santa gave Marysia a chenille bedspread sprinkled with faces of Scooby Doo here and there. Once Sophie saw how drab Addie's cover was in comparison, she invited her youngest to join her so they could shop for a matching spread. A few hours after they left, Irina began chopping sirloin for a batch of *pierogi* she was going to freeze for later in the week. When out of the blue, Addie darted into the house, wailing. "Babcia! Mommy fell at the store. The saleslady wanted an amblance to come. Mommy hit me!" Addie pointed to the red blotch that resembled a handprint on her cheek. "Mommy's mad at me ... it was me who made her fall. I didn't get my bedspread. I wasn't supposed to tell you or daddy." Addie plunged her head in her grandmother's apron.

Irina was appalled when she examined the red mark more closely. As Irina craned her neck to see where Sophie was, she heard her walk in the door.

"Addie, I am so sorry I lost my temper." Sophie sank down on her knees before her daughter while she explained to her mother, "Work is getting to me. I'm on edge with these arbitrations between the administration and the union. We have to get these teachers back to the classroom. C'mon, sweetheart. Sit on my lap over here."

Addie cried and she became so rigid she would slip through Sophie's arms when she tried to lift her up. Irina persuaded Addie to go to her matka trying to make sense of what was happening before her.

"Mother, I've been restless at night keeping Frank up. I drank way too much coffee this morning so I'd be able to function today, and on top of that I didn't have breakfast. I was browsing around when I shivered uncontrollably and my stomach became queasy. I fainted."

Irina hurried over to her, placing her hand on her forehead to see if she was warm. "You good."

Sophie kissed Addie as she burrowed her head into her mommy's chest, sucking her thumb. Irina suspected the whole incident was much more than Sophie was willing to admit. As she was about to ask more questions, one of her papa's sayings came to mind: *Ciekawość to pierwszy stopień do piekła.* 'Curiosity is the first step to hell.'

But this time, Irina didn't care about that first step.

"Sophie, you not right. Tell me."

"I'm fine."

"You never hit girls. What wrong? Tell me."

A curtain of hostility descended between them.

"Maybe you go to doctor?"

"Mother, stop. I'm fine. And there's no need to worry Frank about this."

As she lay in bed that night, Irina kept replaying Sophie's denial. Why didn't she insist Sophie go to a doctor? Or why didn't she ask more questions and forget about her papa's hell? Shedding her lumpy pierzyna, she wriggled up against the wooden headboard and began kneading her disfigured fingers which usually proved to be a distraction from her worries, but not tonight. She prayed to the chipped porcelain statue of the Virgin Mary on her dresser resting between old scraps of threadbare lace and her spool from long ago. Would she be blessed with another miracle?

All Irina could picture was Frank and Sophie brawling on the floor and hearing her daughter spitting profanities, kicking, and biting him. She blinked as a way to erase the string of horrifying memories swimming before her. The luminous dial on her clock revealed that it was 2:00 a.m.

Irina tiptoed downstairs and gripped the rail to steady herself as she surveyed the shambles before her. Shaking her head, she snatched her brandy from its hiding place relieved it was intact. She held the glass in both hands and drained the amber-colored liquid.

"Brandy good for heart," she admitted out loud, as if she needed to explain herself to the empty room.

Irina's papa was a brandy drinker, maybe too much so, but he would tell her that *koniak* would cure any ailment. As life in her new country went on, she realized she didn't need any specific ailment to reap its benefits. Her husband, Albert, shared the same opinion, but in his case, Polish vodka was his cure-all. When she learned that he had stumbled from a ladder at work and broke his neck, she suspected he might have been nipping a bit earlier in the day. Still reeling from the death of her papa a few months before, Irina was devastated with the news. She was now simultaneously an orphan and a widow.

Irina prayed silently as she resumed straightening out all the disarray of the night before. In between her heaving and heavy breathing, she right-sided overturned furniture and swept up shards of glass from shattered picture frames and porcelain from the bases of smashed lamps. The knife was lying there amidst the signs of a brawl, but she couldn't touch it. Frank would have to deal with it.

Concealed under an ottoman, Sophie's treasured artificial flower arrangement was slightly damaged. The girls were so excited when they presented it to her on Mother's Day last year pointing out the colorful clusters of bendable blooms. Plastic greenery never appealed to Sophie; nevertheless, she fussed over their gift emphasizing how realistic the flowers were—a sanctioned lie.

As she straightened a few of the stems, Irina agonized about Frank. The police must have released him by now. Pacing from window to window in search of her son-in-law, Irina was losing the tiny amount of patience she was able to muster. All she could see were hazy street lights piercing through the darkness of a moonless sky. *Where is Frank? Where did they take my Sophie? Maybe she is dead. I could never live without her.* She clasped her throat as the lump of fear lodged there began making its way down her body.

Albert's sudden death left her unmoored. For weeks she ricocheted between anger that he left her alone in a country she didn't want to live in to begin with, and grief. Thank God for Sophie. But what now? Her grandchildren were reason enough to keep going, but she was older now, with less stamina. Her whole world was disintegrating.

One of her papa's favorite bedtime stories dealt with how her uncles and their brothers shed blood to grant Poland its rightful place on the world's map after 118 years of being occupied by other countries. With great pride, he would lecture that Polish people were strong and any weakness in her would be a disservice to him and her ancestors who fought in WWI. Opening the window above her bed, he would point to a field of vivid red corn poppies behind their house and explain, *"That beautiful flower is a symbol of Polish strength and resilience. Whenever you're afraid, think of the field of red blossoms."* Right now, she was failing her relatives and disappointing her papa. No matter how hard she tried to picture that sea of red petals, all she saw was an empty parcel of ground.

Cradling her tumbler of brandy, Irina mounted the stairs up to her bedroom, which was across from the girls'. She peeked in and saw Marysia with her arm slung over her sister's waist and the legs of Adelajda's doll stuck out from under the pierzyna. Irina prayed as she heard the gentle rhythms of their breathing and then crept into her room, where she lowered herself onto her bed and wept.

My papa, please forgive me. I'm so sorry, I want to be strong, but I don't have it within me. If you knew my Sophie and her girls, you would understand how hard it is. How so very hard it is.

The phone's jangling wakened Irina in the middle of a dream about her papa playing a game of *kapela* with Sophie. Her papa was guarding a mound of stones with a Biretta on dressed like a priest while Sophie, with blood spurting from her mouth, was throwing knives at him.

Irina gasped and shook her head until the ringing jolted her back into the nightmare that was real.

"Irina. It's Frank."

"*Dzięki Bogu!* My God! I have terrible dream. Sophie. She Ok? I can see her when?" She swiveled out of bed and wobbled as she stood.

"Irina ... please. I'm exhausted. The ordeal at the police station was overwhelming, but I did straighten things out. Sophie became more violent while we were there, so they ordered an ambulance to take her to St. Luke Hospital. The admitting physician sedated her and then asked many questions about her medical and psychiatric history. It took time to sign papers and then a doctor there stitched up my deeper cuts." His speech sounded as if each word weighed a hundred pounds. "How are the girls?"

"They in bed. They good. How long she be there? When she come home?"

"I'm not sure. I'll get more information tomorrow afternoon after I drop off a few of her belongings."

"Frank, that knife on floor ..."

"I'll take care of that when I get home. Now, go to bed and get some sleep."

Irina stood immobile. Sleep? How could she sleep when her daughter, who went berserk and was carted off by the police, ends up in a hospital? *Why didn't Frank insist they bring her home so I could take care of her? Sophie needs her matka.*

TWO

Their room was dark, with the exception of a Mickey Mouse nightlight glowing between the two beds. Strands of her doll's cherry red locks rested on Addie's shoulder as she kissed her. "I love you, Linda."

Addie bit her lip and tippy toed to the bedroom door, hoping to hear her mommy and daddy making-up, but all she heard was Mary's snoring. Holding her own breath, Addie went back to bed and scooched up against her headboard, careful not to rouse the creaky mattress springs.

Whenever she and Mary played their made-up game, "Highest Jumper" on their beds, the groaning of their springs prompted their mommy to sneak up on them.

"Girls! You should be in bed sleeping!"

Addie would shriek and wiggle under the covers while Mary would apologize.

"I promise. We'll sleep now."

But before their mommy kissed them good night, with a grin on her face, she would ask who the winner was.

Her mommy ... she realized her mommy wasn't home. A sharp pain pierced her heart. A sob spilled out, and so as not to wake her sister, Addie hoisted the covers over her head while squeezing Linda. Her whimpers invaded the darkness that encircled them.

"Linda. Don't be sad. Addie's here and will stay here." Her tears trickled onto Linda's head, sliding down the doll's pink plastic cheeks. "You're a good girl, and mommies don't leave good girls. What?" Addie pressed Linda's head to her ear. "No! You're not bad." Addie's face burned red, and she banged Linda's head against her own. "I said you're not bad!"

"Addie? Are you Ok?" Pushing herself from the comfort of sleep, Mary accidentally sent her own doll, Effie, sprawling to the floor.

Addie hurled Linda across the room toppling over a lamp. "No. I hate her! She makes me crazy." Wrapping her face in her bedcovers, Addie whimpered through her fingers as she wept.

Mary retrieved both dolls and scurried back to the warmth of the bed, complaining. "Addie, I can't understand what you're saying. What's wrong?"

"I hate Linda. She's bad. She makes me crazy like Babcia said Mommy was." Addie stuffed the blanket in between her teeth and began chewing it. "Remember the time Mommy and me went for a bedspread?" Addie kicked the covers to the floor.

"Wasn't that the time she fell?"

"It was my fault. She told me so when she hit me!" Addie punched her doll reddening her knuckles. "Ow! Ow! I hurt myself!" She jammed her throbbing fingers into her mouth. Burrowing herself under the covers, Addie lamented over and over, "I didn't mean to. I didn't."

Mary followed, nearly slipping off the bed. "Let me see your fingers." Studying each of them, Mary fussed, "Honestly, Addie. You could've hurt yourself. And Mommy loves you so much."

But no matter how much her sister tried to persuade her, Addie knew it was she who made her mommy crazy.

THREE

Shafts of sunlight peeped through Irina's window shades and landed on her hooded eyelids. In the haze of her sleep, she heard Frank come home and for an instant wondered why he was out so late. Then she remembered.

She wasn't sure whether it was her usual morning aches and pains or the aftermath from the night before that throbbed as she strained to get up. As her muscles loosened, she made her way across the room and knelt before her makeshift altar to the Blessed Virgin, praying for the family ... singling her daughter out for extra blessings.

"Irina?" She could tell that Frank was spent because his voice was laboring too hard to sound normal. "Please come down. We need to talk about last night."

Forcing her dread into a crevice of her heart, she found Frank and the children huddled together on the sofa with him lodged in the middle. In their rumpled pajamas and with their hair swirling in all directions, the girls looked as if they had been swept up into the winds of a hurricane. With white gauze covering his facial wounds, Frank appeared to have been attacked by a feral cat. Addie and Mary entwined their arms around his and peered at the scattered dressings on his face.

"Good morning, Irina."

Irina's breath faltered, stirring up memories of the day she learned of Albert's death. How would Frank ever be able to explain what happened so Adelajada and Marysia could understand? When she last talked with him, he didn't have any answers.

"Last night was a horrific night for us," Frank began slowly.

Addie wiggled down to the floor and interrupted, "Is Mommy going to get better? When will she be home?"

"Yes, Mommy is fine. I don't have the answer to your question right now, but she sends her love and says not to worry about her. She is being well taken care of. Now, I'm sure you're confused why she acted like that ... so different from the mommy you love."

Addie wagged her head so eagerly that a cluster of matted ebony locks spilled onto her face.

"Mommies and daddies have adult worries and problems that children could never understand until they become grownups. What I can tell you is your mommy has been working so hard that she's been unable to sleep for weeks. So, last night, your Mommy mistakenly thought Addie was yelling for help when I was tickling her. She was so tired and wasn't able to see me clearly. She wanted to protect you." Frank leaned down and kissed Addie on the cheek. "It's nothing either of you did or said. So, I took her to a place where she could rest. She'll be home soon."

"Why did the police come?" Addie nuzzled against Frank's knees at the same time sucking her thumb.

"Because your mommy was mixed-up." He grunted as he hoisted his youngest daughter up, settling her on his lap. Prying her thumb out of her mouth, he asked, "Were you biting on those other fingers?" Frank noticed the swelling.

"Addie hit Linda in the face."

"Tattletale!"

"When can we see her, Daddy?" Mary ignored her sister's taunt.

"I have to drop off a few of Mommy's things at the hospital, so I'll find out then. It's up to the doctors."

"Babcia says mommy is crazy," Mary blubbered.

Frank's eyes widened as if he had just swallowed a needle.

Irina was horrified. "No, so sorry. I no mean that! In Polish *zwariowany* ... no? Confused?" She spun her finger in circles snarling it in her hairnet.

"Irina, stop! It means crazy."

"I get mixed up ... I so upset."

"Irina, *zwariowany* is 'crazy.' This"—he imitated Irina's gesture—"means crazy! Tell me you didn't do this!"

"Oh my! No! No crazy! I never say Sophie crazy! Ach! *Zmieszano,* no?" Frank grumbled. "That's *confused*, Irina."

"Ya. I am."

"Girls, Babcia gets mixed up with her English. She didn't mean crazy ... she meant confused."

Irina scratched her head. *Who acts so violent if they're confused?*

FOUR

The inky black leather suitcase lay open on their bed partially filled with well-worn loafers, fuzzy slippers and a few turtlenecks. Frank placed a picture of the girls in a pouch she would see as soon as she opened the bag. It took him longer than he expected to hunt through Sophie's closet and drawers trying to decide what she would need. As he folded her nightgowns, a floral, woodsy scent enveloped him. It was Chanel, the fragrance he gave her for Christmas shortly after they married.

Sophie was mesmerized by the scent of this exotic blend of roses and lily of the valley as she paused at the perfume counter at Field's that year. She spritzed on a sample and when she came home, fluttered her wrist past Frank's face laughing at how ridiculously expensive a teeny bottle was. Sophie could never rationalize spending that much money on herself since Irina had doggedly reminded her, "Too much spending empties heart. Save."

When she recognized the overblown C on the box, Sophie held the bottle to her nose and took a whiff before she dabbed a tiny drop behind her ears and onto her wrists with great caution. "You shouldn't have spent so much on me!"

As he fastened the suitcase, Sophie's face bunched up like a fist flashed before him. Even though he wasn't able to see the black and blue marks that covered him, his muscles felt the pain of their impact. Any movement on his face felt as though the stitches and cuts would pop open. How could this have ever happened?

Addie tapped on the door. "Daddy? When are you leaving? We have presents for Mommy."

His daughters beamed as they held up papers with indiscernible lines and circles filled and outlined with a rainbow of vivid colors.

"Your mommy will love both of these," Frank exclaimed.

"The colors will make her happy!" Mary giggled.

"Ya! Frank, I have special rosary you give from me. I never use except on Sundays."

This crystal rosary sparkling with prisms of blue hues was a gift from a lady friend of Irina's, who made a pilgrimage to Rome. It had been blessed by the Pope to commemorate the first-year anniversary of Albert's death.

Frank placed the beads into his pocket.

"Daddy, I made this one for you. We're flying in a garden."

Two stick figures with disproportionate melon shaped heads were embracing, standing in what appeared to be a heart. Red flowers poking out from dark green slashes lined the bottom of the page in a wavy pattern.

"Daddy, I didn't do a drawing for you because you're here. I hope you know I love you, too." Mary's voice quivered.

"Of course, I know that." Frank knelt on one knee and beckoned her into his arms.

"Wait, Daddy!" Addie commanded. "Here, Mary, use this color and draw another flower over here. That way this will be from both of us." Standing over her sister's shoulder as she colored, Addie grabbed the paper and added more strokes of green.

Mary grimaced.

"Adeladja ... you good sister. But don't be bossy pants with Marysia. Give here. We stick on figerator door."

Frank kissed them both goodbye.

As she watched him back out of the driveway, Irina realized she needed to pick up a few things if they were to have *bigos* for dinner even though fatigue weighed heavily on her, and the last thing she wanted to do was trudge through the grocery store.

Learning to read English was too agonizing, so Irina never had much of an interest in obtaining a driver's license, and since the necessities of her life were within several blocks of the house ... church and the supermarket ... she depended on her legs or the bus.

"Girls! Girls! Come, we get food," Irina gathered their coats, mittens, and hats out of the closet. "We not long."

The sky was sprinkled with fleecy clouds while the sun was flipping in and out from behind them. When it peered out, the heat of its rays made them unbutton their coats and loosen their scarves, and when it retreated, they would redo what they'd undone. The girls skipped ahead, and Irina's thoughts about Sophie flew wildly as though a bird was trapped in her head.

As Irina was reciting the Hail Mary, the girls began quarreling.

"Babcia! She stuck her tongue out at me!"

Not waiting for a response, Mary chased after Addie, pinching her arm. The two of them began whacking one another, shrieking with voices as sharp as porcupine quills.

Their grandmother separated them and pitched her voice decibels above theirs. "*Zamknijcie się, małe złośnic!*"

The girls plunked down on the sidewalk, consoling each other as their bodies trembled. With her mind racing about Sophie, Irina failed to remember how sensitive her *wnuki* were to her Polish admonishments. Since she would never strike them, she would use her native language as other grandmothers used wooden spoons. The harsh and guttural blurts served to get their attention.

"Get up! Get up! Your *bielizna* get dirty!" Irina scolded.

"Please don't be mad! We're sorry. We are," Mary pleaded.

With as much bending as her old body could tolerate, Irina helped them up and kissed their faces on both sides. "I not mad. No. I love you both." She needed to be more patient with them, but patience was a quality she thought took too long.

"What did your Polish mean?" Addie asked.

"*Bielizna?*" She lifted the hem of Addie's coat along with her dress and pointed to her underwear.

"No ... before that. Did you call us bad names?" Mary stood up and straightened the pink plastic barrette that kept her bangs under control.

"I ask you be quiet." Considering what the two of them experienced, Irina decided this was a time for a sanctioned lie. *Shut up, you little shrews!* would never cross her lips.

With her two-wheeled shopping cart, Irina lugged the bags of groceries into the kitchen while the girls danced around her. It seemed that the creaks and groans of the house were louder than usual, almost as if this old building sensed Sophie's absence. Frank owned it when they married: one of those post World War II reddish brick bungalows that Sophie and Irina found to be quite comfortable with the exception of a much needed third bedroom.

"Marysia, take groceries out, please."

Addie knelt on the edge of a blue and white checked window seat in the breakfast nook overlooking the neighbor's fenced in yard loudly swilling her sucker.

"Babcia! Addie needs to sit down," Mary fussed.

"I can do what I want," Addie declared, batting her eyelids.

"No, you can't. Mommy says seats are for your *dupa*, not your knees."

Their bickering brought Irina to the edge of the patience she tried to stockpile during this unstable time in their lives, so Irina couldn't bring herself to use her usual Polish weapon.

"You go watch TV while I cook."

"Daddy says TV will shrink our brains," Mary reminded her.

Addie shushed her sister.

"You watch clown show for one hour."

"Yeah! *Bozo! Bozo!* C'mon, Mary!" The two of them skipped out.

"You no run with Tootsie stick in *usta!* You poke hole in there!"

Her worst fears began prodding her again. *What if Sophie isn't able to recover? Or worse yet, maybe Sophie is so ill she might die?* It was up to her to be a mother to those girls, but that wasn't what preyed upon her. What if she herself became sick or died? Without Sophie, what would happen to them? Children are for young women, not the old.

What's wrong with me? I am Polish! A strong woman. I'll do whatever needs to be done!

A gurgling erupted from the stove. The pot cover jiggled as steam streamed out and swirled around her. She had second thoughts about choosing *bigos* for dinner, since it was such an ordeal to cook at the best of times much less when what she wanted to do was collapse into bed. As she sliced and diced, a hunk of marbled beef escaped her hand and hit the floor. "Be strong! No *depresja!*"

She retrieved it, straightened up and began dropping quarter size chunks of pork, veal, and beef into the stew pot. It didn't take long for the savory and sweet aromas of the *bigos*—Polish sausage, apples, and bacon—to lure the girls back into her domain.

"What time will we eat?" Addie asked.

"When is Daddy coming home?" Mary snatched a chunk of cooked meat that escaped the pot.

"Ach! What about clown?" Irina sampled a taste of her simmering dinner and added more salt and pepper.

"Commercials," Mary muttered.

"I'm Mommy's favorite," Addie blurted while slurping her sucker.

"No, Addie. We both are!"

"No! It's me!"

"What happen to TV?" Irina asked wiping her hands on her apron.

Jumping up, they raced back to the living room.

Irina thanked the Blessed Virgin for the clown with the big red nose.

Resuming her chopping, Irina was overpowered with memories of Albert. The vinegary smell of sauerkraut would remind her of him since he often bragged that she made the best *kapusta* ... better than his own mother's.

How she wished he were here, but then her papa's voice intruded upon her reminiscence: "Wishing is like throwing peas against a wall." But she didn't care ... she would never give up wishing: for Albert; for Sophie to be normal again; for her matka; her papa. No, she would never give up wishing that her family could be spared from suffering and death. Maybe Albert would be alive if they stayed in Poznan.

At the same time Albert made known that he was going to America, he proposed to her. She clasped his face in her hands, gave him a sloppy kiss, and beamed. "Yes" to marriage, but "No" to America. She celebrated her seventeenth birthday the week before. How could she leave her papa? So, Albert threatened that he would have to leave with or without her. Warsaw was in great political turmoil and, with his involvement in the Polish resistance exposed, he was forced to flee.

The time for Albert's departure drew near and she was paralyzed with uncertainty. Her girlfriends advised her to forget about him; others insisted that Albert would send for her later. How could they ever understand how torn she was between her love for Albert and her devotion to her papa?

When she came home from work, her papa urged her to leave. *"If you don't go, you'll disappear. You're nothing but bones! I can take care of myself."*

When she kissed him on both cheeks, the salty taste of his tears filled her with greater uncertainty. What would he do without her? Her papa had no other family. After much debating, Irina agreed on the condition he would join her when they had enough money to send for him.

"I hear America is a nice place. Of course, I will come to visit!" He chortled, patting her cheek.

"Not to visit! But to live, Papa!"

They were to leave the next morning, and there was so much for her to do.

As perspiration speckled her forehead, Irina prepared the last batch of *barszcz* for her papa; that along with two dozen pierogi stuffed with meat and potatoes would keep him well-fed for at least a week. Albert promised her that his cousin, Kasia, whom Irina knew to be a God-awful cook, would prepare meals for her papa, so she need not worry. That made her feel worse.

The day was moving too fast. She flitted from counting her underwear, packing her suitcase, to checking on the *barszcz*, and then back to recounting her underwear.

"Irina, you need to relax! You will have an exciting life in America." Her papa patted her cheek.

"You promised you will come as soon as I send for you, right?"

He kissed her.

As she and Albert boarded the ship, her knees buckled, dropping her to the floor. When she was revived, Albert was crouched over her, promising they would send for her papa as soon as they settled.

It took several years, but when they were financially able to bring him to America, her papa was adamant that he die at home. And so, he did. In her grief, Irina would pretend to function during the day, for Sophie's sake. But at night, in the quiet of her bedroom, she would weep. *Why did I go without him? I should've made him come with us! My papa died without me at his side. What kind of daughter am I?*

There were days that the darkness of her bedroom was her lone comfort. Albert never criticized her if his laundry remained unwashed, or when dinner consisted of cold soup, or when there wasn't any dinner at all. Gazing at the Blessed Mother resting on her handmade altar, Irina clasped the beads of her rosary begging for forgiveness for having left him. Her protector had forsaken her. She was not able to draw upon her usual mainstays right now, not even her papa's red flowers.

What ultimately shook her out of her desolation was Albert's death which left no time to grieve for either man. She willed herself to tap into her Polish strength while comforting a grief-stricken Sophie who was inconsolable until Irina reminded her that they would survive through hard work and prayer. Their prayers were answered in the form of Frank's parents, Helen and Nick Gurin.

FIVE

"*B*ozo is over. Can we watch more TV?"

"No. You brain shrink. Sit. I give you milk."

"Mary. Don't forget what we talked about." Addie nudged her.

"Where is our mommy? Is she ever coming home? If she's so tired, why can't she sleep here? Why did she have to go somewhere else?"

Guiding them to the window seat, Irina motioned for them to sit on either side of her. Mary held her babcia's hand and brushed a kiss on her gnarled fingers. Addie mimicked her sister's loving gesture.

As the three of them clustered together, Babcia proclaimed as if in church, "*Rodzina nie jest czymś ważnym. Jest wszystkim.* I forever tell you: family not important thing. It everything. You must remember this. We stick together no matter what!"

"If that's so, why aren't we sticking with Mommy and taking care of her here?"

That question haunted her: Who better to take care of Sophie than her own mother? Why wasn't her daughter home? Ever since that police car drove off, the many disparate scraps of guilt that made up the essence of her life tormented her: Catholic guilt ... Mother guilt ... Polish guilt. But her mother guilt outstripped the other two when her daughter wasn't able to return home.

Floundering, Irina took a breath. "Marysia sometimes family not enough. Ach!" She mumbled, realizing that wasn't what she meant. "Family forever enough. Your matka need doctor care ... medicine. We be patient and she be home soon."

"I miss her." Addie wept.

"Ya. Babcia, too." Now was the time to reveal the story that her papa shared with her and the one she passed on to Sophie. "When baby girl comes out of matka's body"—she rubbed her belly—"they are ... uh ... *uwiązany*." Irina looped her two index fingers together and although she tried to yank them apart, she squeezed them tighter.

With her hand under her chin, Mary tried to decipher her babcia's hand gestures. "Hmmm? Twisted? No ... held together? Yes!"

"Ya ... held together." Irina paused, "Matkas and daughters held together by beautiful silken thread."

Addie eyebrows squished together as though the wheels in her head couldn't turn fast enough to understand. Elevating her arms straight up, she skipped in circles, her fingers moving frenetically until she suddenly stopped.

"Babcia! No thread anywhere! Why not?" Addie complained.

"Now, now! My *paczkis*."

Whenever their grandmother referred to them as paczkis, they giggled. They loved being referred to as "stuffed doughnuts" filled with a variety of flavored jams: strawberry, raspberry, blackberry. And the pronunciation of the word itself would lighten their mood—*poonch-key*.

But not this time.

"You no feel with fingers, my paczkis! It *magic* thread ... ah ... let's see." Irina tapped her forehead. "English ... magic, no?"

Clapping their hands, the girls chirped in unison. "Magic? What kind of magic?"

"It's *zmieszany* ... She made circles with her index finger while pointing to her head. "Ach! Not that!"

"Confusing ... not crazy!" Mary laughed.

"Ya! Confusing magic. Can't see or feel. Silk thread gift of love from Matka ... it there, but it change. Sometimes long, sometimes short. Many, many colors. Sometimes be light like pierzyna feather or hard like stale paczki. Sometime feel too tight and sometime too loose. It not stay same but forever there."

"If we can't see or feel it, how do we know she still loves us? It's hard when Mommy's not here."

Their grandmother did not have an answer they would understand. *They'll realize in time that the silk thread runs through every action and word*

29

a mother does or says to her daughter. There will be times a daughter will be hurt or disappointed by her mother, even get angry with her. A daughter has to understand her mother is not perfect and that her mother will do her utmost to be the best mother she can be. A daughter has to believe that with her whole heart. When she does, the thread becomes long enough and strong enough so that the daughter will then be able to stitch a quilt of unconditional love to give to her own daughters.

So, instead, Irina instructed the girls, "Stand tall. Stick hand on top of heart." With great care, Irina closed their eyelids.

Standing shoulder to shoulder, the girls obeyed.

"Now, can you remember many times your mommy hold you, cook for you, kiss you, make you feel special?"

Mary's curls jiggled as she bobbed her head.

Addie sucked in a deep breath that ascended from the bottom of her feet.

"That thread. My paczkis ... thread about remembering ... *Pamiętając.* Go to place in heart and remember. That thread of her love."

Mary leaned into Addie, "All I can remember is mommy hitting and kicking our daddy."

Addie brought a hand up to her cheek.

SIX

As Frank drove home from the hospital, his mind was jumbled with the events of the last few days. Sophie intended to kill him with that knife—it was inches from his face. Did she hate him on some level?

The way he justified Sophie's behavior was logical enough, but sleep deprivation and work stress were too simplistic. How could she possibly believe he was hurting Addie? Since his father was more of a visitor in his own life, Frank was intentional about the kind of dad he would be. From bottle-feeding to changing diapers, he took great pride in being unconstrained from the typical stereotypes men were labeled with.

Whenever she complained about the strike, he half-heartedly listened. And yet, he was uncertain as to what more he could've done to help her. Why didn't he insist she take a few days off from work? Or maybe they should have taken a trip?

His mind mercifully carried him to a better place—the day they met. Sunday mass had ended and well-dressed parishioners were spilling out onto the front portico of St. Stanislas church. While conversing with a friend of his, Frank was jostled from behind and lost his footing.

"Uh ... didn't you see that step?" Frank recalled saying as he brushed the knees of his pants.

"I'm so sorry."

Surprised to hear a woman's voice, Frank whipped around. "Oh! No, I should apologize!" His tone of voice reflected a glow of sheer delight.

Sophie had an understated beauty. Her olive skin was flawless, devoid of any makeup other than a touch of rouge and a dab of lipstick that stained her full lips. Her slightly crooked nose was perfectly placed in the middle of her high cheekbones. But it was the flush of her embarrassment coupled with an apologetic smile that captivated him.

"Darn. I just bought these." Sophie twisted around to see how much damage had been done to her nylons.

"I'm happy to replace them for you," Frank said, with mischief reflecting in his smile.

"No need." Her voice was coated with frost.

Once they both agreed that neither of them was hurt, Sophie pivoted to leave.

"Miss?" Frank followed her.

"Yes?" Turning abruptly, she extended her arm to stop him from plowing into her.

"Oops. This might be a bold move, but how about a cup of coffee? Then we could make sure there weren't any delayed injuries."

"Oh, I'm fine." Another parishioner greeted Sophie, and they began gossiping as they crossed the street.

As he made his way toward his car, the lingering scent of rosewater was so strong, Frank was convinced Sophie was following him. Puffing his chest out, he peeked over his shoulder and laughed to see no one there. Shaking his head, he realized her fragrance insinuated itself onto his tweed jacket. He was confident that he would be reveling in this sweet smell again.

With tax season close at hand, Frank was overwhelmed with the number of returns he yet had to complete at his accounting firm. So, he wasn't able to attend the early Sunday Mass for a few weeks but eventually, he saw that same black hat bobbing in the crowd, but this time, she was accompanied by an older woman.

"Mrs. Kysinski! Is that you? I haven't seen you since my father's funeral." *Is this her mother?*

"Ach! Frank! You good looker man." Irina stood on tip toes and patted his face.

"So sorry about Papa and Matka ... so fast ... how come no service for Matka? I make novena for her."

Frank exhaled. Not having a traditional funeral service for a Catholic parishioner was worse than not attending Easter Sunday Mass.

"Mother ... that's a personal question." Sophie furrowed her brows.

"Mrs. Kysinski, you remember what a quiet and reserved woman my mother was, quite the opposite of my dad, who loved center stage. We had a private service for immediate family."

As big as he was in life, Nick, Frank's father, made his final exit in the same fashion causing quite a ruckus when he dropped dead of a heart attack at the communion rail. It wasn't but six months later that Helen, Frank's mother, followed her husband. Church gossip claimed she died of a broken heart.

"Yes. It's been two years. How are you?" Frank kissed Irina on both cheeks.

"Good. You remember my Sophie, no?" Irina nudged her daughter forward.

"This is Sophie? We fell for each other a few weeks ago, didn't we?"

Sophie's neck publicized her embarrassment with blossoming red specks sprouting in visible locations.

"His matka and papa save us from starving when your papa die."

Soon after Irina and Albert arrived in Chicago, Frank's father offered Albert a job at his construction company, apprenticing him as a plasterer while Helen enthusiastically promoted Irina's alteration business to the other Polish women at church. Both families were members of the congregation at St. Stanislaus which was the center of life for Polish immigrants on the northwest side of Chicago. Despite Mr. Gurin being a Russian immigrant, Helen and her family agreed to the marriage along with a partnership in their successful business on the condition that he would adopt Catholicism and the Polish culture. Without hesitation, he did so and became a respected member of the parish and community at large. His generosity extended beyond his friends and employees, and included substantial weekly church offerings, hefty donations to any school fund drive, and capital improvements for the buildings. Recognition was as sure-fire way to keep the coffers full so his name appeared regularly in the church bulletin as well as from the priest at the pulpit.

Life was good then, until Sophie's daddy fell off a ladder and broke his neck, leaving Irina penniless. Her mind remained trapped in fear. *I have no family here. I am all alone. How will I feed and clothe Sophie?*

On the day of Albert's funeral, Mr. Gurin gave Irina a check for $1,000 explaining that since her husband's death occurred on a job site, he was able to compensate her through insurance. He also introduced Irina to a gentleman who owned a ladies' dress shop in Logan Square and served as a reference for her. She was hired that very day.

Irina thanked God since her worries were settled within a week of Albert's death ... except for Sophie. Who would take care of her while Irina worked? Paying for child care would leave her without any discretionary money. But more importantly, who could she trust?

While she was praying for an answer at church, Helen Gurin contacted Irina and offered her services at no cost. Irina was adamant that she would pay her, but Helen insisted since Albert's accident occurred on her husband's work site. In spite of that, the Polish community at St. Stanislas was a tight knit group and more than willing to help anyone in need. After much debate, Irina agreed under the condition that if Helen needed any alterations, Irina would do so at no charge. A deal was struck.

"Sophie, you remember him?" Irina tapped Sophie's arm.

She didn't ... that whole period of her life was an empty space in her memory bank. Her mind wheeled about searching for a way to take charge of the conversation. "I was playing with dolls while you, I imagine, were interested in real dolls," Sophie declared in a mocking tone.

"That's right! I was used to being the center of attention until you came along. But, I have to say, you were a cute kid!"

Irina affectionately patted Frank on the shoulder. "I tell your matka stop spoiling my girl. So many gifts she give ... Sophie, remember Charlotte Clark Mickey Mouse doll? I want to buy for your birthday, but Helen bought before me."

Sophie waved at another church member whizzing past them.

"I never imagined the little girl I often caught chewing on one or the other of her braids would become such a beauty."

It wasn't easy for Sophie to hear compliments about herself because she didn't think she deserved them but more importantly she believed lurking in the shadows of the flattery was a self-serving form of manipulation.

"Mrs. Kysinski, may I have your permission to take your lovely daughter out for dinner this evening?"

"Wait a minute! I make my own dates," Sophie's face slammed shut like the trunk of a car.

Irina blurted, "Ya! That be good."

"Great! I'll pick you up at seven." Frank winked at his potential dinner date.

"Mother! I beg your pardon! But it's *not* good."

Irina harped at Sophie about her dating life, which was nil but wasn't the result of any laziness on her part until her encounters with boys became too agonizing. Just like then, her unwelcome ruby red splotches of humiliation began covering her neck.

"Apparently, my mother is free, so I hope the two of you have a good time." Glowering at Irina, she snarled, "Good-bye," and strutted off.

"Ach! Sorry, Frank. Sophie not that way."

"Not a problem, Mrs. Kysinski. It was great seeing you and I'm hoping it won't be the last time."

Frank wasn't sure what his next move would be, but he did know he would have to be patient. He suspected Sophie needed time to recover from her mother's indelicate actions.

It had been a few years since his fiancée ended their engagement, and he hadn't been with a woman or interested in any since. When that relationship ended, Frank entered the seminary and not long after, his spiritual director informed him that the ministry wasn't the place to heal broken hearts and suggested he rethink his commitment. Withdrawing from the institution, he was recruited back to his former place of employment, a prominent accounting firm, where his career thrived; but not so for his love life until he reached for Sophie on those church steps.

But maybe she was too young for him, or he was too old for her. Dismissing that idea, he thought of Jack, a partner at the firm who married a much younger woman and was quite happy after twenty years. To further build his case, with humility, he realized that for a man his age, he was as energetic and active as any 30-year-old. Quite a few women had flirted with him and several had approached him for a date. Standing at over six feet tall, he had rugged features and a shock of lustrous, velvet black hair. Maybe his hairline was receding a bit but his smile accentuated dimples that made round hollows in his cheeks, frequently referred to as sexy by more than a few women. But it didn't matter what his opinion was about their age difference. What did Sophie think?

Sophie found herself smitten with Frank on the day they tumbled into each other ... but she assumed nothing would come of it, which was par for the course. But as that week wore on, fantasies about Frank became more and more of a distraction. Dillydallying after Sunday mass, she lingered longer than usual with friends hoping Frank would appear. After the last churchgoer straggled out, Sophie plodded to her car, dropping her church bulletin as a way to make sure she stalled long enough. No Frank.

It worried her that she would end up being an old maid as her mother feared. She dreamt about getting married and having children, but the truth was her prospects were slim and her opinion of herself was even slimmer.

When memories of her teen years surfaced, there brewed a pool of self-loathing. Socializing with boys was a burden because of her hands: Any time she was on a date or within close proximity of the opposite sex, they perspired profusely. So much so that the hankies she used to hide her embarrassment were soaked within the hour. Parties or dances required two such helpmates.

Whenever her occasional dates deposited her back home, she would engage in replays of her ineptness.

He probably thinks I'm ugly.

Was that a joke? Should I laugh now?

Why am I so clumsy?

Why can't I be cleverer? More witty?

She would laugh when nothing was funny and make apologies when it was. She would say "sorry" if she talked too much or if she didn't talk enough. If she was out in a restaurant, either with a boy or in a mixed group, she would never order food that might result in sauce on her face, or food stuck in her teeth. So, no spaghetti, pizza, or burgers unless she was with her girlfriends. Those mind games were exhausting. Staying home was much easier.

So, when Frank finally asked Sophie for a date, her voice caught at the back of her throat. "Well ... ah ... that would be nice."

"Great. There's a concert at Grant Park on Saturday. How about if I pick you up, say, six o'clock, and we can have dinner first?"

"Ok. See you then."

Her usual self-recriminations came into play, but this time, she prayed to the Blessed Virgin to transform her into Doris Day ... clever, interesting, perky.

That concert was the beginning of their romance. Early on, they agreed that they would alternate planning their dates. Sophie was intimidated the night Frank drove up to Chez Paree, where they had amongst other dishes oysters Rockefeller, filet on the bone, and bananas flambee for dinner, sitting so close to Louis Armstrong they could see glistening droplets of perspiration rolling down his face.

What can I plan that would be as much fun? Trying to be creative as possible and wanting to impress Frank gave her many sleepless nights. After surveying the faculty at her school, the principal gave her a great suggestion. Frank was stupefied when Sophie surprised him with tickets at The Blue Note Jazz Club for a Duke Ellington show which nearly depleted her savings account. That would have to be the last of the extravagant date nights.

A few weeks later, Frank bowled her over when he prepared a dinner of Polish kielbasa, bacon-infused *kapusta* along with cucumbers in sour cream with sprigs of dill sprinkled on top. She savored the juices from the sausage along with the salty taste of the bacon. His Polish cuisine was as flavorful as her grandmother's.

"You can thank my mother for bribing me to help her in the kitchen." Frank laughed. "My friends used to call me a 'girl' because of it, but that didn't bother me because my mom focused on the chemistry of cooking which I found fascinating."

As they snuggled watching Milton Berle performing his slapstick antics on TV, Frank squirmed in his seat. "Soph, uh ... how about if we start doing normal things together? We're past having to impress each another. Am I right?"

"What do you mean? You impressed me tonight!"

"I'm glad! Are we moving into the next stage of our relationship where we can relax and be confident there'll be another date?" Frank asked.

As she studied his face, she searched for any hint of insincerity. Feeling the warmth of his body next to hers, she forbade herself to doubt his intentions.

Freeing her hand from his, she held it up. It was bone dry!

"Yes, Frank. I'm thinking many more dates."

Frank's caresses and probing touches intensified Sophie's desire for him, but when he would explore certain areas of her body, her muscles would constrict. Perplexed at her physical reactions to what began as pleasure born from love, Sophie chalked it up to her Catholic upbringing. *Sex before marriage is a sin. It's up to the woman to stay in control.* It was obvious Catholic boys weren't given the same lectures.

As the months passed, Sophie would fantasize holding a bouquet of fragrant lilies as she made her way to Frank in a silk organza wedding gown ... or friends and family would be tossing rice in their direction as they stood on the church steps. More times than not, those daydreams would have bittersweet nuances when she would suppress them as being ridiculous. Since their last serious discussion about moving forward, Frank appeared quite content with the way things were.

When he invited her for dinner at the Colonnade Room at the Edgewater Beach Hotel, Sophie accepted, but kept pointing out how expensive the restaurant was. "Are you needing to impress me? I thought we weren't doing that anymore." Her voice was as casual as the edge of a dull knife.

"Ha! Aren't you the Scrooge? Isn't about time we splurged? We can catch a movie afterwards. *Dial M for Murder* is at the Esquire."

"I'll be ready."

A valet wearing a deep red jacket opened Sophie's car door and directed them to the dining area where the maître d', dressed in a tuxedo, led them to a romantic table covered with a crisp linen cloth sporting white roses in a red tinted cut glass bowl, and an array of stemmed crystal glasses. How would she ever know which glass was for what? Sophie's curiosity was piqued when she situated herself before a beautifully wrapped gift larger than a magazine resting on her charger plate.

"What is this?" Sophie wiggled the box, holding it up to her ear, and giggled.

"Go on ... open it."

The waiter placed a bottle of champagne in an ice stand by their table while straightening flutes that were nestled in between the red and white wine glasses.

"Frank! What's this about? How did you get this here? And why the champagne?" Sophie resisted the urge to think maybe it could be ...

"Well, I delivered the gift earlier today, so you'd be surprised. Go ahead. Open it." With his elbows on the table, Frank rested his chin on his steepled fingers.

Sophie untied the satin ribbon, peeled off the tape on the icy blue wrapping paper, and removed the box. Inside were a dozen seamless nylon stockings.

"Nylons?" Her smile was in direct contradiction to her rheumy eyes. "Well, I only ruined one pair that day at church ..."

Sophie's heart sank. A few hours before Frank's arrival time, she was twirling before her mother in the umpteenth outfit she tried on, and blurted that maybe tonight, he would propose to her.

"Sophie, I know you like Frank ... maybe more than like. My papa use to tell me, '*Nie popychaj rzeki, która sama popłynie.*' Do not push river, it flow by itself."

Her mother was right.

"Before you say anything else, take all of them out." Frank insisted.

When she did, a sparkling solitaire diamond rested on top of a platinum band scotch-taped to the bottom of the box. "Oh my!" Holding the ring up to the light, she was dazzled by the prisms of blue and silver that radiated from its center. *The river is flowing, mother!*

"Sophie, it was love at first sight on the day we fell on those church steps. This past year has sealed the deal. And keep in mind, as an accountant, I don't make decisions impulsively! You'd better say 'yes' so I can pop the champagne!"

Without hesitation, Sophie wiggled her flute and replied, "Start pouring."

SEVEN

Nearly home from the hospital after attempting to visit Sophie, Frank wondered how his parents would have reacted to his choice of a wife. It was difficult for him to admit that he was jealous of the attention Sophie received from his mother: cookies, dolls, toys. His father was never happy with most of what Frank did, but since his dad helped the Kysinskis when they arrived in the US, he might have approved. But then again, he came to the aid of many immigrants.

Frank slowed down as he steered into the driveway and saw Mary flying down the street on her two-wheeler with Addie chasing after her. When they heard his familiar honking, the bike landed on a plot of grass and they scurried toward him, racing to see who would reach him first.

Mary won. "How's Mommy?"

"She's getting better and she sends oodles of love. Hey there!" Frank pointed his finger into Mary's face. "Not so fast on that bike! And you, too!"

With bowed heads, they promised never again.

"Daddy, did mommy like our drawings?"

It took Frank a minute to remember what he said and to whom. He hated all these lies not to mention any future ones he was certain would have to pass his lips. Sophie couldn't have visitors until the next day but at least he was able to give their artwork and the suitcase he packed to an orderly.

"Of course!"

A sanctioned lie, as Irina or Sophie would say. In spite of Irina's disagreements, Frank argued that fathers had the same privilege.

Shielding her eyes from the sun, Mary asked when they could see her.

"I don't know, honey. It's up to her doctor. I'll tell you as soon as I can. Now go on and play." Frank paused for a few minutes, watching the girls retrieve Mary's bicycle.

They were so innocent. How could they make any sense of this when he couldn't? Would they be scarred for life? The ache in his chest was a jumble of fear and confusion as this was uncharted territory. He had an appointment with Sophie's psychiatrist the next day and intended to discuss what her opinion was on the matter.

"*Jestem w domu*! I'm home, Irina," Frank announced. The blended savory aromas of frying bacon, sausage, cabbage, and apples rippled throughout the house. Irina made this dish so often that he had had no difficulty discerning the various ingredients. His dimples made an appearance as he brought to mind Sophie's description of *bigos* as "everything but the kitchen sink" stew.

Irina dashed into the living room and helped Frank off with his coat. "How is she?"

"I didn't see her."

"What? Why not? What wrong?" Irina followed him, stepping onto the heel of his shoe. "Ach. Sorry."

"We can see her tomorrow. The head nurse met with me and explained that it will take time for her to adjust to the medications, and that Sophie is making attempts to mingle with the other patients. So that's positive. We will meet with Dr. Meizner, her psychiatrist, tomorrow."

The staff hadn't offered a good report. No matter how much they prodded Sophie to leave her room and join the other patients, she refused. Trying to be upbeat with Irina, he left that part out.

"Ya. Good. Frank, I worry so."

"Irina, she'll be fine. Sophie takes after you ... strong and determined ... *ustalona*. Where's your faith?" Frank wasn't up to dwelling on Irina's fears. The last time he saw Sophie she was slurring her speech, raving about blue flowers and other nonsense. Would she ever be normal again? His thoughts were jumbled and thorny with questions he wasn't sure could ever be answered.

"What did the girls do today?"

"Ach ... they watch me cook and watch clown show ... you no like TV for girls. But I need break, no?" Irina stirred the stew and dipped her nose closer to the pot, surprised that this batch would be one of her best.

"Yes, of course you do, Irina."

"Frank ... you good husband and father. Not bad son-in-law."

He chuckled.

"You let me live here since Marysia born, so I help Sophie. I can be ... *uparty* ... how you say?"

"Stubborn."

"I try to mind my business, but you know, my *usta* has own mind. I lucky to have *wnucki* all by myself. I wish my matka live to care for Sophie, but my papa use to say, 'Wishes like throwing peas against wall.'"

"Wow, that's an old Polish proverb I heard from my grandfather!" A snippet of his *jaja* smoking a fat cigar popped into Frank's mind. "I am grateful you're here ... and that my girls have you, even though we haven't seen eye to eye."

"Ya, with girls. Otherwise, we good."

Irina glanced at the red and white plastic clock in the shape of a rooster hanging above the sink. "It's four o'clock ... how about brandy?"

"Great idea." Pouring two tumblers full, Frank pondered how he and Irina would be able to care for the girls together. He downed his drink in one swig.

EIGHT

On the drive to see Sophie, Irina relied on her usual source of comfort—her rosary. Frank parked the car a few blocks away, and they walked in the same apprehensive quiet that surrounded them on the way there. Hospitals were a curiosity to Irina, but any apprehensions that troubled her were masked by a need to have answers about her daughter. *What will they do to her? Operations ... that's what they do. How will they help her? How long will she be here?*

As she shuffled through the sliding door, a draft of air caressed her face, giving off an odor of disinfectant laced with a hint of evergreen. Potted plants with large glossy leaves were scattered here and there, and the ceiling soared overhead to a height she'd never seen before. As she inspected the gleaming lobby, highlighted by the polished tile floors and walls that gave the impression that they had been bleached, Irina exhaled. *Maybe not so bad.*

Frank tapped her shoulder and pointed in the direction of the elevators. As he placed her leathery hand in the crook of his arm, she was relieved to see a statue of the Blessed Virgin in an alcove near the gift shop. Frank reminded Irina that before seeing Sophie, they would first meet with her psychiatrist.

"Here it is." Frank knocked on a door that identified *Dr. Meizner* on a walnut plaque several inches above the feather on Irina' felt hat.

An attractive middle-aged woman wearing the customary white jacket and lacquered name tag pinned below her left shoulder introduced herself.

"Where doctor?" Irina asked as she scanned the room.

"I'm Dr. Meizner. Please have a seat."

Irina was startled to see a woman.

The office was large and disorderly in an orderly way. Leather bound books were stacked haphazardly on bookshelves that pressed against a wall across from two large windows overseeing the expressway. The tasseled shams on the maroon corduroy armchairs were lopsided and were so close to the edge, it looked as if they were going to slide off. Dr. Meizner's oversized mahogany desk was overflowing with stacks of files and creamy yellow folders that were bursting with papers.

Psychiatrists were unheard of in the old country, and Irina didn't know of anyone here who needed this kind of doctor. It baffled her that, from what Frank explained, their job was to prescribe medicine and listen to patients. It didn't make sense that talking would get to the bottom of her daughter's violence.

The discussion between Frank and Dr. Meizner was happening so quickly, Irina was lost. Without warning, Frank thanked the physician and supported Irina as she got up. Before she could say a word, they were hurrying down the corridor.

Irina tugged on his arm. "Frank ... what happen? I don't get—"

"We're late. I'll explain later."

When they arrived at the visitor's lounge, Irina breathed in the sharp scent of an antiseptic fused with the fading fragrance of days old flowers that were crowded into vases and placed on a few tables near the window. Ornately framed photos of stony-faced nuns listed as "President" followed by their years in office, lined up above the wainscoting.

Irina shuffled over to a brownish leather couch and settled herself into the cushion, which was surprisingly soft, while Frank peered out the window when the door swung open.

Irina rasped as if she saw a dead person stumble in. Sophie's blue robe sagged loosely on her body, which made her bones protrude. A few bright purple smears dotted her face, along with lumps and beads of dried blood. Her hair was tied in a knot on top of her head, with messy and greasy strands dangling in all directions.

Irina walked gingerly toward her daughter with arms outstretched, but Sophie slumped down into a chair staring at nothing. Snatching a hanky from her purse, Irina saw Sophie push Frank as he tried to sit next to her.

"What am I doing here?" Sophie clenched her jaw. "I think they told me but it's so fuzzy." She lowered her head into her discolored and swollen hands. "Oh, my God. Addie ... Mary ... how are they? They saw didn't they?" Her voice was thick with emotion. Bolting up, she gripped the lapels of Frank's jacket and demanded answers to her questions. "What did you do that made me attack you? And Mother, where were you? Why in God's name didn't you stop me?"

Irina eyed Frank praying he would defend her.

Sophie glared at him while she tensed up, ready to pounce.

Since the truth might set her off again and flip her into another reality, her psychiatrist advised him to step into her world by agreeing with her and acknowledging her perceptions of the attack.

"We're sorry, Sophie, aren't we Irina? Dr. Meizner plans to talk with you about this."

Sophie squirmed as she stared out the window and in a flat, unemotional voice asked once again how the girls were doing.

Before they left the house, Frank and Irina agreed that she would remain in the background until he could get a sense of Sophie's mood. Unable to contain her frustration, Irina blurted. "They no good, Sophie. They want you home. They want to know what wrong. I say you sick."

Sophie bounded up and came face-to-face with her mother. "Did you have to tell them I'm fucking *sick?* Why would you do that? I am not sick! How will they ever trust me? Know they are safe with me? Respect me?" She scowled at her mother with unconcealed resentment.

Irina blanched when the word 'fuck' thundered from her daughter, and teetered several feet back.

Frank touched his wife's shoulder which she brushed off. "Sophie, please calm down. The girls believe you have been working hard on the strike and not getting much sleep so you needed to rest. Your mother gets her words mixed up. She didn't say 'sick' ... what she meant to say was 'confused'."

"Ya. Confused I say confused. Not sick. I confused." Irina wiped her forehead with her hanky.

"Jesus, Mother, learn English!"

Irina's earrings jiggled as she nodded.

"Soph, the girls are fine. They miss you. Can you call them tomorrow?" Frank's voice was soft and gentle as if speaking to Addie or Mary.

Sophie's anger transformed into an eerie calm. "Let me see what Dr. Meizner says about that. I have a session with her in the morning, and if she says I'm ready, I can probably do that in the afternoon. She'll let you know."

"Soph, I wasn't able to discuss this with Dr. Meizner today but I think the girls should talk to a therapist ..."

"Absolutely not! And don't bring that up again, ever." As she spewed the last word out, she swayed back onto a sofa mumbling.

At that moment, Frank realized he wasn't up to dealing with Sophie's mercurial reactions. There were times he imagined the horror of that night wasn't as awful as it was, but this visit dispelled that fantasy for good. Sophie was sick. Thoughts fumbled into each other as he ventured to keep the conversation as nonthreatening as possible.

"I miss them so. But I have to be sure to say the right things." Sophie's voice was low and monotonous as if her emotions had dried up.

The rest of their time together was filled with inane chit chat initiated by Frank. "How was the staff?" "The food?" "How was the chaplain?" which resulted in one-word responses: "Fine ... Ok ... nice."

As they were getting ready to leave, Sophie made a few unusual demands, which she characterized as promises: she didn't want visits or phone calls from anyone, including the two of them, for as long as she was in treatment. Irina's eyebrows shot up as she turned toward Frank. Sophie insisted, "No debate!"

They both were speechless as Sophie shared another disturbing and intractable decision. "Dr. Meizner expects me to be in treatment for several months." As Sophie coiled the belt on her robe, words jetted from her with increasing speed. "And I don't want the girls to know any of this. They would never feel the same about me if they knew I had been locked up in a psych ward. Exhaustion is more acceptable, especially with the strike. One other request, and I've given this a lot of thought. Prayed over it. Let's say a week from now, you tell them I was better, but I couldn't come home because a relative in Poznan was sick without any family and that I had to leave urgently to care for her." Irina was confused about what her daughter was asking. The demand rushed out so fast that it appeared Sophie had her own doubts about what she was insisting upon.

"Sophie, they'll ask questions and want to know why you didn't come home and tell them yourself. They need to see and hear from you."

"I'm too emotional right now. I'm not sure I can ..." Sophie crossed her arms, bent over and rested her head on her knees.

"Then, I'll have to write fictitious letters from you and pretend you've phoned them? I can't lie to them." Frank regretted saying anything when Sophie's face turned crimson.

"God damn it, Frank!" Sophie shot up and was within inches of his face. "Tell them it was an emergency ... fake it ... make up letters. They're young ... they won't remember. When I come home, we'll get back to normal."

Sophie withdrew a grainy leather Bible the size of a missal with gold lettering on the cover from the pocket of her robe and handed it to her mother instructing her to swear the girls would never know the truth. Unable to meet Sophie's gaze, Irina did so. Frank hesitated until she grabbed his hand and pressed it against the book.

As the two of them were leaving, Irina stared at Sophie as she stood in the doorway, not knowing if she would ever see or talk to her again. It didn't seem their magic thread was so magical anymore.

NINE

The next day Irina suggested that Frank take the girls out for breakfast to determine how they were doing and to get some inkling as to what they thought about the violence they witnessed.

As they were directed toward a booth, the hostess placed a steaming pot of coffee and a cup before Frank and handed the girls placemats with pictures of animals at a circus along with a pack of crayons. Standing up and bending over their largesse, they dug their fingers into the box and searched for the right colors to make the wildlife before them come alive. As Addie launched into shading her bear, her strokes were so bold, her crayon broke in half.

"Daddy! Look what I did!" she cried.

"Addie, go easy on that. Use the bigger end."

As the nutty aroma of his coffee filled his nostrils, Frank suspected that they, too, were upset that their mommy wasn't at home baking or watching TV.

"Daddy! See! My bear is purple like the grapes I love to eat!" Addie giggled.

"Wow! Aren't you clever? Any old bear is brown!"

Mary's head darted up from coloring the elephant on her placemat a dark gray and dipped her head in agreement with her daddy.

"And any old elephant is gray!" Addie snickered.

"Shut-up!" Mary threw her sister's broken crayon at her head.

"Girls!" Frank said that louder than he intended.

"We're sorry, daddy."

The sound of their crayons shading their paper animals was too loud for Frank. It seemed his edginess would not be tamed regardless of his efforts to distract himself from the purpose of his mission.

As they waited for their orders, the girls gabbed about Bozo and how funny he was and about Joanie, the neighbor girl next door, who wouldn't share any of her toys with them. As Addie babbled on and on about that, Frank fiddled with his wedding band until the waitress asked the girls to make room for their food.

When a plate with two sunny-side eggs, crispy hash browns and toast were placed before him, he sighed. When the waitress deposited strawberry pancakes, topped with mountains of whipped cream before the girls, they clapped.

It wasn't long before Addie's face was splattered with peaks of white which brought chuckles from their server. Dabbing away the froth, Mary complained that her sister ate way too fast. It would appear that this was a normal breakfast with a father and his two daughters fighting, laughing, and teasing each other. But it wasn't normal at all.

"Daddy? Aren't you going to eat?"

"Oh, sure."

"Daddy, you shouldn't play with your food!" Addie reminded him.

Dwelling on whether he should bring up what he wanted to forget, a bit of wisdom his mother repeated many times over when he was growing up came to mind. "Ignorance is bliss." How is there any bliss in not knowing how his girls were dealing with this crisis? Time to push aside the procrastination.

"When you talk to your mommy, keep it short. I want you to remember, she needs a lot of rest so she can get better." Frank was uncertain if Sophie could hold it together for long without freaking out on them.

"Do you miss Mommy?" Addie asked.

"Oh, my yes. I miss her terribly. Babcia does, too."

"Are you mad at her, Daddy?" Addie squirmed in her seat leaning over to see how fast Mary was eating her pancakes.

"Of course not. I love your mommy. Remember ... 'Family is not an important thing. It's everything.' No matter what ... family sticks together.'"

Frank chomped on a forkful of eggs grimacing as the cold yolks slid down his throat. Taking a breath, he blurted out, "So, Mary, what do you think about what happened the other night with Mommy and me?"

Resting her crayon on her chin, she reluctantly admitted, "I was scared, Daddy. But Babcia helped us. How are you?" She leaned across the table as she tried to pat a blue-green bump on one side of his face.

"These aren't as bad as you think." His daughter's touch gave him the strength of will to do what needed to be done. "You must have been scared when mommy was, uh, so angry with me."

"I was scared, too!" Addie interrupted.

"I was mixed up. I hoped you and Mommy would kiss and make-up. I was scared I wouldn't see you and Mommy again." Mary squeezed her eyelids shut. Noticing her sister's wet face, Addie began shaking as she tried to muffle her blubs with the hem of her dress.

"Girls. Of course, you were scared. Mommy was not well that night. We love you both so much. We will never leave you again." He bit his lower lip cursing himself since that's exactly what Sophie intended to do ... not leave but hide. That was the next conversation he was dreading.

Taking a clean napkin, he dried both of their faces. Their questions, considering the violence they witnessed, proved to be less worrisome than Frank expected which was a relief. Frank assured them that their mommy would get better, that he wasn't mad at her, and that she was being well taken care of. Maybe they weren't as affected by it. *Wishful thinking. But I can hope.* When Sophie's deceitful plan played before him, he swept it aside counting on his ability to convince her how dangerous it was when they next talked.

"Daddy, can we go so if the doctor lets mommy call, we'll be home? And Daddy, shouldn't we bring breakfast back for Babcia? She loves those things stuffed with fruit."

"Great idea, Mary. Addie, please take your finger out of your nose."

Addie was half-way through the door when she presented their colored animals as gifts to their babcia. Surveying the refrigerator door that was plastered with their creativity, Irina squished these latest works of art near the top so she wouldn't have to bend down.

Mary handed the carry-out bag to her babcia who thanked her profusely.

When Frank angled himself closer to Irina, she informed him that the doctor called and said that the girls would hear from Sophie at 2:00, and in the next breath asked how the morning went. Giving the barest of details, he bowed his head and squeezed her arm.

"Babcia. Your food will get cold."

"Marysia, thank you!" Irina crouched down and cuddled her. Addie pushed herself between them and blurted, "It was my idea!"

"No, it wasn't! Was it, Daddy?"

"Addie ... what have we told you about lying?"

"Well, I wanted to." Addie murmured.

"Ya. Adelajda ... you must tell truth. Marysia, you both go make-up beds."

A rosary was a constant companion to Irina and was housed in her pocket. She clasped a bead between her fingers and prayed but she suspected that the Blessed Virgin would never consider the lies she promised to tell her *wnucki* as sanctioned.

As a way to keep the girls distracted, Frank agreed to let them watch TV for longer than usual. "Girls! You can hear the phone from in there," he explained.

Addie's and Mary's dolls were propped up on their laps while they watched *Scooby-Doo*. Frank kept checking his watch hopeful they would hear from Sophie as scheduled and yet at the same time, he was worried, wondering if this was such a good idea. Too soon, perhaps?

Irina carried in a plate of *chrusciki*. "Ach. Too much powdered sugar," she complained as tiny white motes flitted in a ray of sunlight.

"When will we hear from Mommy?" Mary stopped combing Effie's hair which resembled shiny amber corkscrews sticking up and out of her head.

"After *Scooby-Doo*." Frank checked his watch for the hundredth time.

"Babcia, may I have one?" Addie was standing over the plate, holding her hand in mid-air, ready to strike as soon as she got the Ok.

Irina offered her a napkin. "You take. I make for you."

Licking the sugary coating from her mouth, Addie skipped over to her doll and kissed her.

"Ha! Look at Linda! She ..."

The jingling of the phone immobilized them.

"I'll get it," Frank leaped up.

The girls scampered behind him.

"Hell-o Sophie." Frank asked how she was doing as both girls tugged on his pants leg.

"Yes ... they're right here!" Mary placed the receiver between their ears.

"Mommy, we miss you."

"Yeah. Mommy, where are you? We want you home. Babcia and Daddy told us you're tired. You need rest. Did I make you tired?" Addie spouted.

Sophie, along with Dr. Meizner, prepared written responses she could rely on if at any time her anxiety threatened her ability to remain stable. "No, my dearest. You did not make me tired." The spaces between Sophie's words were full of uncertainty.

"And Daddy's not mad at you," Addie trumpeted into the receiver.

"I know he's not. I'm getting the rest I need. It's work, girls. Work has made me so tired."

"Mommy, come home and we'll take care of you." Mary insisted.

"I wish I could, but I need medicine, and a doctor must give it to me. You be good girls and listen to Daddy and your babcia. I love you forever and ever." A surge of adrenaline began overtaking her. *Breathe! Breathe! Slow it down.* "I know Babcia told you about the magic thread. Remember I feel your love through it in my heart. Can you feel mine?"

"Yes, Mommy. I can." Mary tried hard to remember.

"Do you love me, Mommy?" Addie's voice wobbled.

"Of course, I do! Can't you feel the magic thread?"

"Well, I don't if I can't see you, Mommy."

"Addie, ask your daddy for a picture of me. That will help. Your daddy packed one of the two of you, and it's right here on my dresser. Mary, you're standing behind Addie smiling from ear to ear. And Addie, you're staring up at her. Your tongue is sticking out between the gaping hole where you lost another front tooth. I took that last summer at Cedar Lake."

"I remember!" Mary and Addie both chimed in.

"Those beautiful drawings you made for me are taped above that picture. So, you're both with me day and night. Ask Daddy for a photo of me, Ok? I love you both with my whole heart. Is he there?" Sophie needed to escape.

"Daddy! Mommy's asking for you!"

"Thank you." He signaled for them to go watch TV.

"How did it go?" he asked uncertain if this was a good question to ask.

"I needed to cut it short. I started to ... never mind." Too much information would lead to more questions.

"We promised not to visit, Sophie, but this is tormenting your mother and me."

"This isn't about either of you. It's what I need. Do you hear me?" she snapped.

Lowering his voice and with his back to the girls, he pleaded. "Will you at least reconsider this lie about Poznan? You can't disappear for God knows how long! Think of the girls." The receiver was slippery ... wet from his sweaty hands. He knew he was treading on dangerous and unknown waters, but he felt as though he didn't have a choice.

"God damn it! Stop!" Sophie's breath became labored. "Give the girls a picture of me."

"Yes ... I will. Soph, can't you please reconsider what you're planning to do? Wouldn't it be better if the girls heard about Poznan from you?"

"Damn it, Frank, I'm not discussing this again!" Sophie spat out those words like razor blades.

"Please don't get upset. Your mother is waiting to talk to you."

Sophie hung up.

Irina stood next to Frank, holding her hand out.

"I'm sorry. But you have to realize we have no idea what she is dealing with. We have to be patient."

Although disappointed, Irina agreed and started for her room when she heard the girls quarrelling. Addie wrenched Mary's doll away from her, and threw her own doll on the floor while declaring Effie was hers now and Mary could have Linda because she was a bad girl.

"Babcia ... Addie took Effie and won't give her back to me." Mary gripped Effie's legs.

"I don't want Linda. I want Effie," Addie trilled.

And before Irina could interrupt them, the girls were relentlessly kicking one another. Frank dashed in to see what the ruckus was as Irina jerked Mary's doll away from her.

"*Zatrzymaj to teraz!*" *Stop this right now!* She made an all-out effort to soften her tone, but her words came out like a stifled sneeze. She wanted to rein in her anger and be firm yet sensitive to what prompted this outburst; however, her restrained rebuke flew over their heads. Addie continued whacking and spitting at her sister when they collided on the floor with arms and legs pretzeled over each other.

"Stop this right now!" Frank echoed Irina's command and carried Mary upstairs.

"Why do I have to go to my room? I didn't start it. Addie's mean!"

Irina steered Addie toward the sofa. "Adelajda, no fight!"

With a few red streaks on her legs, Addie yawned, snuggled next to Babcia, and within minutes, was asleep. Irina knew that hearing their mother's voice would unleash what they weren't able to put words to.

Once they apologized, the girls received permission to visit their friend next door as soon as dinner was over. "You can stay an hour, and then I'll come and get you," Frank informed them.

Frank was stooped over the sink scouring the broiler pan, trying to scrape the crusts of pork drippings from its bottom. He took charge when he heard Irina's huffing as she tackled her usual after dinner chore.

"Have another slice of *babka*, Irina, and sit down. I can do this."

Insisting he leave her be, she cursed her aging body.

"Can't I do a good deed? And I'll bet you'd rather have another brandy instead."

She was won over. "How about both?"

"More *babka* and brandy?"

"Ya. *babka* stale, so brandy make it soft for teeth." She popped her upper denture out for a minute. Dunking a slice of the dried cake into her glass, she dipped it vigorously permitting crumbs to float free and swim in the amber liquid. She scooped the intruders out with a spoon.

"Girls tired from talking to Sophie and doll fight. Ach! They make up."

"God, Irina ... what did you do to make this so hard to clean?" The next minutes were filled with the scraping of metal on metal along with Frank's grunts.

"What you think about call?"

"Better than I thought it would be."

"What you think about yesterday visit?"

"I thought her therapist with those diplomas and awards scattered on her office wall was more than qualified."

Frank wiped the pan dry and wedged it in the cabinet next to the oven.

"You did a great job on dinner tonight ... the pork tenderloin was juicy, mashed potatoes had the right amount of butter, and the sour cream and cheese-filled *pierogi* was ... well, outstanding!" Frank took hold of the bottle of brandy and poured himself a tumbler-full, straight up.

"Ya? But you didn't eat much. Try *babka*. Frank, what doctor say?" Irina rattled the ice in her glass.

Frank guzzled his fortitude and then poured another.

"Sophie suffered a psychotic break, Irina ... *przerwa psychotyczna*. It's a condition that affects the way the brain processes information and can cause a person to lose touch with reality. That's why she attacked me ... understand so far?"

"Talk Polish. Easier for me." Irina switched to her mother tongue. *"How did it happen so quickly?"*

"The doctor explained that it might have been caused by a possible trauma or a mental illness. She ruled out any physical cause, but was uncertain if or when another episode might occur. She was hopeful that therapy would be able to help her determine a more definitive diagnosis. It will take time."

"But there's no mental illness in our family, and Frank, she didn't have any problems growing up. Maybe her papa's death was too much for her. She wouldn't eat and she cried all of the time. Then when I had to go to work, she begged me to stay home. But I couldn't. I had to work. Frank, what do you remember about the times she came to your house while your mother took care of her?"

"Why would you ask that?" Frank drained his glass of brandy.

"I've been trying so hard to understand. And then I remember. Once she came home and threw her favorite doll ... the one your mother gave her ... in the trash can." A fragment of an uninvited memory—Sophie refusing to ride

her tricycle from out of nowhere. Irina's reflections detached and traveled to fragments of her mind that she was unable to grasp. Kneading the back of her neck, she added, *"I just wondered."*

"I wasn't home much, Irina."

"I failed as her mother."

"No time for self-pity. We have to focus on getting Sophie well and helping the girls through this."

"Frank? What about those promises? Not to tell the girls she is sick like she is? Forbidding us to visit her while she's there? Not to talk with her on the phone?

And the worse ... that lie about Poznan?"

"Irina, if that's what she wants then we have to respect her wishes." Those promises made no sense so he wanted to avoid any more discussions about them. What needled him was that he had to have contributed to her breakdown, so he wanted to know what he could've done. And what about the girls? Irina? How could she get better without any of their involvement?

Yesterday he phoned Dr. Meizner who agreed with him about family participation but she suggested they wait until Sophie was further along in treatment. "We don't know what we're dealing with, Mr. Gurin."

"Ach! Crazy is the same as mental illness." The effects of the brandy loosened Irina's tongue.

"Irina! Przestan! Stop!" Taking a hard swig of his drink, Frank didn't need his mother-in-law saying what he did not want to acknowledge as a possibility.

What Sophie planned to do was crazy ... yes ... crazy, and this time he meant crazy. *"It's as though the Sophie I married is dead. What happened to her?"*

TEN

For months, the depression continued to weigh her down as if there was a 50-pound barbell screwed to her back. As she began revealing fragments of her nightmares to Dr. Meizner, Sophie became increasingly fearful as to what else might be prowling in the recesses of her mind. Her detachments were becoming increasingly persistent. She couldn't control them—it was like a magnet was drawing her to another place in her brain. The reason she remained in the hospital was to rid herself of the unknown terror that had a stranglehold on her. All she longed for was to be with her girls ... to go home.

Pleading with God to take this burden from her, Sophie began to believe that she was being punished, and yet she wasn't able to pinpoint what her transgression might be. Any time she would reveal details of her splintered memories, a hardness churned in her chest. It felt as if the stone of a cherry was trying to climb up and lodge itself in her throat. Her breathing became so labored during the last group session that the nurse began transporting an oxygen cart in the unit for Sophie.

There were days she was positive these remembrances never occurred, that in fact they were hallucinations caused by the myriad pills she was taking. But as soon as she relaxed into that comforting mindset, this perspective would disintegrate in therapy when she had to verbalize what prowled in and out of that dark pit of her brain—hearing the words made it real. It could not be denied. A staff member recommended that she keep a journal, so she could write about her recollections instead of reliving the painful experiences by having to talk about them. The desperation to purge herself of the reels of images that plagued her compelled her fingers to write what she wasn't able to speak.

Group therapy was essential to her recovery and she dreaded it. The other patients would not permit her to remain silent and coerced her to participate. One of them told her, "If we have to spill our guts, you do, too." Sophie suspected their interest was driven by a perverse curiosity about her since none of them experienced her symptoms. When she was able to share a snippet of a nightmare, a few of them were speechless.

According to Dr. Meizner, she continued to hold back and stay stuck. "You have to walk through the fire to get to the other side, Sophie. I understand it's painful to share what's been dormant for so long, but if you want to heal, this is what you need to do," Dr. Meizner repeated over and over.

Minutes before group therapy was to begin, Sophie prayed to God to give her the strength to delve into her darkness. At the end of the last session, Sophie was the final patient to share any difficulties she was experiencing. Scanning the room, she lingered on the large round clock lodged between a patient bulletin board filled with assorted scraps of paper and a colorful wall calendar of Lake Michigan.

The roaring in her head was all she could hear. Unaware, her eyes bounced off the faces of the other patients who freely talked about the quagmires of their depressions, anxieties, and suicidal thoughts.

The metal chairs were scraping against the colorless tiled floor and people were coughing, shuffling their feet, when she realized they were impatiently waiting for her to say something. She willed herself to speak but scarcely a croak came out. Her shoulders started to quake and hot tears began to trickle down her cheeks.

"Take your time," Dr. Meizner said.

"Well, I have these recurring nightmares." Sophie bit the inside of her cheek. "This little girl is terrified of a sour smell that's makes her gag. She's choking." Sophie stammered. "I want to help her but, in my dream, I'm paralyzed."

"All you're talking about is a kid. Who?" Another patient asked.

"Her face is a blur. She has no mouth. She's so little. There is a shadow as if a storm cloud was hanging over her." Sophie starts to whimper.

"Maybe that little girl is you, Sophie." Dr. Meizner placed her hand on Sophie's knee.

"Probably is," another patient blurted.

"No! No! Why would you say that?" Sophie leapt up. Sucking in air as fast as her lungs would tolerate, she maneuvered herself to face the lopsided circle of women staring at her.

"No! No! It's not me!" She fled the room.

For three days, afterwards, she shrouded herself from head to toe in bedcovers, and refused to leave her room. When the nurses tried to physically remove her, she screamed obscenities and kicked savagely. Months ago, Sophie discovered that if the outside world was too difficult to live in, all she had to do was befriend an object ... clock, a picture, a door knob ... and lose herself by absorbing her complete awareness into it. Her body became a shell as she tunneled into her safe place where it was as quiet as a cemetery. On this day her descent was darker and more cavernous than the first one she experienced while she and Addie were at Field's on the hunt for a bedspread and that was the one that unlocked her long-forgotten past.

Sophie spiraled, entombed underwater, and as she glimpsed up toward the surface, she was lured to the light. Dr. Meizner was holding her, providing reassurance that no one would harm her. But Sophie's soul knew otherwise. An unknown person had already damaged her and she would never let that happen again. Those black holes, the darkness that protected her, provided a brief respite from the reminders that she endured unspeakable violence.

And now she knew. It *was* her. She needed to get out of this place and away from these people. She cursed herself for staying as long as she has.

The staff insisted Sophie remain in treatment. Dr. Meizner met with her, explaining that her resistance to continuing was an indication she was on the verge of a breakthrough in her recovery.

"Bullshit!" Her voice reverberated throughout the unit. "It's been a year. I'm getting worse. I want to go home a whole person. Instead, I'm more of a mess than before I came in here. Why did I need to remember this crap? Whenever I dredge up these memories, I can't sleep, I go into panic mode as if a switch flipped, and it feels as if I'm dying. It's not getting any better. It's killing me."

And so, she gathered her things, signed herself out Against Medical Advice, and hired a cab to the Sheridan-Chase Hotel. She and Frank had celebrated an anniversary there years ago.

Sophie paused outside the entrance to the building and peered into the lobby, surprised and grateful that it was empty. Her absence from the real world depleted her confidence in being able to deal with normal people. Overhead, a cloud shielded the sun which cast a pall over the building, adding to her despair. Doubt began to overpower her. Was she capable of putting herself back together the way she once was? Maybe she should go back. She dug her fingers into her temples wanting to rip the sharp pains from her head hoping her headache would dull itself.

"Ma'm. Are you going in or out?"

"Ah ... in."

As the revolving doors deposited her into the lobby, she whiffed the sweet smell of Bazooka bubble gum wafting from the receptionist, a girl with apple red hair. Bazooka girl popped a bubble in Sophie's face and asked her to complete a registration form while cracking her gum nonstop. Those shattering noises felt as if firecrackers were exploding in her ears. Sophie's edginess diluted her fragile confidence about leaving the hospital so her feet teetered toward the twirling entrance door as people came in and out.

"How long will you be staying?"

With her back to the desk Sophie stammered, "Ah, maybe four or five days."

After Bazooka girl recited the rate, Sophie grabbed her suitcase and started toward the exit. *Go back to the hospital! I'm not ready to be out yet.*

"Ma'am? Something the matter?" *Pop.* "How about I get some water for you?"

"Maybe that little girl is you, Sophie," echoed in her head. *I can't go back.*

"No, thank you. How much did you say it was?" She hoisted her baggage onto the counter and began shuffling through a messy pile of her things searching for her checkbook. The packet of journal pages she'd written while in treatment appeared and seemed to want her attention. Annoyed as she leafed through them, she began hunting for a trash can but after considering the contents, she decided to destroy them. Without any receptacle nearby, Sophie stuffed them back in, and continued foraging through her belongings. In doing so her bag crept closer and closer to the edge of the counter crashing to the floor. Embarrassed, she stooped down to collect her possessions and hurled them back into her bag.

"Hey. Need help?" The Bazooka girl bent over the counter, staring at the jumble of clothes on the floor.

Sophie swallowed the four-letter expletive that was about to fly into the face of that stupid receptionist.

"You sure got a mess there." *Pop!*

Kneeling and with arms crossed, Sophie restrained herself from lunging at this girl and shoving that gum down her throat. "I'm sure you have more important things to do."

"I think you were trying to find a check." *Pop!*

"I know! Here it is!"

Once in her room, she placed her luggage on the bed and hunted for the photo of her girls, trying to picture how they might have changed. No doubt they would be taller and maybe they had filled out more with their grandmother's cooking and baking. *Was Addie any feistier? And Mary, she couldn't get any kinder.*

She agonized about how their reunion would unfold and she recollected how Dr. Meizner prepared her for an "unwelcoming" welcome home, assuring her that rejection is typical when a parent has been absent even for a short period of time. Of course, it would take a while for them to warm up to her, but Sophie believed the fictitious letters and calls Frank conjured up would insure a smoother reunion. With great care, she placed their photo on the nightstand next to the digital clock along with their drawings.

Not being able to control that unknown portion of her mind was what gave her the strength to avoid all contact with them. Considering how she attacked Frank which was still a mystery to her, how could she trust what she might say or do to them? She would rather die than have Mary or Addie exposed to that damaged phantom residing within her again. *I'm the mommy who doesn't know why I tried to kill your daddy.*

She attended daily Mass in the hospital's tiny chapel and prayed to God about the pros and cons of her decision. If she let them visit her, they would ask questions, questions she had no answers for. Their visits would confirm that she was sick ... weak. And, yes, this would be hard on them, but Sophie had faith in the magic thread. At least when it came to her daughters.

Her arms shot up in a defensive posture when the buzzing of the phone startled her awake. *Breathe! No one's here.* It was Bazooka girl checking to see if her room was satisfactory.

"Yes. Please don't bother me anymore."

Sophie watched the storm-tossed waves on Lake Michigan from the filmy oversized windows in her room. She tried to visualize how she would react to her mother and Frank after so long, but all she saw was the tortured face in the painting, *The Scream*. Closing the drapes, she paced from one end of her room to the other. Then she flopped on the bed for a few minutes, and as if she sat on a hot poker, bolted up and resumed her prowling.

Who abused her? Why didn't her mother protect her? And, Frank? Why did she loathe him? He's been a loving dad and husband. Dr. Meizner suggested that her shame and guilt for battering him could be related. "It's much easier to be angry at him then face the inexplicable rage that lives within you." Those words frightened Sophie. What would happen when she did face it?

But at this moment, all she cared about was that they kept their promises. Under no circumstances were her girls ever to know the truth about her breakdown including the last eleven months.

Splashing cold water on her face, she recalled one of Irina's many stories about the natural determination of Polish people and their inner strength. Having been in a psych ward meant a quintessential failure that marked her as a flawed person, a weak person. The hours of therapy with Meizner, the groups, and the nurses, left her feeling as though her insides had been ripped out and scattered to places impossible to find. She had expected those grueling hours of treatment to do the opposite.

That shopping trip with Addie loomed before her. That's when it all began. The two of them were browsing for a new bedspread at Field's. Skipping over to her mommy, Addie hoisted up a lemony yellow quilt scattered with tiny blue cornflowers and jabbered about how much she loved it. As she lifted it to her mother's face, a patchwork of murky shadows overpowered Sophie. She fought to catch a breath. She was oozing with perspiration. The entire room began orbiting in all directions. The color yellow blinded her—it was so harsh—then it faded into black, and she was alone. An oppressive crush of terror seized her and she blacked out.

"Mommy! Mommy! Wake up! Please! I'm happy with my old bedspread!" Addie knelt down, buried her head on Sophie's chest and begged her to wake up.

As a few bystanders helped Sophie to her feet, Addie shook her mother's hand and kept kissing it. The saleslady insisted on calling an ambulance, but Sophie kept repeating in a shaky voice that she was fine. As the heat of embarrassment colored her cheeks, she and Addie hurried past the crowd that circled them.

Alarmed about this incident, Sophie replayed her morning routine, and decided that it must have been the caffeine. But then again, she'd only had one cup of coffee. Maybe it was a seizure. But that yellow color was so harsh and blinding. Maybe there was a growth affecting her vision. *What's wrong with me?*

Once in the car, Addie locked herself into her mother's arms so forcibly, Sophie couldn't drive.

"Mommy! What happened to you?"

"Addie, honey, I'm Ok. I was dizzy. Nothing for you to worry about. Here, please move over a bit. It's hard for me to drive with you so close."

"Mommy! You don't look so good. Maybe call daddy or Babcia," Addie pleaded.

"Oh no! I'm fine. How about opening your window a bit?" Sophie hated to see her so frightened, but when she tried to mollify her, Addie continued to pummel her with more questions.

"Mommy, I'm scared. Will you get dizzy again? What happens if you get dizzy now? Mommy! I'm scared. Did you hurt yourself?" Addie's incessant questioning felt as though Sophie was being cross-examined for a murder she didn't commit. "It was my fault, wasn't it? Wasn't it?"

Sophie kept an ear on Addie's blabbering, but lurking in the back of her mind was the possibility of brain cancer. No matter how she tried to calm herself, Sophie's fears thrust her into a head trip of future occurrences: doctors, chemotherapy, nurses poking at her, her family sobbing before her coffin.

Addie's shrill voice stung her eardrums like needles. "Mommy!"

"SHUT UP! Can't you ever keep your mouth shut? You drive me crazy with these questions!" Sophie slapped her. When she saw Addie's stricken face ... her puffy eyes swiveling from side to side searching for a way to escape, Sophie was horrified. *What's happening to me?*

After a series of blood tests, x-rays and multiple visits to doctors, Sophie was shocked when she was told that she was perfectly healthy with the exception of hypoglycemia. From then on, she convinced herself the episode was caused by too much coffee and low blood sugar. However, her rationalizations wore thin.

A few months after that day, the barriers of her past ruptured within her, devouring any joyfulness she ever knew or would know. Sophie began experiencing terrifying splinters of flashbacks and night terrors, blaming any number of things for their occurrences—what she ate, stress, insomnia—but they became more vivid. These fragmented mirages appeared at inappropriate times ... at home and at work, giving her no warning.

A formless darkness loomed over this faceless child. A man that stunk of cigars and grease purred how special she was to him. He covered her with a moth-eaten yellow blanket with blue flowers on it.

That awful night she heard Addie scream: "Stop!" It was as if a marauder drove her out of her own body and viciously attacked Frank.

Loud voices outside her door brought her back, back to her hotel room—to the present. These emotions were chasing one another, wrestling and fighting within her. Without any effort on her part, her legs dragged her out the door. She needed to move—it felt as though her muscles were filled with crawling insects. Sprinting through the corridor didn't free her from those terrifying emotions. Neither did jogging up and down two flights of stairs. Panting as if her lungs collapsed, she found her way back to her room and sagged onto her bed.

Digging her finger nails into her forehead, she tried to scratch the life out of these terrors, but they were so much stronger than her resolve. In desperation, she hammered her fist onto the nightstand, and as she massaged her knuckles, she caught sight of four perfect right angles of paper sticking out of her suitcase. Without hesitation, she began to read.

January 28
I dreamt of a frightened child. A man was looming over her. I can't make out who he is. Who made her do such horrible things? ... this faceless shadow. He says no one will believe her if she tells. Where is this dream coming from? Who could imagine such violence being done to a child? How could God let this happen?

February 6
I ... I don't know why I can't talk in group. I'm all by myself inside my room, and I'm afraid to let myself be heard. This pain slips through me. I see her, the innocent child in the corner without a mouth to scream. How do I pick her up and give her a voice? I'm alone.

February 25
My God! It can't be me. It couldn't have been me. I don't want it to be me. It's coming back in pieces. But now I remember ... the times I couldn't make any noise. He was hurting me. Why didn't I scream? I didn't have a voice. He said I wanted him to. Did I? I had to be quiet. I tried to stop him but that made it worse. I can't remember all of it. That's when I learned to leave my body. I found an object ... any object to fixate my attention on—the blue flowers on the blanket, a picture frame—but then I was back feeling the terror of him. I remember begging him not to do it. Or maybe it never happened.

Staring into nothingness, Sophie prayed that she had made it all up. What human being could rape and brutalize a child? Rob her of her innocence? Her anger was like bits of glass tunneling throughout her insides. *Why didn't I fight more? What's wrong with me that I let it continue. But then he told me no one would believe me.*

A day before she left, Dr. Meizner tried to convince her that children who have been sexually abused are not at fault, but Sophie would not accept that.

"Sophie, children have to blame themselves because it's a way to believe they have some control over adults who are out of control. The child thinks that if she was a 'good' girl, then this wouldn't be happening to her. Being a 'good girl' is in her control."

Whenever Dr. Meizner encouraged her to have compassion for "Sophie, the child" who was an innocent victim, Sophie would speak haltingly. "That little girl is a stranger to me. She means nothing to me." *If I let myself have feelings for her, I would disintegrate.*

The maid rapped on the door, waking Sophie from a sleep that insinuated itself into her very bones. Disoriented until she touched the plush mattress beneath her, she recalled where she was. Nothing as uncomfortable as that paper thin hospital bed.

The growling in her stomach reminded her she hadn't eaten. After ordering coffee and juice from room service, she took a long, hot shower and dressed. Wiping the steam from the mirror, Sophie was jarred at her reflection. Her shame was so great she couldn't tolerate seeing herself in a mirror the entire time she was in the hospital.

As she swept away the tendrils of wet hair sticking to her face, she pressed closer to examine the veins of silver that were beginning to obscure her natural shade. That along with the grayish half-circles beneath her eyes and the fine lines nuzzling up to her mouth made her forty-four years seem a blatant lie. How could she let her girls see her like this?

Removing the cumbersome Yellow Pages from the nightstand, she fingered the flimsy pages until she found a salon and a clothing boutique nearby.

As she was leaving to hail a cab, she was delighted that the gift shop near the elevators showcased red and gold boxes of the girls' favorite peppermint candy. What a nice surprise that will be!

After Sophie paid the cabbie, she mustered up the energy to push herself through the lobby, to the elevator, and back to her room surprised that shopping would take so much out of her. Trudging to the bathroom to get her medications, she lingered a few minutes to view her do-over.

As she tilted her head side-to-side, she grinned at her bobbed hair style and how it swayed filling the room with the clean, refreshing scent of the citrus shampoo the salon used. The auburn shade that cloaked her gray reduced her age by ten years. At least that was her opinion. Never much for makeup, at the sales lady's insistence, Sophie did purchase a beige cream foundation, mascara along with her rose colored lipstick and a pinkish rouge, all of which she hoped would be symbols of her new beginning. The salmon pink blouse and the paisley scarf, along with charcoal gray slacks, weren't too far off from her "old Sophie" style ... much more colorful though.

She laughed as she held another of her splurges—a cobalt blue pullover—against her body and was able to admire herself in the mirror without feeling ashamed, if only for a few minutes. A new person would be coming back home by the end of the week.

Room service delivered dinner: a plate of wilted lettuce, a hamburger that resembled a hockey puck, and soggy French fries none of which were that much more appetizing than what she was used to these past months. The flickering monochrome movies on TV lulled her to sleep when another of those nightmares seized her.

She sprung up, moaning. Her heart pumped with such speed, she pressed down on her chest hoping to keep it from bursting. The nightgown she wore stuck to her body as if she had been swimming in it. Her head swiveled frantically from one end of the room to the other. *Where am I?*

And then it struck her. Slamming her head against the headboard, she couldn't shake the night terror from her brain.

"Oh my God! The faceless man, the man who covered that child's face to muffle her screams. I saw him! It was Frank's father! And Frank barged in. He witnessed what was happening. That little girl ... it's me ... I AM that child." At first, those words lingered in her head waiting for her to acquiesce to the grisly truth but as her resistance continued to hammer against what she couldn't tolerate facing, her inner self—the self that kept the violence she endured from being real—began to break apart.

Feverishly searching her suitcase for a sharp object, she found nothing. *God damn it.*

The only items she found in the drawers were a Bible and a pad of hotel stationery. *Where is the pen? There should be a pen in here!*

Terrified she would be swallowed up in her pain, she desperately tried to quell the searing rage that was scorching her insides by injuring another part of her body. Taking her fingernail, she doggedly scraped her arm, leaving lines of crimson poke through her flesh. A bit of relief, but not enough. She wailed so violently that someone knocked on the door.

"Go away! Leave me alone!"

Why didn't I remember it was him before?

Dr. Meizner once cautioned her, "More memories of abuse could surface when your body and mind are ready to receive them."

How could anyone be ready to endure such suffering?

Those missing years unfolded as if she was watching a movie. That doll ... it wasn't Helen who gave it to her. It was Mr. Gurin, and he bought it as a gift for being such a good girl.

Frank ... why didn't Frank stop him or get help? Is that why he married me? Out of guilt? Pity? I think I told my mother? Why didn't she help me? And if I didn't, she should have known. Did Mrs. Gurin know what her husband was doing? Where was she? Did they all know? Why didn't they stop it? Why didn't I fight more? Why didn't I tell?

The agony of it thickened in her stomach like a clump of cold mud.

No one cared enough to protect me. I was invisible and worthless to all of them, including God.

At first, she thought she heard screaming, but it was sirens on Sheridan Road that woke her. The weight of the truth was paralyzing. She yearned to set fire to her thoughts until they became ash and before they charged recklessly down that dark and desolate passageway she was so familiar with. Before she left, Meizner insisted that by leaving, she was resisting going deeper into her trauma. Was this deep enough?

She rubbed her eyelids in circular motions to expel the reality of what happened. Her mother, Frank, and Frank's mother shielded that pedophile to protect themselves from shame and embarrassment. But what about that little girl?

Picking up her journal notes, she hesitated at first, but when her pen brushed the paper, it felt as though the lines and squiggles travelled of their own volition, revealing this latest trauma.

"... I was sure I would die the first time. The second time, I blamed myself for it. If I did what he said. Resisting made it worse. So, I lay there ... like a rag doll. I hate that person who didn't fight. I hate that person who did what he wanted. I hate the person who has no voice. I hate that person who was so afraid."

Since she had kept the curtains in her room tightly drawn Sophie wasn't sure what day or time it was. When she phoned Bazooka Girl, she was astonished to learn two days had passed since she had checked in. Straining, she raised herself up and was troubled by the sluggishness that weighed her down. Twisting her head around, she smiled when she saw her two girls splashing in a pool having a rip-roaring time that only children that age are privy to. She wanted to dive into the picture and run off with them to a place where they would be safe from the world. "I would kill anyone who hurt them."

An unanticipated vision of that night ... Addie screaming, the police, the blood ... snapped that final puzzle piece into place. A slight wave of relief washed over her ... she wasn't crazy. She was trying to help a little girl who seemed to be in distress. Something no one had done for her.

Two conflicting compulsions clashed inside of Sophie: one was urging her to open up, to breathe, to let go, to go back to the hospital while the other, the stronger of the two, goaded her to constrict, to keep squeezing those memories into oblivion, to masquerade as if that shopping trip never happened, to revert to the person she once was. This was the way to keep her family from breaking apart.

Her outside may have presented an attractive and confident person, but the inside was tormented. She leafed through a magazine. She wandered along the lakeshore. She knelt and prayed. She cursed God. Guilt prompted her to beg for His forgiveness. Her body was as taut as a piano wire.

It's time to go home and take care of my girls. Now that I know, maybe it won't haunt me anymore. I will drown my past in the cesspool it has lived in for so long, and if and when those memories surface, I will beat them down again and again.

ELEVEN

During Sophie's hospitalization, Frank phoned Dr. Meizner weekly to see how she was progressing, and he received the same answer: due to Sophie's refusal to sign a release, the doctor was unable to disclose any information. However, Frank insisted that Sophie be told about his calls and how much the family loved and missed her.

Frank despised being so deceptive with Mary and Addie, but he had promised. How could he refuse Sophie? What would happen when she came back home? Meizner didn't approve of the secrets either, but Sophie was adamant. So, he continued to lie and tell the girls that their mommy had called and wanted to know everything about them. Mary was curious as to why she did that while they were in school. More lies. Frank would fabricate letters from Sophie and in response, the girls gave him notes and drawings to mail back. He stashed these fictitious messages in a lockbox which he concealed at his office.

Addie was now in second grade and Mary, fourth, busy with homework, friends, and choir practice. They both volunteered to help the nuns after school with sweeping and dusting classrooms, and once in a while, they would collect the hymnals in church while their grandmother replaced burned out candles in the red votive holders.

The longer Sophie was absent, the less the girls would ask about her. Addie's closest friend, Mags, came over to play and wondered where Addie's mommy was. Irina overheard her explain that her mommy was across the ocean helping an aunt who was sick. After Mags left, Addie wandered up to her grandmother and watched her sift flour.

"Babcia, is Mommy ever coming back home?"

"Ya. She be back. She love and miss you."

"Will that aunt mommy's taking care of come back with her?"

"That Mags nice girl."

Many nights found Irina and Frank wrestling about those promises, but they came to the same conclusion: at least Sophie was in a safe place and getting treatment.

While Irina was peeling potatoes for dinner, out of nowhere, the phone rang.

"*O Jesza! O Jesza*! Sophie! Is that you? How are you? When you come home?"

"Yes, it's me. I'm coming home tomorrow in the late afternoon."

"Tomorrow? Ya? *O Jesza*! The girls be so happy. Frank, too! Dinner? We have dinner, no? Good to have family dinner together."

"No. I need to spend time reconnecting with my girls—the three of us. You can eat without me."

"No dinner with family? Sophie! How come no?"

"Mother, please. No dinner, at least not tomorrow."

Ever since Sophie left, Irina's imagination created various homecoming scenes. The recurrent one was where the family occupied their usual places at the dining room table as she would proudly march in carrying steaming platters of Sophie's favorite foods: a juicy pork loin, *pierogi* stuffed with mushrooms, homemade applesauce, green beans with almonds, and champagne! The girls would be giggling, and Frank would kiss Sophie. The house would be filled with the life of a whole family once again.

"I make dinner to celebrate. Can you give time?"

"Forget dinner, Mother. I should be there at about seven thirty or so. Ah, the girls believe I've been in Poznan these months, right? And you kept your word on our secret about my ... ah, illness?"

"Ya, Sophie. I never break promise. Frank, too."

"I have to go. I'll see you tomorrow."

Irina made her way to the living room and puzzled over that call. *Was that Sophie? Was that her? She is supposed to be better, more the way she was. I could tell she was annoyed with me. Why? What good did that hospital do? All those months, and what?*

Frank was frightened when he found Irina slouched on the sofa, clasping her rosary.

"Are the girls Ok?"

She blubbered and nodded.

"Is it Sophie?"

It took a few minutes for Irina to gather herself. "Ya. She call while ago. She home tomorrow."

"What? I can't believe her psychiatrist wouldn't have let us know." His irritation about Sophie's refusal to allow any staff communication with him resurfaced with a vengeance. In contradiction to his usual self-control, he wanted to throw something, anything.

"You think she be happy, no? This not same Sophie."

"Irina," he talked slowly hoping to calm himself. "We have to adjust to this. Keep in mind that after she left, we needed to fill her place in the family. Now we have to make room and let her fit back in at her own comfort level. She won't be the same Sophie considering the months of intense therapy she's had."

"I don't get this terapy. What it do?"

"Well, it's a way to get to the bottom of her breakdown, so it doesn't happen again."

"I scared, Frank. How I act? What we talk about?"

"I don't know, Irina. I just don't know."

TWELVE

When Frank announced that their mommy was coming home, Addie and Mary both stopped doing their homework, eyed one another, then glanced up at him for a few moments.

"No! I don't want to see her, Daddy." Addie trembled. "Don't make us."

Mary put her hands up to her face.

Frank suspected they would have to warm up to Sophie and reacquaint themselves with her, but this reaction never entered his mind. A day didn't go by that he or Irina didn't talk about their mother, how she loved and missed them.

"What? She is so excited to see you guys. What's going on?"

"We love you, Daddy, and Babcia, too. Don't be mad," Mary pleaded.

"I'm not mad. Can you please try and be happy to see her?"

"Can we build a snowman?"

He didn't realize a layer of snow carpeted the ground. The three of them changed into their winter coats, boots, hats, and gloves and hustled outside in the biting cold, and not another word was spoken about their mother. Frank could understand that they needed time, but this would be a blow to Sophie.

Irina and Frank were pacing back and forth, anticipating Sophie's arrival when they heard a jangle of keys. Sophie strode through the door.

Frank declared how happy he was that she was home. His voice was a blend of anger tempered with sincerity.

"Sophie! Sophie! I miss you so!" As Irina reached for her, Sophie motioned for her to stop.

She scanned the living room. "Where are my girls?"

"Sophie, you are absolutely beautiful," Frank smiled.

"Mary! Addie! It's Mommy! I'm home!" she shouted as she tore through the house.

Following closely behind her, Frank warned, "Soph. They're in their room. Don't expect too much. This is an adjustment for them."

"I know!" she snapped as she inhaled a lungful of air. "My therapist prepared me for their reaction. I can deal with it."

As she ascended the stairs, the weight of her footsteps became lighter and her pace slower. The hall was dark, and she tripped on a toy, letting out a yelp. Doubtless the girls would surprise her and jump out any minute now. Nothing.

She opened the door to an empty room but then heard a barrage of blubbers gushing from underneath Addie's bed. Squatting down, she raised the lacey bed skirt to see both of them clinging to each other as if they were on a sinking ship.

"Girls. It's Mommy. I'm home. I brought you those peppermint bars you love!" This time she wedged herself under the frame.

"Go away!" yelled Addie. "Go away! But leave the candy."

"Please come out." Bits and pieces of Dr. Meizner's advice repeated themselves. *Sophie, they will be upset with you. This is normal when a mother has been absent for a period of time.* What amount of time? Biting down hard on the truth of this moment, Sophie started toward the door.

Mary wrenched herself out of Addie's chokehold, mopped her tears with the palm of her hand, and paused a distance from Sophie. Wearing a creamy pink ruffled dress that had a few dust balls clinging to the hem, Mary straightened her shoulders, and interlaced her fingers while her attention remained focused on her mother. In the midst of Addie's earsplitting screams begging her sister to come back, Sophie stepped toward her oldest daughter wanting to feel her skin, smell her hair, but Mary backed away. Without relenting, Addie began kicking the box springs.

"I missed you. So did Addie, but she's mad right now. Don't worry, Mommy. I'm happy you're home." Mary shouted so she could be heard above the din of her sister's rants. "I'm sure Aunt Catherine must have really needed you. Is she Ok now?"

Sophie nodded but diverted her gaze a little too quickly. "Mary. I love you. I'm sorry. Forgive me. But I had to leave ... I had to."

"Mommy, what's wrong? You're shaking."

The bed creaked as Sophie gave way to her trembling legs. "I'm Ok my love. Will you come here and let me hold you?"

Wavering for a few minutes, Mary rushed to her mother where the two of them swayed in tandem while Sophie hummed *Katki Dwa, Two Kittens,* a Polish lullaby she would sing to her girls when they were babies. Mary peeked up at Sophie, scrutinizing her face while touching her skin.

Feeling Mary's body against her own made Sophie yearn for the times she'd missed touching her, kissing her. The penance the chaplain dispensed at her weekly confessions assuaged her guilt for a few hours, but whenever the burden of her decisions troubled her beyond that respite, the only other way to appease her conscience was to convince herself that these were sanctioned lies.

In between her wailing, Addie kept shrieking. "Go away! I wish you were dead!"

In the homecoming scenes she entertained over the past months, Sophie was dazed by Addie's reaction. If her daughter knew how many times Sophie had come close to what she wished for: the events of the past year had filled her with an overwhelming desire to harm herself. If she had stopped him. If her fear hadn't prevented her from telling someone.

One of Mary's shoes lying near the dresser offered a way out: fixating on the silver buckle, she began slipping into the darkness. Voices were garbling above her and vibrated as though they were underwater.

"Addie! Come out from under there and be quiet!" Mary pleaded. "I think Mommy's sick."

Addie wriggled out from her hiding place and wiped a clump of snot from her chin, dangling Linda by the neck. Wearing her Bullwinkle pajamas, Addie closely examined her mother and scrunched up her nose so tightly that her dimples disappeared. When her mouth dropped open, she sucked in as much air as she could getting ready to scream, when Mary tossed a peppermint bar at her and demanded she shut up.

Sophie prayed to be fully alive to herself and to her girls. The sharp scent of that peppermint clung to her nostrils and nudged her back to the present.

"What's wrong with you?" Addie asked chewing her candy.

"Addie, Mommy's tired. Let's help her go to bed."

Sophie tried to speak, but nothing came out. Her tongue was thick and rigid.

"No! I hate her!" Addie blabbered and crawled back under the bed.

Sophie began sinking back again at the same time Mary touched her face.

"Mommy, I'll help you. You must be tired."

Fighting hard to focus on her daughter, Sophie uttered, "You are my anchor, Mary." And at that moment, Sophie knew her oldest daughter would never hurt her, ever. A crushing pain in the back of her head, roused her enough to ask Mary if she could tuck her in for the night.

"No, Mommy. I'll take care of Addie."

Her sister settled down to sniffling from her hiding place.

"Would you want me to sleep with you tonight?" Sophie patted her head.

The waif beneath them threatened to run away if she did.

"Maybe another night this week," Mary's voice was as soft as a hummingbird's wings.

Before she closed the door to their room, Sophie paused. Mary was standing there, arms flattened stiffly against her sides, like a wooden soldier and Addie, wailing and thrashing about as if she had been doused with a pot cold water.

Mary and Addie, I hope you can forgive me.

Frank was waiting for her in the living room smoking his pipe, a habit when he was tense. "Your suitcase is in our room."

With stooped shoulders and bleary eyes, she ignored Frank and stepped around him.

"How are you doing, Sophie?" Having overheard the heated exchanges, the kicking, and the bawling, Frank had an impulse to run interference with the girls but then his better judgment restrained him. How would Sophie react to that? Would it upset her? Would she lose control of herself? She was now facing the consequences of her decision to leave them. And for what? He endured many sleepless nights trying to understand how any mother could do that.

"Sophie ..."

As though he were non-existent, she remained silent and isolated herself in their bedroom.

"Sophie! Did you hear me?" Without tamping his pipe down, he tossed it into the ashtray and strode toward the closed door. He hesitated as he tried to calm himself down.

Sophie was facing the window, unbuttoning her blouse and glaring at the darkening sky.

"So, you decide to come back without any discussion? Do you have any idea how your absence has affected us? The empty hole you left behind? I don't know what you're dealing with or why you came home, but I can't live with a zombie. Soph, I will help you, whatever it takes, but you have to let me in, you have to." When he searched her eyes, Frank realized he could see right through them. "Oh my God, Sophie? What has happened to you?"

His arms caressed a stiff, nonresponsive wife. *Why did you come home if you're not any better? Why?*

The next day, Frank peeked into the bedroom carrying a cup of coffee along with a slice of *babka* resting on a plate. Greeting Sophie with a cheerful "Good morning," he apologized for losing his temper the night before. Sophie didn't acknowledge his regret and with her head obscured by a pillow muttered that she wasn't hungry and mumbled a perfunctory thank you.

"Are you home for good?"

"Yes."

"Soph, it's important you tell me what you went through these past eleven months. Won't you please let me in? I love you. We've both changed, and if you shut me out, we'll become complete strangers. Our marriage won't have a chance. The girls have been through so much disruption."

Completely absorbed in her own emotional suffering, Sophie didn't consider how she would deal with Frank once she came home. How long would he tolerate her covert anger and resentments? They rested beneath the surface—formidable and biting. Growing up without a father had left a hole within her, and although she despised Frank for knowing about the abuse, he was a kind and loving dad.

"I discharged myself from the hospital against staff advice, but I'm much better and don't see how staying any longer would have helped me." Sophie hiked up her covers, closer to her face. "Any more time there would have been damaging. And right now, I need to be a mother to my girls."

"What? They weren't ready to discharge you? Soph, are you sure leaving was a good idea? You will continue to see your psychiatrist at least?"

"No."

"Can I please talk to Dr. Meizner—"

"No!" *This will be hard. I have to settle myself.*

In a breathy voice, she said, "Trust me. The hospital helped me as much as it could, Frank. Now, please, tell me all about the girls—school, friends, any hobbies?"

With slouched shoulders, he opened the blinds to see that the rain had slowed to a gentle drizzle as dark clouds scudded across the sky. His voice was brittle as he detailed their motherless days—each word strung together with a blend of grief and resentment.

"They asked about you constantly." A sanctioned lie.

"What else?" Sophie stood.

They both knew that it was the big lie she was referring to, the one that resulted in sleepless nights and many acts of contrition before God.

"As far as the story about Poznan goes, I typed letters from you to the girls, and they answered." How could he tell her that as the months passed, their enthusiasm to write back waned significantly? "I kept them simple. I have them in a lockbox at my office. Do you want me to bring them home?"

"Yes." A flicker of fear stopped her from asking how the girls reacted to that fabrication.

"I'll be as patient as possible, Sophie, but I'm about at the end of my rope." Frank left the room.

A slow but steady throbbing snaked across her skull. Reading those letters would split open the anguish of having left them, but she would read all of them.

Sophie slid back down under the covers. In order to preserve her family, she needed to sacrifice herself, at least until the girls were grown and on their own. She couldn't let the rage and bitterness that scorched her soul corrode the security that only a family can provide Addie and Mary at their tender ages. She realized her memories could not be crushed, but she would do whatever it took to cram them back into their original lair.

What else might be lurking in that dark cache of memories? She'd have to create more secrets to keep the other ones safe. How in God's name did she get here? In this hell?

Any time Sophie slept more than her usual 8 hours, her depression demanded more. She lifted herself up with a low moan and dumped the contents of her suitcase on the bed. When she noticed her folder, she rammed it a drawer. After showering and dressing, she switched on the radio and lip-synced *Que Sera Sera*! with Doris Day, which boosted her spirits a tad until that folder transported her back to her less desirable feelings. Gathering up her trauma from the drawer, she leafed through the pages, surprised that she had so many entries.

Sophie didn't want this journal of horrors to belong to her, but then again, she would never want another woman to experience such suffering. Maybe after the girls are gone, she might consider resuming therapy. No matter how horrific, these were significant periods of her life that explained her erratic moods and outbursts ... that she wasn't a crazy lunatic. Would she trick herself into forgetting she was the innocent victim?

Sneaking into the kitchen, she retrieved a roll of adhesive tape and made her way back to her room without being seen. She secured several strips over the flap of the envelope and as she scribbled *Sophie Gurin, 1965 to1966—Confidential and Personal*—on the front, she began rummaging through her drawers, under the bed, all over for the safest hiding place and came across the perfect one.

"That little girl will have to be invisible to me if I'm to survive," she declared as she stowed her secrets between Frank's bureau and the wall.

Satisfied with herself for locating a refuge for her notes, Sophie breezed into the kitchen and was startled to see Irina sitting stock still, gazing at the half-eaten *babka* smeared with peaches before her.

"How about breakfast? I make eggs ... I have *babka*—"

"I'll have more coffee. Sit. I'll get it." *What to say? Mother, did you know about ... no! I have to pretend. None of it ever happened. We are a normal family. It's up to me to make it so.*

Staring at a spray of crumbs on the table, Sophie thrummed her fingers on the rim of her cup. "Sophie? You mad at me? I love you. What I do wrong?" Irina begged in a shaky voice.

Let it go ... I have to let it go ... Sophie reminded herself. *Pretend ... pretend.*

"No, I'm not mad at you. Please be patient with me. Will you be fixing dinner tonight?" That request was a surefire way to keep her mother happy and distracted.

"Ya. You missed good food last night."

"I'm sure I did." Sophie drained her coffee cup.

"Sophie, we ever go back to way we were? My heart tell me I do wrong to you. Maybe when your papa died, and I had to work ... leave you ... or maybe something else. I so sorry."

"Please, Mother! There's nothing," Sophie sneered, but then immediately softened her tone as if she was in the confessional divulging her sins. "Truly, nothing."

"Well, can you tell about hospital ... what you do ... did it help?"

"Yes. It did. I'm home now, Mother. All I want to do is live my life—be a mother to my girls."

Toying with whether to stay or leave, Sophie resorted to diving into the area of her life the two of them could easily interact about. Other than Addie and Mary, Sophie's career was free from any emotional triggers.

Her rise from secondary school teacher to assistant superintendent was alacritous and a source of great pride for Irina, who didn't complete sixth grade. Without her mother's sacrifices, Sophie would have never thought to compete for a high-level administrative position. Scanning the wrinkles embedded into her mother's face, Sophie was taken aback by how much she had aged.

"May I get you more coffee?" For a brief moment, Sophie wished she could erase the past year and wrap her arms around her mother until that little girl hiding in a closet poked at her.

"No, no more." Irina nibbled on the last of her *babka*.

God, how she hated this. She needed to overcome this barrier of resentments to want to be in the same room as this woman. Where was she while Mr. Gurin was raping her? A mother is supposed to be tuned into her children. Certainly, a mother would have sensed if her child was being abused. If her own mother had, she wouldn't be suffering so.

"When you go back to work?"

When her family doctor questioned her sudden departure from the hospital, Sophie convinced him that the last three months of her medical leave would be more beneficial if she were to spend it at home.

She debated whether or not that was a good idea, since those memories would have too much freedom to roam about. Making up for lost time with her girls was her priority; so, she would have to figure out how to tame her mind's willful nature. Besides, at this point, her job was the least of her concerns.

"Not until August. What time will the girls be home from school?"

THIRTEEN

About a week after returning home, Sophie was finishing up breakfast when Addie, with egg yolk streaming down her chin, blurted, "Mommy, do you love me?"

Disbelieving what she heard, Sophie said a silent prayer of gratitude to the Blessed Virgin. "How about a hug?" Since this was the first overture her youngest daughter had made, Sophie's enthusiasm was excessive even to her own ears.

Addie held out her arm stiff as a board to keep her mommy at bay.

Sophie inhaled sharply.

"Yes, Addie. I love you with my whole heart. And I'm sorry I was gone for such a long time."

"Why did you try and hurt Daddy?"

It took Sophie a minute to breathe at all.

"Addie, I believed someone was hurting you. I couldn't see it was your daddy. It was dark, and I became terribly frightened for your safety." Sophie's stomach swooped from fear to despair. This was the moment Dr. Meizner's advice rumbled in her head. *Answer the questions asked. Nothing more, nothing less.*

"Do I make you crazy?"

You sure do. An interesting question from her.

"Of course not." *A mini-sanctioned lie,* Sophie concluded.

Addie began kicking a leg of the table. "What was wrong with Aunt Catherine? Why did it take so long for you to come home?"

Those letters Frank saved had rescued her several times before in answering their questions. "Don't you remember? I wrote you that her heart wasn't working the way it should. She needed to have surgery." How she detested these lies, but the images of what she did ... of having pleasurable feelings with Frank's father, devoured her guilt. Sophie hoped that would appease her daughter's curiosity but then Addie threw a grenade.

"Why was Aunt Catherine more important than me and Mary?"

"Ah ... well, of course you're both important ..." Her possible excuses were ricocheting at every crossroad of her brain. Fidgeting with her coffee cup, Sophie tipped it over.

Mary sprang to her feet and hurried over to her mother, embracing her. "Mommy knew Babcia would take good care of us—as good as she would have. Jesus says we have to help others who are in trouble. Aunt Catherine didn't have anyone else to help her, Addie. Right, Mommy?"

A sticky wetness from under her arms discolored her blouse. "Yes, that's right."

Addie sat there, resting her chin in her chubby hands. Sophie could see from her crumpled brow that she was mulling this over.

After a few minutes, she proclaimed, "Mommy, I can let you hug me now."

It didn't take long for Sophie to get the family into a routine because she understood how important that would be in creating stability as well as re-establishing family relationships, particularly with the girls.

Irina would attend Mass and then afterwards, polish chalices to a sparkle, straighten the priest's vestments preventing any unnecessary creases, and whatever else the Ladies Altar Society required of her. Frank would leave for work at eight-thirty and be home for dinner at five-thirty. Sophie would prepare breakfast for the girls ... either pancakes without syrup or poached eggs with toast ... after which she would drop them off at school.

For most of the day, Sophie did what she could to stave off the sinfulness that vibrated in her gut: jogging, laundering, reading, and running errands. Three o'clock, when the girls came barreling through the door, never came fast enough.

Trying to replicate their lives before she left, Sophie would ask about school as the girls gobbled their afternoon snack, check to see about homework, and find out if they needed any help. Depending on the day, the three of them would play "Pick Up Sticks," "Fish," or "War." Linda and Effie were low priority ever since Sophie came back.

Mary stayed pretty close to her mother and, on weekends, was her assistant baker and vegetable peeler at dinner time.

Once Addie decided to come out from under her bed, and after she granted permission for that hug, there were times she wouldn't speak to her mother—would ignore her presence or refuse to play with Mary and her. These actions ripped into Sophie's greatest vulnerability – being invisible.

Frank suggested she be patient with Addie, which resulted in a snarky response from Sophie. If she and Frank spent too much time together, her ability to "pretend" wore thin.

On occasion, Sophie was able to step into her former self and behave as Frank and Irina expected, but on other days, it was impossible. Often, those were the times she was drawn into her safe place. Early on, Sophie's detachments were met with various reactions from the family—giving her water, gently shaking her, or asking if she needed anything until her blank face became like the proverbial "elephant in the room." In an inexplicable way, Sophie was relieved that her family, at least for now, tried their hardest to live around her secret. It was one way they could have some connection, no matter how tenuous.

PART II

*Some Fifteen Years After
Sophie's Return Home*

Chicago
1981

FOURTEEN

It happened so quickly, and all because Irina went overboard with her brandy.

Since it wasn't often she had her granddaughters to herself, Irina was overjoyed when Addie surprised her with a visit before heading back to her apartment as she and Mary were chopping and dicing lettuce, cucumbers and tomatoes. Addie began juggling a large head of ruby red cabbage with two brownish potatoes until her grandmother plucked the vegetables from the air.

"*Przestań! Stop!*" You squash them." Irina hollered.

"Then I'll set the table." Addie blew her grandmother a kiss.

The three of them jabbered about *Titantic,* an old movie they'd watched a few days before, as Babcia poured them a swig of her favorite physic.

"Gosh, weren't Barbara Stanwyck and Clifton Webb great? I can't imagine what it would have felt like to be on a sinking ship." Mary sliced the rye bread while her babcia took a bite out of a piece, loosening her denture.

"Ya, I remember big news. When me and Jaja come here, I scare we sink with weather." Irina dropped the sliced cucumbers into the sour cream, sprinkling them with sprigs of dill. "I so happy three of us cook."

As they rattled on about the end of the film, Sophie barged in, sporting red blots on her neck. Irina braced herself to face Sophie's wrath for being excluded whenever her daughters were involved with their grandmother.

With hands cocked on her hips, Sophie scowled at her mother and asked if she could join the party she hadn't been invited to.

"Oh, Mother, don't blame Babcia," Mary grunted.

"Stop. Your grandmother can do no wrong! Having dinner as a family is important to me. Your grandmother is well aware of this. This is my house, and she needs to honor my wishes."

These past years, Irina lived on a precipice of grief, teetering back and forth between mourning the relationship she once had with her daughter or grieving over what took its place.

She was never able to land anywhere, stuck in a perpetual cycle of misery. Once in a while, she saw traces of the old Sophie but at as soon as Irina relaxed into that space, she was reminded that version of her daughter was dead.

Tired of pretending all these years and disgusted with herself for lying, Irina guzzled her tumbler of brandy.

"Sophie, why you so mad? You not nice to me or Frank or Adelajda. We love you." After she poured herself more brandy, Irina slammed the bottle down. "Sophie, why you go *zwariowany* with Frank? I forever want to know. Oh no! I not to say nothing!" Irina narrowed her eyes into slits. "Why you hate him? He good husband. Why you hate me? I good matka. Why such secrets we must keep? Doctor say you break in here." Irina points to her head. "You there long time. Why so long? We Polish people are fighters ... why you not fight? I have hard times, but I not give up. I fight!"

"You will pay for this!" Sophie retreated to her bedroom, and as she slammed the door shut a picture on a nearby wall crashed to the floor.

"Babcia ... Mother didn't stay in the hospital ... she was there a few days before she left for Poznan," Mary corrected her grandmother.

"And what break?" Addie repeated her grandmother's gesture. "She suffered from exhaustion, didn't she? At least that's what you and dad told us."

"Ya ... I should stop my *usta!* My mouth. My brandy give me trouble."

When Addie demanded more answers from her grandmother the next day, Irina confessed it was her medicine that jumbled her mind, that whatever she said was drunk talk.

More determined than ever, Addie and a reluctant Mary confronted their dad about what they heard as soon as he arrived home from his business trip.

"Dad, how long was mother in the hospital?"

"That's an odd question after all this time. Why?"

"Don't answer a question with a question," Addie blurted. "C'mon, dad. How long?"

"According to Babcia, she had a kind of breakdown. Your version about exhaustion doesn't quite jive with hers," Mary interjected.

"And what's this thing about keeping secrets? What secrets?" Addie demanded.

"Girls! Girls! Please give me a minute here." Frank flung open the liquor cabinet, filled his glass with ice and poured Irina's brandy to the tip of the highest cube.

"I have a question for you. And, yes, Addie, I'm answering with a question." He sipped his drink. "Had your grandmother been into the booze when this came up?"

"Well, yes ... but ..."

"I suspected that. She's old. When people get older, they can't consume as much alcohol as they once did. She gets mixed up." He guzzled the rest of his drink, and rinsed his glass out.

"Dad ...what are you hiding?"

"Girls. I'm not repeating myself."

"Wait! All these years Mary and I've been stuck living with a story that we thought explained that terrifying night. You know the one that's been dumped into that abyss of forgotten family disasters. Thanks to Babica, drunk or not, we were able to get dribs and drabs of the truth and it had to be the truth because she pissed off Sophie to no end."

"Watch the language, please. I'm exhausted. It's been a long week. Good night."

Addie and Mary were in disbelief.

Reminding her sister of another of Babcia's tidbits of Polish wisdom—*Curiosity is the first step to hell*—Mary encouraged her to let it go.

"What does it matter? I'm going to hell anyway."

Irina's sudden exile to an "old people's home" a few weeks later was not received well by any family member, but she reassured them it was better this way.

"Please no forget me."

FIFTEEN

Some Months Later

The digital clock on Mary's nightstand warned her that if she didn't get moving, she'd have to deal with an unhappy mother. Dragging herself out of bed, she dressed in her usual Saturday attire: jeans, a light reddish cardigan, and gym shoes. She twisted her shoulder-length, nut brown tresses into a bun at the nape of her neck. When her mother informed her that they would have to meet at the café since she had errands to run, Mary was relieved. She could listen to the radio without criticism about her choice of music. *What's not to like about Blondie?*

These weekly Saturday lunches with her mother passed like a movie on a continuous loop—the same monotony, the same conversation about Mary's dating prospects with the only variation being the weather. Rain, snow, temps below 60 degrees or above 85 brought them inside the restaurant to "their" table which displayed a reserved sign warding off any potential intruders.

Parking close to the café was difficult, so Mary was delighted when a car whipped out of a spot right in front. She could make a quick getaway if things became too tense. Lime green striped umbrellas shading round tables adorned with roses in multi-colored bud vases dotted the oblong patio. Orange porcelain containers of budding geraniums, ivy, and asparagus ferns were situated in various corners ... announcing that spring was on its way.

Lee, their regular server, waved as soon as she saw Mary. As she started toward the table, her feet felt as though they were trudging through quicksand, but Mary bullied herself to keep moving and ordered her usual beverage, sweet tea.

Do other daughters cringe at the thought of spending time with their mothers? It wasn't that she didn't love her mother. Of course she did. *Do other daughters walk on eggshells to avoid upsetting their mothers?*

"Mary! Mary!" Sophie signaled to get her attention.

Mary's hand wagged with more enthusiasm than she possessed. When she jutted her face out so her mother could kiss her on both cheeks, Sophie tossed a few shopping bags on the ground and breathlessly plopped next to her daughter.

"Look at us!" Sophie gloated. "People will think we're twins!"

Mary bit the inside of her cheek. It was uncanny how her mother often chose similar outfits to her own but today, she mirrored Mary's hairstyle as well, only Sophie's bun was slicked back tighter as if she were punishing her face—not a single fly-away strand.

"How are you doing, Sophie?" Lee's voice lilted as she placed silverware in rolled up white linen napkins in front of them. "We have a few specials today—"

Mary's mother interrupted her. "Oh, we're good with our usual, aren't we, Mary? She'll have the Greek salad with extra olives and feta, and I'll have your famous Reuben."

Sophie rattled on about her morning in detail, gossiping about Mrs. Wingate, a neighbor she had bumped into. Mary yawned.

"Mary! Please! Cover your mouth." Without missing a breath, Sophie kept on prattling.

What about my morning? Are you at all interested in me? These musings were never verbalized since Mary was designated as the daughter who listened, the pillar.

"Weatherman might be right this time." Lee pronounced as she squinted up at the darkening sky. "Here you go, girls." Placing their orders before them, she said, "I'll stop by in a few and check on you guys."

"Sit up straight, Mary. I worry about you. You remind me of me when I was your age. I can tell you're not dating. Just because I was older when I married your father, doesn't mean you should follow my example," Sophie complained while picking at Mary's salad, stockpiling the olives on her own plate. "Thank God you didn't get my sweaty hands."

Mary would try to convince herself she was perfectly happy being single until another voice in her head blared ... *liar*. Her greatest problem was her mother who never approved of any man she brought home. After a while, she gave up playing the *Dating Game* where her mother was the judge.

As far as her love life went, Mary knew that providing her mother with grandchildren was the hidden agenda. *What bothers you is not having control over that part of my life. I know mother, your happiness is all that matters.* Straightening up and fixating on her mother's moving lips, Mary pushed her plate aside. "Mother, I'm only twenty-four—"

"What about that nice fellow you work with? I've seen him flirting with you whenever I stop by. He must have asked you on a date by now. Why aren't you eating?" Sophie squirted lemon into her tea.

Scanning the patio, taking in the activity, Mary pondered how the other diners would react if she stabbed her mother in her left eye with the fork closest to her plate. Her fantasy spawned an image of her twisting that fork several times before she could pop her mother's eyeball fully out. She pictured people cupping their hands over their open mouths, as her mother screamed and clutched at her empty socket. And there sat Mary with a smirk as she studied the punctured gray sphere that oozed a clear jelly-like substance sliding down the weapon ever so sluggishly. She saw herself plucking out the iris and placing it right on top of the pile of olives on her mother's overloaded plate. The pupil would stare emptily at her. The pierced remains would be deflated and squashed next to the robust kalamata olives.

"Mary? I'm speaking to you, dear." Sophie speared an olive with a toothpick. "Such a nice young man, that teacher, do you flirt with him? How else will he know you're available?"

Much to her dismay, her mother's shrill voice interrupted her momentary glimmer of pleasure. Twirling her fork, she decided to twist Sophie's chain in real time. "Uh-uh. He would've never fit in with our bizarre family."

That comment ended any veneer of niceties between them.

"Mary!" Her mother bristled, spilling her glass of tea. The people in the surrounding area registered their disapproval for the noisy interruption. Mary enjoyed a perverse sense of satisfaction as a flush bloomed on her mother's face. Sophie rifled through her purse, as Lee began to clean-up, during which time, she remained impassive until the table was spotless.

"Mary! You have been spending too much time with your sister!"

Playing with the unused fork, Mary smirked. "Addie is the only normal one among us."

"Mary! What is wrong with you today?"

It didn't take long, as Mary knew it wouldn't. Her few minutes of amusement were followed by crushing feelings of guilt, feelings she had worn like a heavy, wool overcoat ever since she could remember.

"I'm sorry, Mother. Babcia's motto is etched on my psyche. 'Family is not an important thing. It's *ev-er-y-thing*." Mary hammered out the syllables as if her mother was hearing it for the first time. "*Rodzina nie jest czymś ważnym. Jest wszystkim.*" The explosions of raucous sounds driveling from Mary made Sophie wince. Her babcia joked she and Addie "murdered" the language any time they attempted to speak a phrase or two of it.

Interesting, she mulled over. *If family was ev-er-y-thing, why is my grandmother living in a nursing home where she doesn't belong? And then there's my dad. Why does he spend his non-working time in the basement? And last but not least, there's Addie.*

Focusing her attention onto the speckled patio tiles, she took a breath. "But we are kind of peculiar, don't you think?"

"Stop!" Sophie hissed. Mary could see the muscles in her mother's face tighten so that her usual lines and wrinkles disappeared momentarily. "There is no room for criticism or name calling in our family. This is not the Mary I love."

There may not be room in your family, but that isn't the case in mine.

Mary sucked in air through her teeth. "I'm truly sorry." As she extended her hand toward her mother's, Sophie yanked hers aside before their fingers could touch. Removing a clip-on earring, she massaged her puffy earlobe while manipulating her half-eaten sandwich without a word. Mary's rebellion, as usual, was defeated by her mother's aloofness.

Mary set the fork down.

Whenever Sophie was displeased with her daughters, she would withdraw into what they referred to as her "frigid zone" and remain silent, as if her voice went on strike. This passive-aggressive reaction started at the time Mary and Addie began to have minds of their own. The angrier Sophie was, the more hostile her nonverbals were: slamming doors, getting up and leaving the room, and throwing things, which were more times than not Addie's books, shoes, or clothes.

Sophie's weird withdrawals could last anywhere from ten minutes to several days. Their length depended on who the offender was. When they were in high school, Addie screamed that she hated Sophie and this entire "fucked up" family. Mary begged her sister to apologize for weeks to no avail, until she bribed her with ten dollars. Then all was back to normal or what was normal in the Gurin household.

Addie timed her mother's non-verbal stints if she was the offending family member. On a sleepless night, Addie devised a scheme in which the two of them would keep a daily diary recording who and what would set Sophie off, and how long it took their mother to return to normal if she wasn't coaxed out of her funk. The longest withdrawal was five days and, of course, Addie was the perpetrator. But when Sophie tossed out a few benign comments to the culprit as an ice breaker, the frost barely melted.

"What would you like to watch on TV tonight?"

"Me? Are you talking to me?" Addie arched an eyebrow.

"I suppose. I don't see anyone else here."

"I dunno. What are you up for?"

"Well, nothing, really," Sophie replied as she'd leave the room.

As they tallied who was the worst offender, Addie was at the top of the list, followed by their grandmother and then their dad. Addie was proud of her superior status and taunted Mary for being so perfect. Never having paid attention to this before, they were disturbed to see the other two right behind the winner.

"Family is everything, huh?" Addie quipped sarcastically. "Well, Mary, you are *The Family* by yourself. She hates the rest of us."

Once this conclusion was drawn, Addie became bored and could not care less about her mother's freeze-outs. As a matter of fact, she became more masterful at pissing her off.

The scariest of their mother's defections were those that were unpredictable and occurred for no apparent reason. Sophie's face would become as colorless as a winter frost glazing a window.

Mary's earliest memory of that hollow expression was the day her mother came back from Poznan, Poland. Addie was having a fit under the bed in their room. Since Mary's arms were too short to reach around her mother, she stretched them desperately wanting to ease the pain and disappointment of her sister's behavior. Her mother felt soft and limp as if her bones had turned into dough. Her face was white almost as white as the powdered sugar that dusted her babcia's pastries, and her eyes like steel gray flecks of ice. Mary assumed she was exhausted; but these bizarre occurrences appeared more often and affected Mary profoundly.

Fearful of disturbing her mother in the midst of those times, Mary would cradle herself while coiling a thick lock of her hair between her fingers. *It's Ok. She'll be Ok. I have to be patient.* These spells were erratic and when her mother would return to normal, it was as if she had never left.

Sophie's eerie stupors unlocked the terror that Mary endured during her mother's episodes. At first, she would imagine striking her, but gradually her fantasies became more violent. Initially, before her guilt would consume her, she recognized that in a strange way, they comforted her. It was as if this mammoth clump of sludge that was lodged inside of her was liberated, freeing her to breathe until the next time her mother infuriated her. *Do other daughters have such fantasies?* Whenever she was about to confess to Addie, her throat would close up.

"I'll be back with more tea," Lee said bringing her back to the frosty silence between Sophie and her.

"Well, Mother, it's pretty difficult to have a relationship of any kind considering you were dead-set against Jeff Bowman." Mary wasn't finished with her yet. Her earlier apology couldn't assuage the resentment she harbored inside.

"What?" Sophie brought her hands to her forehead. "How on earth can you say such a thing? You knew he wasn't right for you. A divorced man? With a daughter? I can't imagine why you would get involved with someone like that! A criminal lawyer ... I believe those people to be unscrupulous. Besides, he wouldn't have fit in with our family. And if his daughter attends that uppity school you teach at ... well, he lives in another world."

The clattering of plates and glasses along with servers whizzing past, were front and center of the sullenness that consumed the space between them.

Mary could no longer tolerate seeing her mother's crossed arms and legs—a trigger that whisked her back to being an eight-year-old. Their implicit agreement held to the expectation that if she repented, Mary could return her mother to normal. But right now, she wanted to return to the comfort of her unmade bed.

"I'm sorry, mother." Mary's voice sounded like a raindrop.

Sophie relaxed. Excusing herself to "powder her nose," Sophie toddled off. Her way of escaping unpleasant interactions.

Mary frequently made bets with herself as to whether or not Sophie would reappear from her hiatuses. Today, she prayed her mother would just go home.

Feeling drops of water splash her arm, she craned her neck to see if it was raining, only to glimpse a striped patio umbrella hovering above her instead of the open sky. Standing behind her was the infamous sister flinging droplets of water from a glass.

"Addie! What are you doing here?"

"Bless you, my child!" Addie pronounced reverently, making an exaggerated sign of the cross.

One way people could tell that she and Mary were related was by the blast of their identical laughter. It began rumbling in their bellies and rushed up through their throats like a big sneeze.

Tall as her mother and sister, Addie was leaner, her legs longer. Her oval face held her childhood dimples that resembled knotholes but over the years, they became less pronounced. Whenever the mood struck her, her face would be adorned with wire-rimmed glasses although she didn't need them. Having a barrier parked on her nose was a way to make certain people weren't able to peer into "the windows of her soul." And they spoke of her affinity for John Lennon.

It seemed as though a bag of shiny crow feathers had been dumped over Addie's head. Brushing her hair only occurred to her when she caught her reflection in a mirror which was infrequent. The oversized plaid shirt that drooped far below the waist of her jeans gave the appearance that she was heavier than the 135 pounds she carried.

"How did you know where we were?"

A laugh boomed out of Addie. Bending over, she gave her sister a hearty squeeze. "Today's Saturday, isn't it? Hey, I saw Babcia this morning."

Neither Mary nor Addie found any pleasure in their alternating visits to "The Orphanage of Old People," as Irina referred to it. Whenever Addie meandered down the dimly lit corridor lined with uneven rows of wheelchairs containing the elderly beaten down by the ravages of time, she would present each of them a bag of Pop Rocks. The staff was never happy with the incessant popping or the fizz bubbling down the residents' chins. No number of warnings deterred Addie since the old folks loved them ... and her.

Quite the opposite of the other cast offs—as Addie referred to them—her babcia was mentally alert and sassy with arthritis being her singular physical limitation which made walking a bit of a challenge.

"How is she doing today?" Mary straightened up.

"Well, she pretends quite well. Like the rest of us. I'm pissed that she's been dumped by the same woman who left us! The secret gets ejected from the house, but not out of my mind!"

"Addie, maybe that's why I don't want to talk about any of that. I can't deal with you if you start ranting."

"I've been seeing a therapist ever since she exiled her own mother, and this shrink keeps probing into my past that I'm clueless about. I'm trying to make sense out of the nonsensical! Doesn't this bother you, Miss Ostrich?"

"Addie, please. Saturdays are never easy for me." Mary took a long sip of her tea. "You were particularly upbeat when you baptized me."

Addie rested her chin on her hands and grinned. "I have a surprise for you which is the reason I crashed your lunch. Babcia has been expelled from the orphanage because she gatecrashed a staff meeting, presented a list of their inadequacies, and threatened to report them to the health department. Get this! She presented the administrator an invoice for the work she did while the staff was loafing."

Addie's snarky laughter brought murmurs of irritation from nearby diners. "Unloading her mother didn't do the trick for Sophie. They want the naughty old lady out of there by next Saturday. Ain't that great?"

Mary beamed until she thought of her mother. *She'll be furious.*

"We'll have to deal with the aftershocks. I was planning on getting my own place next month, but I won't be able to now. You will come home, right? I need your spunk in dealing with mother," Mary declared.

"Of course. I'll talk to Mags later and tell her I'll be moving out. And by the way, I'll be able to torture Sophie on a more regular basis!" Placing her finger on the middle of her lowered chin, Addie gave Mary the *this is what being so nice gets you* face.

"Of course. I'll have to do the dirty work."

"Hey, speaking of the devil, where is Sophie?"

"When will you stop calling her that?"

"Never!"

Mary relived the disastrous morning Sophie became "Sophie" to her youngest daughter because Addie didn't believe she deserved to be called "mother." In the middle of a dream, Mary was awakened by what appeared to be a barroom brawl beneath her bedroom. When she rushed into the chaos, she was shocked at what was before her.

Addie was crouched down, projectile vomiting over the furniture, the walls, the rug. Along with the foul stench of vomit, the sour smells of urine permeated the house.

Her sister was intermittently blubbering and laughing hysterically amidst Sophie's belligerent threats to ground her for the rest of her life for breaking curfew and being so drunk.

Trying to keep Addie from the belt Sophie whipped out from the loops on her slacks, Frank seized Addie by the shoulders, and aimed her in the direction of her bedroom, insisting she get some sleep.

As he tried to run interference with Sophie, he tripped on Addie's purse.

Sophie lunged for her daughter before Frank hit the floor.

"You think you're so smart, don't you?" Sophie looped a clump of Addie's ponytail in one hand and walloped her with the other but before another landed, Addie's arms flailed up. She ducked, dropping to her knees. As she tried to crawl between her mother's legs, Addie took a nosedive.

Sophie hauled her up by the scarf draped around her neck continuing with her rants declaring Addie as "a worthless human being." Frank regained his balance as Mary screamed, "Mother! What are you doing?"

Shrinking back, Sophie flushed scarlet as she gaped at Addie face down on the floor, huffing and puffing. "Uh, I don't know what came over me ... I shouldn't have reacted so harshly."

Frank's face registered déjà-vu as he clasped his wife's shoulders. "Are you all right? You're not ..."

She glowered at him and backed away, quickly turning to Mary. "I'm sorry."

"Don't apologize to *me*, for God's sake!"

Before another word was spoken, Sophie disappeared into her bedroom.

Since Mary never defied her mother, she carried the anguish of culpability for this beating and the other abuse Addie endured. Whenever the two of them would engage in warfare, Mary's loyalties were sliced in half until she decided to lean toward whoever was being unfairly treated by the other. Then there were times she played the Switzerland card and remained neutral.

Not being able to focus clearly, Addie slinked toward her own room, deposited a pool of vomit on the carpet, and passed out.

"Dad, is Mother having another breakdown?" Mary prayed it wasn't.

"No, I don't believe so. She was able to control herself and end it. You take care of Addie, and I'll check in on her."

Stripping her sister of her clothes, Mary manhandled her into the tub with great effort where she shivered and yelped that the water was too cold.

"You stink!" Mary dumped shampoo over her head, giving the vomit and beer that was caked into her hair a good scrubbing, along with the rest of her.

"Do you love me? Am I a bad person?" Addie choked on her tears. "Why does she hate me?"

Mary held her up as they stumbled to Addie's room and maneuvered her body, covered with goosebumps, under the covers as if she were a porcelain doll. Cupping Addie's face in her hands, flattening their foreheads together, Mary confessed, "Of course, I love you, you dumb shit. I wish I could be more like you!"

"Wow! And, I swish I could be, too! More like you, not me," Addie mumbled.

The Gurin family had a tradition of pretending bad things never happened in their house so this event would be archived into the abyss of nonexistence.

It took a few minutes to shake this memory off and bring her attention back to her sister.

"Hey! Mary, stop staring at that dried up lemon. Here! I'm right in front of you. You didn't answer my question, dearest. Where is Sophie? She's been MIA for quite a while." Addie scanned the patio.

"She needed to powder her nose."

"Of course. I take it you must have upset her royally."

As a server rushed by, Addie signaled for her attention, and ordered a loaded spicy Bloody Mary with extra horseradish in her "Irma the Pig" voice.

"Oh my. Lee won't mind if I take your order. Can you say 'Bloody Mary' again? In that same voice?"

Modulating her vocal cords, and scrunching her face to resemble a pig, Addie repeated her request.

"Oh, no! You're that pig my kids love! Can I have your autograph?"

Nothing gave Addie greater joy than being recognized as Irma or *that pig*.

While she was a theater major in college, she dreamt of making it big in New York but after spending a summer there as an intern, she quickly learned how unrealistic her dream was. So, she decided a big dream needed another lesser dream, but after leaving the Big Apple, she remained dreamless until she serendipitously came across an ad in the paper announcing voice-over tryouts for a big Chicago ad agency. To her delight, she was offered the job which transformed her into a pig—Irma—doing a series of cartoons named *Pig Tales*, which became a success. Although Addie's appearance in the cartoon hadn't made her as famous as Popeye, she was a minor celebrity.

"Of course!" On a paper napkin, she squiggled a line. "Tell them that's Irma's tail."

The muscles in Addie's face relaxed and her voice switched into normal mode. "I get that I bug you with this, and I promised I would stop, but why can't you say *no* to these Saturday rituals with her?" Addie snatched the last olive on Mary's plate.

"If I hear your lecture again, I will scream!" Mary's hands covered her ears.

"Ok! Ok! You're the nice daughter, I'm the bitch."

"Stop. Please!"

"I'm sorry. My opinion will never be heard again!"

Taking hold of her tea, Mary played with the lemon wedge resting against the damp glass. If Addie could see what Mary's pleaser façade was hiding. *Maybe she'd realize I'm not that perfect.*

"Ah ... Addie, I need to ask you a question. Have you ever ... ah ... considered harming our mother?"

"Harming her how?"

Mary wasn't sure if she could reveal her cruel fantasies but since Addie's relationship with their mother was so antagonistic, she hoped she might find relief if they shared the same dark side.

"Oh ... um ..." Mary stammered. Tapping her finger on the tines of her fork, she was about to confess.

"I just want to slap the shit out of her whenever I'm with her," Addie replied. "Why do you ask?"

"No reason." Mary sucked in a long breath more convinced that she was abnormal. Murdering and slapping were poles apart on her fantasy spectrum.

"Here she comes."

Addie nabbed a nearby wrought iron patio chair, grinning as she dragged it across the speckled cobblestone floor so that the screeching sounded as if a cat had been stepped on. A barrage of "tsk! tsk's darted toward Addie from nearby lunch ladies.

"Addie! Stop," Mary pleaded.

"Did you have to do that? You're making a scene, Adelajda."

Ever since Addie refused to refer to Sophie as "Mother," Sophie responded in kind by using her daughter's Polish name strictly reserved for her grandmother's use alone.

Addie snickered as Mary made an excuse for her. "It's the texture of these tiles, Mother."

Scooching down in her seat, Mary kicked her sister, reminding her what she needed to do.

Stroking the air that surrounded her mother without touching her, Addie puckered her lips and made a smacking noise. Sophie flicked her wrist. "As usual your hair ... ah ... it's awful and that outfit ..."

"Can't you ever say something nice to me?"

Mary interrupted the banter and stationed herself between them. "The patio is so festive, isn't it?"

Servers swished past while Sophie fiddled with her earrings. Addie crouched over and nabbed a flower petal that landed on her shoe. The rustling of Sophie's shopping bags as she rummaged through them invaded the prickliness until the server deposited Addie's cocktail.

"So glad you're delighted to see me, Sophie. I'm sure you're dying to know how long you'll be honored with my presence. It depends on your behavior. Have you finished badgering Mary about her love life? She bit into half of the shrimp that was gripping the lip of her glass and then decided to devour the whole thing.

Mary's smile was like a light switch: on for her mother and off for sister, replaced by a wave of her hand commenting on what a nice time they were having.

"Well, in case you care, Sophie, *my* dating life is equally unpromising. Why? My psychiatrist refers to my flaw as a mood disorder. And guess what? Men can't deal with that. Hell, *I* can't deal with it! I began therapy when Babcia let the cat out of the bag before you banished her. Oops! Is that a permissible topic?" Addie jammed her index finger into her chin at the same time she wagged her head. "We're at a point where he's asking questions about my childhood. At my appointment today, he implied I was fearful of having intimate relationships. And guess what the good doctor inquired about?"

"Lee was right about the rain. The sky is darkening ..." Mary interrupted.

"I couldn't understand why you deserted us to take care of a mysterious Polish relative we never heard of before. Those letters of yours that Dad read to us, I now question who the real author was. And how convenient that the mystery woman died not long after you came home."

A burst of off-key voices singing "Happy Birthday" interrupted Addie's vent, but not for long.

"What are you hiding? My doctor says secrets, Sophie, are a fucking breeding ground for shame."

"Adelajda, first of all, using such foul language is an indication you lack the intelligence to have a more sophisticated vocabulary. Secondly, it appears to me your therapy is not working if you wallow in the past. As a matter of fact, it appears to be doing more harm than good." Bringing her purse to her lap, Sophie found a file and began to square off a nail. "You need to get on with your life."

"Well, you carted me there when I was in high school Sophie and then expected my therapist to 'fix' me when you were my biggest problem."

"My memory has a different version. It was your school counselor who recommended it. I was never a fan of therapy, my dear," Sophie replied, placing her purse beneath her.

"Back to my question. What are you hiding?"

Wheeling around, Sophie sipped her tea.

"As usual, no answer. I'm not surprised. But whatever it is, it's the answer to the mystery that would un-fuck both of your daughters when it comes to men and to life.

"But what's more disturbing is how you changed after you came back from wherever the hell you were. It was a slow process, but you weren't the same. Your relationship with Dad is odd: the two of you don't do anything together or have much to say to one another. And you were horrible to your own mother! You've hardened as if your insides were packed in ice!"

Addie lowered her voice. "Where were you? Having an affair? Tired of being a mother? I can't have a normal life until I know ... my therapist needs to know."

"Addie, she's not here," Mary waved her hand in front of her sister's face.

"Oh, damn. I'm so fired up I didn't notice. All that for nothing! When did she go?"

"It was the F word that did it. Addie, why do you insist on harassing her now? Maybe Babcia did have too much to drink that night and Mother is right ..."

More screeching as Addie jostled her seat out from under the table.

"Fuck off, Mary. She has a secret. Even though Babcia took care of us, thank God, Sophie's disappearance screwed us up. Why is it such a secret?

She was MIA for a year and then popped back into our lives as if nothing happened. Normal mothers don't *do* that! Mothers aren't *supposed* to do that. She's a bitch, but you keep defending her," Addie blurted, storming off, leaving Mary quite alone at the table.

SIXTEEN

With the exception of a large antique wooden crucifix displayed above their bed, the walls in Frank and Sophie's bedroom were bare and painted with a butterscotch shade of beige. A mahogany dresser covered with a lace doily, which protected its surface from Sophie's jewelry box, was nearest to the door. The mirror centered above it reflected their queen bed with its taupe coverlet, as well as Frank's bureau that displayed a large, framed photo of Sophie in her wedding gown. The nightstands with matching bedside lights were crammed in on either side of the headboard.

A blood-red love seat cradling beige velvet shams at either end was nestled against the foot of their bed. This was Sophie's sanctuary, where she would flee any time she was unable to cope with the outside world. Without any discussions, Frank recognized her need for space and never bothered her if the door was closed. Now that she thought about it, other than sharing their bed at night and attending family meals, he lived in the basement. She wished their relationship could be more real, but those fragments of him bursting into the room where she was being abused by this enormous and foul-smelling man—his father—bit into her heart. Over the years, there were cracks in the anger she clung to. A few times these spaces let in the ghosts of their previous life together. But never for long.

A clap of thunder startled her. The rain that had threatened their lunch earlier in the day bore down mercilessly, pounding hard and heavy against their bedroom window.

Sophie glanced out and, amidst the darkening sky, saw tree limbs quiver in the strong winds. With a quilt covering her and an unopened book by her side, she worried: *I'm concerned about Addie. What do I do about her?* Furious that her boozed up mother had violated her promises, Sophie was compelled to ship her off. She continued to hope her family would reoccupy their places behind the constructed façade she worked hard to hold up, but now Addie was stirring the pot.

It angered Sophie that her daughter's outbursts affected her so. *What kind of mother would let her daughter talk to her so disrespectfully? How can I stop this cruel badgering?* But then, overriding these questions was one which prodded at Sophie's most blistering fears: *How can I keep my girls from finding out who I truly am? Where I've been? What I've done?*

Out of all of Addie's ranting today, the words "hardened" and "secrets breed shame" shook her to the bone. Hardened? Reflecting back on these past years, she knew Addie was right. She was right about a lot of things.

Secrets breed shame. That's what's hardened me, my secret.

Why couldn't people understand that giving voice to the violence and cruelty she had endured awakened the trauma with a fury? Memories of his hands exploring her body roused her in the middle of the night with a racing heart, sticky wet pajamas, and short sharp dry heaves.

That innocent child whimpering and cowering in a closet served to remind her to detach ... to never trust anyone, ever. *If my own mother didn't love me enough to save me from the horrific violence I endured, who could ever love me? Who can I ever feel safe with? And what about Frank? I'm sure he married me out of guilt.*

Her mind slipped back to their wedding, an intimate, elegant affair at the Edgewater Beach Hotel towering across from Lake Michigan. In spite of her excitement, like a magnet she would be sucked into an unknown chasm which would send a shiver up her spine. The uneasiness of it nudged her to go to confession. But for what sins? Praying before a looming statue of Christ at St. Stanislas, she recited the rosary and lit a votive candle.

As the wedding day grew closer, she found herself ironing her lacey panties, her satin slip and the peignoir set that the faculty had given her as a shower gift. Imagining herself being naked in front of her husband-to-be drove her to washing the kitchen floor.

While they dated, she had strict limits as to which zones of her body were untouchable. *This isn't normal. I don't know of any bride who's terrified of having sex on her wedding night. Maybe those nuns brainwashed me so much that it will take time to undo the damage. That must be it! I'm sure of that.*

And before she knew it, the wedding was over. In the elevator that would deposit them into their suite, they stared up at the luminous numbers announcing each floor in an awkward silence. Twirling around their room in her beaded wedding gown, sifting through the gifts, and opening envelopes, she babbled about the flowers, the guests and the reception while Frank sat on the bed minus his coat jacket.

With nothing else to say or do, in a breathy voice Sophie proclaimed that she was going to the bathroom. Hunching on the toilet seat, she picked at her fingers, counted the tiles on the floor for an hour, and tortured herself about how sex was sinful one night and poof! ... an act of love the next. With reluctance, she changed into the negligee and blushed at her reflection in the mirror.

"Sophie, the lights are off, and I will be in bed. Be careful you don't trip when you come out."

The stream of light peeping out from under the door vanished.

"And Soph, this is the happiest day of my life ... I love you."

She hated herself, knowing that Frank didn't deserve this. "I'll be out in a few minutes." When she caught her image in the mirror again, an elusive sensation lurked in the back of her mind that kept needling her. *What is it?*

Trembling, she tiptoed into an inky blackness, save for a trickle of light glowing from a dresser lamp on the floor.

As she crawled into bed, Frank caressed her, enveloping her into a soft sheet.

"How did you know?"

"Hmmm, let's see ... Father Wojcik warned us guys about 'bad girls.' And you aren't one of them."

While the rain pelted her bedroom window, she mulled over why her behavior was so bizarre that night and being a good girl was far from the real reason. Her ploys ––headaches, exhaustion from work, or drifting off to sleep were pretexts to avoid being sexual with Frank. Certainly not what a good wife does. But her guilt evaporated the day the blurred visions of Frank and her abuser became crystal clear ... that day in the hotel.

My life, destroyed by one man's sick selfishness. And what about my mother? Frank? Helen? If they had stopped him. They harbored their own secrets, too.

In spite of the years, Sophie's memories and nightmares persisted. At first, she would try to avoid them by watching TV, reading, cooking, volunteering at St. Stanislas. When those failed her, she would go to church at night, light a votive candle, and pray in the semi-darkness,

Whenever the sexual acts she did as a child occupied her mind, she was filled with disgust for herself. Often a memory would stimulate sexual feelings, and even with Dr. Meizner's assurances that those times of arousal were a physiological response common among women who had suffered from abuse and not any perversion on her part, she would shake her head. From Sophie's perspective, those words were a therapeutic act of kindness.

She remembered Mr. Gurin's warnings. His hot breath whirling in her ear when he threatened her to keep their game a secret. Where was her mother? How could she not know? Whenever she came home from there, Sophie scrubbed herself so vigorously, her skin took on the shade of a rug burn. Since she was so young, she wasn't able to describe what was happening to her, but an inexplicable dark suspicion bored inside of her that these horrible games were wrong. Why didn't she try to help herself and tell someone ... anyone? Why? That question never released its grip from her mind and became unyielding at night when quiet and darkness mercilessly surrounded her.

Hundreds of times she had contemplated freeing herself from this suffering. She'd stockpiled the medications her family doctor prescribed for her nerves after she came back. It was draining to pretend she was normal. If her nightmares plagued her or if she didn't have the energy to go through the motions of living, that cache of stockpiled pills was her safety net. They were her way out.

That bride's face in the photo on Frank's bureau had glimmers of promise, but when Sophie caught her reflection now in her dresser mirror, all she could see was a woman without hope, clutching her secrets.

Sophie was startled by a tapping on her bedroom door.

"It stopped raining. How about a walk in the park?" Frank stuck his head in.

"No thanks." As she pretended to read, she curled the corner of the page.

"Addie mentioned your mother is coming back here to live."

Sophie snickered. "Addie's trying to get a rise out of me. No way in hell is my mother coming back here. She is too old. She needs more help than we can give her."

Frank tightened his jaw in an attempt to control the smoldering emotions and unspoken words from being unleashed because, as always, he was fearful of another breakdown.

Why did Sophie lump Irina and him together treating them as though they were evil interlopers in her life? Did she hate them because they colluded in her lies? As he edged around Sophie's slippers, something broke inside of him. He was startled by what he heard himself speak next ... the words crashed out, unfiltered. "Sophie, you have an amazing ability to create fictional outcomes any time you don't want to deal with what's real. Do you even remember why you shipped your mother off to a nursing home?"

Flipping a page in her book, she ignored him.

"I'll remind you. Your mother cracked open our secrets of long ago to the girls. They came to me and demanded answers about your disappearance."

"Well! What did you tell them?" Sophie slammed the book shut.

"I blamed it on your mother's drinking."

"Good." She resumed reading.

"If I know our daughters, they will bring their grandmother back here with or without your consent. Remember, she took care of them when you ..." Realizing the impact of that comment, he apologized.

Droplets of rain randomly splattered onto their window.

"May I please sit down next to you?"

"I'd rather you didn't."

"Sophie, I have avoided asking any questions all these many years about that night or your hospital stay. I'm terrified I'll say the wrong thing, sending you into a depression or worse yet, another breakdown. This entire family has been pretending that night never happened, that you hadn't disappeared for those many months. We went on living your lie to protect you, and we still don't know what we've been protecting you from! We can't do that anymore. Addie won't."

"I'll deal with her."

"If it hadn't been for your psychiatrist who explained that you suffered from a psychotic break of some kind, because of a mental illness or a trauma, I would know absolutely nothing. And that happened because I met with her before you decided to shut me out. Which is it? Why are you so secretive? If it's mental illness, I don't care. I love you. If it's trauma, I can support ..."

"My God, Frank! Shut up! I could kill my mother! She's dangerous. She's betrayed me ag—" Sophie coughed mid-sentence. "The past is the past." She threw her book across the room.

"Unfortunately, our past is a living ghost between us. Sophie, it's eating me up. When you—"

"When I *what*, Frank, went crazy?" Sophie wrested the blanket off.

"I wasn't going to say that. Soph, I'm getting close to my breaking point."

Ever since his mother-in-law exposed what had been exorcised from the past, the questions and uncertainties that he had blotted out those years ago were slicing through his denial.

"Why did you shut us out all those months? Did you give a thought as to how that affected us? You've been punishing your mother and me for what, Sophie? For what?" Frank raked his fingers through his disheveled hair. "I have to ask you this, what's the difference between a secret and a lie? And I don't mean that sanctioned crap you and Irina used on the girls."

"Well ..." she shrugged. "I suppose a secret is a way to protect people, while a lie ... well, a lie is about deception. It breaks the eighth commandment."

"Maybe secrets are a way to protect the secret keeper. How about mulling that over?" His nostrils flared as he continued to press her. "Or how about this? When is a secret a lie, Sophie? Huh? When?"

As he kept needling her, his cheeks flushed as his own secrets reared up. When he recognized that her eyes were clouding over like a thick morning fog, he uttered, "Sophie. Sophie. I'm sorry. I love you so. Please don't leave, I can't fix this as much as I want to. I can't fix this without help from you."

SEVENTEEN

It's exhausting, spending time with my mother and my sister. Mary climbed the worn carpeted stairs to her room. Her bed beckoned to her, but if she obeyed, she would feel worse berating herself for being lazy. And until she made-up her bed that feeling would continue to harangue her, so she did and clapped when she saw no lumps and bumps under the bedspread.

Sinking into her sofa, Mary glimpsed the shrine to the Blessed Virgin she and her grandmother had constructed so long ago.

Mary's childhood memories had been sketchy but this one of her grandmother's giving her this multi-colored bud vase along with the worn, wooden statue of the Virgin Mary was vivid. After the two of them cleared an area for the altar, Babcia offered her a tattered prayer card featuring a beautiful image of Mary in a sky-blue robe with a golden halo floating above her head.

"Ya, you stick new flower in front of Her, light candle, and say novena on back of picture for seven days if you want to try for miracle." Irina bowed her head and kissed the worn silver crucifix dangling from her rosary.

"Me and you do this while your matka not here?"

The next day after they prayed, Irina mumbled in Mary's ear about being good to her matka and that she must take care of her, and then in Polish whispered, *"Rodzina nie jest czymś ważnym. Jest wszystkim.* Family everything." Her babcia kissed both of her cheeks. "Don't never forget magic thread."

Any time this remembrance surfaced, a hollowness would accompany it, a hollowness so vast that she could taste the darkness it occupied; a mystery so elusive it frightened her. What a crushing responsibility to take care of her mother when she could hardly take care of herself. She grew up at lightning speed in order to keep her mother safe. What if she failed and her mother left again? It would be her fault.

Remembering the thread became more of a challenge as time weakened those early recollections of reading together, playing games, and cuddling and were replaced with the realities of her mother's need to control her life: which dress to wear was replaced with which man to date. So now keeping her mother happy meant sacrificing herself. Hope flickered within her when she recollected Babcia's explanation about the thread being everchanging. Well, it clearly was and right now, the thread between her and her mother was more like a noose and it was choking her.

Striking a match, Mary lit the blackened wick of the votive candle and placed a red rosebud that she had plucked from their neighbor's flower garden into Babcia's bud vase. The acrid smell of sulfur brought a mental picture of her grandmother on her knees petitioning the Virgin Mary for an intercession of some sort.

A day didn't pass without Mary asking for forgiveness from Her as well, her sole confident for the imagined violence she visualized inflicting on her mother. Kissing the symbol of her faith, Mary pleaded, "Give us the strength to deal with what is burdening this family. Especially my mother," she implored fervently until the subject of her prayers hollered up the stairs.

"Mary! What are you doing up there? Come down and keep me company while I cook dinner. You can peel the potatoes," Sophie commanded while searching for a peeler.

"I'm grading papers that are due on Monday. I'll be down as soon as I'm finished.

Her mother would never interfere while Mary was reviewing her lesson plans or doing any prep work for her classes. An alibi that rescued her many, many times from the inane babbling and criticisms that monopolized their mother/daughter conversations.

Back to business. Which room would her grandmother have?

Ever since Mary could remember, she and Addie had shared a room, while the other bedroom across the hall was their grandmother's. As the girls became teens, Sophie decided instead of moving to a bigger house, a better financial decision would be to build a large addition to the existing structure. The architect designed a bedroom with a bath on the first floor and updated the master and second floor bathrooms.

After a number of disagreements between Sophie and Frank about which family member would relocate to the new addition, Frank unilaterally decided it would be Addie. Mary assumed this was her dad's way of making up for her mother's cruelties. He made an effort to offset Sophie's mistreatment of their youngest daughter by complimenting her or defending her. The fact that he didn't carry any real power as far as Sophie was concerned made Addie's status equally inconsequential, but as he described it to Irina, "At least the two of us are irrelevant together." And her retort was, "Make it three."

Soon after Sophie banished her grandmother, Mary's freedom was unchained for the same amount of time it takes to sneeze. When she mentioned another teacher was interested in sharing an apartment with her, Sophie became relentless in trying to dissuade her.

"Why pay rent? You can live here and save your money. Then buy a house. Now that your grandmother is gone, you can have the entire second floor to yourself. Of course, you can decorate it any way you want."

After hours and days of debating the benefits of staying and the need to be independent, Mary caved in promising herself that it would be for a few months, but here she was, a year later.

Any time she expressed her desire to have her own place, Sophie would whip up a sales pitch on the advantages of living at home. Life would be much less complicated if she listened to her mother. At least one of them would be happy. But now, with her grandmother's circumstances, she wasn't going anywhere.

Throughout the day Mary pondered over the least painful way to break the news about her grandmother. *Do I gradually tell her? Mother, Addie stopped in to visit Babcia today. No. No. Never mention Addie and Babcia in the same sentence. Mother, I miss Babcia. No, she'll tell me to visit her more often. Maybe I should just drop the bomb?*

"Mary! Mary! Dinner is ready, although I have no idea where your sister is. But then again, why am I surprised?"

It will be the bomb drop.

115

The flavorful aromas of Sophie's cooking aroused her appetite: beef tenderloin, pickled beets, *pierogi* filled with potatoes, onions, and cheese along with *kapusta* and mushrooms.

"Were you able to catch up on your reading after lunch?" Mary didn't care, but was trying to dismiss the guilt that stalked her for being so joyful about her grandmother's homecoming.

"Yes, but I'm far from finished." Sophie pointed to the vegetables. "These go in the pan but throw the chopped shallots in as well."

Somewhere in her memory cache, Mary could hear her sister, her grandmother, and herself singing a Polish song along with the sizzling of onions in a frying pan. As their eyes burned and leaked, Addie and Mary would watch their babcia chop them while they sang this Polish children's rhyme but because the girls massacred the language, Babcia would pat their cheeks and say, "We do English."

Ślimak, ślimak pokaż rogi,	Snail, snail show me your horns,
Dam ci sera na pierogi,	I'll give you cheese for pierogi,
Jak nie sera, to kapusty,	If not cheese then cabbage,
Od kapusty będziesz tłusty.	Of cabbage you'll be plump.

"If you sing song, onion be happy!" She'd blink. "No fire in here." When they would complain it wasn't working, she'd say, "You sing no good."

"Mary? Do you know what your sister was doing after our lunch?"

And before Mary could respond in the negative, her mother hollered for Frank.

"Dinner is ready. Are you down there?"

Nothing but the ticking of the kitchen clock answered her.

"Well, Mary it's the two of us tonight. I have no idea where anyone else is," Sophie complained, as she brought in two steaming plates of food.

Mary loved her dad dearly, or, at least, the dad he was before her mother's long hiatus. His usual spritely step became ponderous and his spontaneous tweaks and teases that she would pretend annoyed her, faded over time and disappeared. When Sophie came back, he morphed into a stranger. There was truth to what Addie noticed about their mother, but the same was true for him. He molded a shroud around himself.

Prayers were said and then Sophie grumbled. "Those two are so inconsiderate. I'll have to pack up the extra food separately."

She couldn't wait for Addie any longer.

"I have something to tell you, Mother." Mary was crushing her peas with her knife and burying them in her mashed potatoes.

"Mary, what are you doing? Please stop that."

Sliding back in her seat, Mary took hold of her knife.

"Well, what is it?"

"Babcia has been expelled from that prison for unwanted old people that you stuck her in." The announcement jetted out quickly and landed on her mother's contorting face. "She'll have to come back home. And I will not go through any arguing again when you decided to ship her off to begin with! That was a nightmare for us." She saved the more palatable news for last. "And I won't be moving out, so I'll take care of her. You won't have to do a thing."

Since her tolerance for her mother's reactions was limited, Mary decided to save the news about her notorious daughter's new living arrangements for another day.

"Your father informed me, but I'm certain it's another of Addie's ploys to irritate me. No. That can't happen. I'll find another place for her." Sophie began touching her neck, which was beginning to flourish with purple-red blots.

"No, you won't. She belongs here with us. Family is everything, right? Addie and I will work out the specifics of the move." Mary stood and began clearing the dishes.

"Sit. I'll do that. What about your father? Shouldn't he have some say in this?"

Mary's eyebrows tilted up in an awkward angle. "What?" Her father's opinions had never held any significance with her mother. "Well, I'm pretty sure he won't have a problem with it. If you remember, he was as angry as we were when you exiled her."

"But—"

"We'll take care of her. Period." Mary was quite proud of herself for being straightforward and firm with her mother. Addie's abrasive energy was contagious, at least for a while. "The administrator gave us a week to pack her up, so I'm going over there later to get her started. Not nice ... didn't give us much time."

"Well, the rain was quite torrential this afternoon, wasn't it? The ground soaked it up which will make my flowers happy. Have you seen the daffodils popping up?" Sophie straightened the napkin on her lap.

Mary didn't pay much attention to the noise coming from her mother until she heard her say, "On my way home from our lunch, I ran into Mrs. Szwencky at the grocery store, and she was telling me about her successful unmarried nephew ..."

Gazing at the ivory candle flickering in front her, Mary imagined picking it up and setting her mother on fire.

As Mary was driving to the nursing home, her guilt felt as if a thousand bee stings pricked every bit of her insides. Those horrifying fantasies began when her mother resembled a living corpse. Is that justification enough? She couldn't imagine other daughters having such gruesome thoughts no matter what a mother did. But then again, who would ever admit to it? This was her secret.

She'd bet Addie didn't have any secrets. *Addie lives her own life. There isn't a person alive who doesn't know how she feels about Sophie because she lets it fly. I hide behind my morbid fantasies, cruel and punishing as they may be. Addie's raging outbursts aren't as brutal as my visions ... or are they?*

These thoughts were draining her so she switched on the radio. The gravelly voice of Rod Stewart spilled out. *"If you want my body and think I'm sexy..."*

Jeff Bowman's face popped up. She has not seen or talked to Jeff since right before her grandmother's exile. A day didn't go by that she didn't regret their last evening together. Maybe if she hadn't been such a coward, she wouldn't have succumbed to the path of least resistance.

Mary's anguished mind carried her back to the happiest time of her life.

EIGHTEEN

Since Mary taught in an elite private school, the parents who attended parent-teacher meetings were obsessed with grades and would pummel her with questions. This was more of a hassle if their "exceptional" child did not receive straight A's. The outlier was Katie's father, Jeff Bowman, a divorced, successful criminal attorney.

He dressed like a stereotypical lawyer—a GQ cover model—expensive gray pinstriped suit, crisp, pastel shirt with a multi-colored tie, and polished wingtips. A lock of glossy and dense black hair rested on his forehead, giving him a less than perfect exterior which added to his magnetism. Gliding into the room, he bypassed the que and zipped in front of the parent Mary was saying good-bye to.

"Excuse me. I'm due in court in 45 minutes for a trial. May I please speak with you next? I'm Katie Bowman's dad, Jeff. I'm sure it won't take long." He deposited his briefcase on the floor, eyed his watch, and peeled his lips back in a sly smile that flashed like a flirtatious wink.

With a tilted head, Mary's attention flitted from this interloper to the couple standing a few feet away when one of them mumbled and stepped back.

"Thanks." As if he were on overdrive, Jeff began babbling about Katie's mother having the flu and ended with a question about his daughter's progress.

Mary knew she should have insisted he get in line, but her voice abandoned her. It wasn't his attractiveness that appealed to her but the way he took charge of the situation—a male version of Addie but a bit more polished.

"Let's see here. Mr. Bowman, Katie is not doing that well. Assignments late, incomplete, or missing. Right now, she's holding on to a D minus by her fingernails." Mary then asked how often he reviewed Katie's writing assignments, knowing full well this wasn't a priority in his life or her mother's … Katie commented on this a few weeks before.

"Ah, well, my ex-wife and I try to stay on top of her, but she often tells us she doesn't have any homework. I'm sure that can't be true. As I said, my ex-wife would be here today, but she's down with the flu. I'll be sure to tell her about Katie's D." His Rolex caught his attention. "I have to be back in court." He rushed off as another set of parents introduced themselves to her.

As she was locking up her classroom, Mary kept ruminating on Katie's dad and what an ass he was. Her initial impression of Jeff Bowman was typical of uninvolved parents. That opinion skidded into another. *He is quite full of himself, arrogant and rude.* But by the time she started her car, her criticisms morphed into curiosity about him until, without warning, she was overcome by this blur of sexual feelings.

The extent of Mary's physical intimacies was limited thanks to Sophie's browbeating about sex which was reinforced by the good nuns. "Boys want one thing. And guess what happens after they get it? They disappear." But the clincher, "sex before marriage is a mortal sin," tattooed itself in every brain cell.

Mary's job never failed to provide a distraction from any of life's frustrations including those with her mother until Jeff Bowman. Whenever Katie strolled into class, Mary's fantasies about him would strike with a vengeance, more so at night disturbing the little sleep she could snatch. Her students began referring to her as the "bitch" and her co-workers opted to have lunch without her.

"Mary! You've been impossible to deal with these past weeks. Either sullen or openly disagreeable. Are you on your period? You should go see Dr. Wysnewski," Sophie ordered as she filled Tupperware containers with leftovers. Fondling her dinner knife, Mary debated if it was sharp enough to slit Sophie's throat cleanly. She didn't want her mother to suffer, just to be dead and out of her life. In her mind's eye, Mary saw blood spilling out of the neat incision that resembled a thin smile around her neck, and then it bubbled out like a red spring, and spurted out over her mother's newly waxed floor.

Addie shot up before Mary's guilt began to bulldoze her.

"Oh Sophie, lay off," Addie quipped. "You have the empathy of a camel."

Sophie stormed off.

"Another fun family dinner," Mary grumbled.

The Gurin living room was more of a museum crammed with Victorian antiques, leather wingbacks, and faux Tiffany lamps. It kind of smelled like the parish rectory to Addie, a lemony waxy scent mixed with the slightest hint of coffee. With the last of the dishes finished, Addie wanted to check on Mary and lingered when she saw Sophie moored on the velvet divan, staring wide-eyed into space. Another of her hiatuses.

For a brief moment, Addie's heart softened as she observed her mother who in a strange way appeared as fragile as the last petal on a dying flower. Taking a few halting steps toward her, she longed to hold her and tell her that she loved her, but as she was about to, Addie's breath locked up. It never failed. When she described this reaction to her therapist, she was zapped with a question. "What are you afraid of?"

As she approached Mary's room she thought her therapist needed a therapist.

"Mary, it's me. Open the door."

Addie headed straight for the ottoman in the alcove and plopped down. The wavering flame on Babcia's altar candle imbued the room with the scent of sandalwood, but it was the porcelain bowl filled to the brim with wrappers of Bull's Eye candies that snagged her attention. "Hey! I see you're not worried about having your teeth rot and fall out someday." When they were kids this was Sophie's fearmongering tactic whenever she saw their cheeks bulging with caramel.

Addie took in the whole room and noted that nothing matched, and yet, everything appeared to be living happily together. "You did a nice job furnishing our old bedroom given the little space you had to work with. I can't understand why you decided to live here, Mary. Are you ever going to get a life and let go of your mother?"

"Shut-up!"

Addie was talented in dishing out lightning quick jabs. These barbs came out of nowhere and would spill out before she could stop them. There were times she badgered her tongue to shut the fuck up. Staring at her bare feet, Addie stammered an apology when Mary lifted up her chin, and said in a thick voice, "Addie, I appreciate your *mea culpa* because I know those words feel like needles in your mouth."

"Oh, Mary! Lighten up!"

"Oh, Addie! You laugh when you're uncomfortable." Mary mocked her.

"As you well know, I'm not comfortable with your dear mother," Addie complained. "Sophie's a bitch, but you are *not* yourself, my dear, sweet sister. It pains me to say this but you are mutating into a mini-Sophie, and I could not tolerate two of you! What's been bothering you?"

Mary kept chomping on a Bull's Eye as she stared at her wooden statue—her sole confidante when it came to her confusing and uneventful sex life as well as those crimes against her mother. Popping another candy in, she knew what troubled her required a more immediate solution than prayer was able to provide.

Sitting cross-legged on the floor, Mary began with her first meeting with Jeff, and then babbled on and on about the patchwork of emotions she was bombarded with—annoyance at his arrogance, shocked by his rudeness.

"Does he turn you on? Are you sexually interested?"

"Addie!"

"I'm no Sophie, Mary. C'mon, let's get down to it."

Mary buried her face in the fringed silk scarf draped over her shoulders.

"That says it all." Addie swiped Mary's shield and tied it in a bow. "You having the hots for a man! I'm happier than a pig in shit. Wait, maybe not a pig."

"Oh, Addie. How can I get him to ask me out?"

"Oh, for God's sake! You don't get him to ask you out. You ask him out!"

Mary blathered on about the Bowman family and how they breathed the air from an elite orbit. "Why would he consider dating me?"

"You're always leaning to the left—the loser side. You have this dumbass habit of judging yourself and end up feeling bad about yourself. Are you a masochist? Lean to the right—your radiant side! Fight for what you want! You say you want to be more like me. For chrissakes Mary, remember what a president whose name I can't remember proclaimed, *'Never give in ... never give in ... never ... never ... never in nothing great or small, large or petty ... never give in.'* A quote I live by!"

"It wasn't a president. It was Winston Churchill," Mary corrected her.

"Hmmm. That's right. It must be why I got a D in history. Well, do it! Take charge!" Using her talent for mimicking accents, Addie let out a perfect Cockney lilt and pumped the air with her fist.

"You're right!" Mary jumped up.

By the time Addie left, Mary's enthusiasm waned. As she observed her reflection in the mirror, she began nitpicking, starting with her stomach. She pinched a lump of flesh and yelled, "Fat!" Then her quibbling attacked the size of her nose which was, "crooked as a zucchini."

Stop! I can't keep doing this to myself. Addie's right about that negative crap I get muddled up in. As she began to dial Jeff's number, she hesitated. He's a divorcee. The church's stand on divorce was quite clear on the issue: a hell's fire mortal sin. From her mother's viewpoint, it was a double dose of third-degree burns.

Praying before her statue, Mary waited for a sign. When her spiritual confidante remained silent, she reprimanded herself for getting in such a tizzy about asking a man out for a simple drink. She sat across from her phone, picked up the receiver and then put it down. She leaned to the right, and heard Addie's mantra. "Never give up ... never ..."

"Jeff, this is Mary Gurin, Katie's teacher. I'm sure you don't remember me ..."

"Of course, I do! Any problems with Katie?" Papers rustled, a voice in the background suggested that he'd better hurry.

"No. No. I was calling to see if you're free to ah, meet for a drink. I'm sure you're busy ..."

"Would love to! Let me get back to you. I'm late for a court hearing."
Mary chuckled. *And to think I put myself through hell for nothing!*

When Mary entered the Red Door Tavern, a place Jeff suggested, she
was greeted with a great blast of deafening music blended with intermittent
orders for drinks and eruptions of laughter. The intense smell of smoke,
grilled meat, and stale beer oozed from the wooden interiors and the 1920s
memorabilia that decorated the walls.

Wearing a navy pair of close-fitting Ralph Lauren jeans, an ivory
V-neck silk shirt, and an oversized navy jacket, Mary absorbed the
unfamiliar ambience until she felt a gentle tapping on her shoulder. She
reeled around, saw Jeff, and experienced an abrupt rush of excitement
which tickled her toes, swirled up through her entire body, settled on her
face, and ended with a smile.

"Hi! Any trouble finding the place?"

"No. You gave me perfect directions." Since it had been several weeks
since those parent meetings, she tried to be nonchalant as she gave him
the once over. He was attractive in a brooding sort of way, inky black hair
with gray streaks perfectly placed as though they had been painted on by
hand. The lines on his face etched a story of a relatively stressful life. When
he smiled though, the crinkles embracing the corners of his eyes suggested
that he didn't take life too seriously. Similar to his meticulous professional
attire, his casual clothing was just as worthy of a GQ cover—a light blue
button-down oxford shirt, a blue and white argyle V-neck tied loosely
across his shoulders, cuffed khakis, and penny loafers.

Jeff escorted her to a table in a quiet alcove of the restaurant. Crowded
with bottles of ketchup, mustard, salt and pepper, an ashtray, menus,
and napkins, the antiquated pub table didn't leave room for much else. It
resembled an Andy Warhol painting—all the items were placed exactly
where they needed to be.

Katie, their sole common interest, occupied their conversation through
the first round of drinks. Sliding into a discussion about his divorce, Jeff
wanted to know if Mary thought his daughter had adjusted to the split.

Explaining that Katie attended only one of her classes, she went on to say that she didn't feel comfortable making a judgement about that.

Once they exhausted Katie's performance in English and her tendency to seek sympathy for her procrastination around homework, they voiced their political views, shifting into a wider layer of personal info—work, family. After ordering a couple of burgers, a martini with two olives for himself, and a glass of red wine for Mary, Jeff asked, "Why did you ask me out?"

"Why do you think?" Answering a question with a question was what she did with students. A great way to buy time if she didn't know the answer.

"Ah, good response. It's obvious. I'm handsome, intelligent, successful," he replied without missing a beat.

"Hmmm. So, why did you agree to my invite?" Mary asked.

"Why do you think?"

"Because I'm attractive, smart, and successful." Their faces were inches apart when the waitress deposited their food without moving a thing. They both dissolved into laughter.

"Well, whatever your reason, I'm glad you did." He winked.

Mary's customary anxieties about herself faded, but she was clueless as to where they may have disappeared. "I'm curious Why did you decide to become an attorney?"

"It's in the Bowman blood!"

His entire family including the aunts, sisters, and mothers, were barristers, judges, or politicians. His great-grandfather was a well-respected Congressman.

As he disclosed more about his family and his passion for work, she brooded. *My God, I am out of this guy's league. Why did I let Addie talk me into this?*

Mary asked the server where the ladies' room was using the same ploy as her mother when she was uncomfortable. As she came near the door with a gold **W** plastered on it, those anxieties that had vanished earlier, niggled at her again. *I can't imagine the kind of women Jeff would socialize with let alone date. Probably those Winnetka debs whose families dripped in wealth.*

According to her mother, gloom and doom were an inherited mindset which she referred to as their "Eastern European moroseness." A curse, for sure. However, Addie's quote hammered nonstop at her ... "never give in ... never give in," so right then and there, Mary resolved Sophie's quip was an old wives' tale, and besides, her grandmother never mentioned such an affliction. As a matter of fact, Babcia repeatedly spoke about Polish strength. That, along with the effects of two glasses of wine loosened her up enough so that she was able to shake off the pessimistic outlook, replacing it with the opinion that Jeff would adore her by the time the check was paid.

As soon as she neared the table, Jeff stood, touching her shoulder as she sat down. A pleasant shiver flooded her body.

"Can I ask what your favorite book is? And movie?" Circling her fingers around her wine glass, she smiled a smile invisible to him. On the opening day of school, she would pose these two questions to her students and was amazed at the personal information she learned about them.

"Ah. On the book front, *The American Constitution* by Tribe. I could read that again and again, which I have! On the movie front, have you seen *The Deer Hunter*? Outstanding.

Interesting questions. What about you?"

Mary mouthed the word "check" and pointed to herself as the server scuttled by. Emboldened by her new attitude and the wine, she replied, "I'll answer that the next time we get together. This date leads me to suspect there will be another ... if you agree."

"With that cliff hanger? Without a doubt! But you're not paying for this."

On the drive home, Mary rewound the entire night analyzing it bit by bit. His book choice revealed he was committed to his profession, had a strong sense of justice, and could be boring. Didn't seem boring, though. *The Deer Hunter* might mean a lot of things. Her observations circled in many directions. *He shouldn't be so darn serious. A movie about the Vietnam war? Lots of pretty violent scenes. He must be anti-war. That's good.*

By the way he gave her the once over, Mary sensed he was pleased when he caught sight of her ... not the bland teacher he met at school. Sizing up herself in the rear-view mirror, she beamed. But as she relaxed into a bit of self-admiration, her old friend, self-doubt, rubbed it out. *Am I clever enough for him? I wonder how I compare to the other women he's dated.* Addie's voice crashed into her musings. *Stop it! He's lucky you called him ... damn lucky.*

Without warning, Sophie's face loomed before her. *Oh, what does it matter? I could never become involved with a divorced man. So what, if he's divorced? Why can't I go out with a man I like for once? But, do I like him? Seems to have a high opinion of himself. Kind of uppity. Who reads* The American Constitution? *Maybe he needs to impress people with his brilliance. Maybe he's not that great. Why am I making excuses?*

Mary dropped down the visor and stated to her reflection, "I am an adult and will live my own life! And furthermore, he is lucky I suggested another date!"

A honk from the car behind startled her. As she sped off into the night, she began fabricating a story as to her whereabouts that would pacify her mother.

As they spent more time together, Mary was able to relax into herself. But it wasn't easy trying to maneuver this relationship without her mother finding out. Even with Babcia's attempts to change the subject, Sophie drilled her with a million questions whenever she left the house and pumped her for more detailed information when she came home. In spite of the fact that her venial sin of lying was of a lesser nature, Mary bumped up her monthly confessions to weekly.

The rosary the priest assigned to her as penance was a blessing compared to what her mother would do if she detected her perfect daughter was dating a divorced man with a child and ten years her senior—her mother's double standard about age differences annoyed her.

Being quite familiar with her mother's control tactics—the threats, the icy nonverbal punishments, the piercing, accusatory voice—Mary was not going to leave herself open to that anguish. *Nope. Not worth it.* And Jeff was the other motive for being a regular penitent since she lied to him, as well. What adult woman would ever admit to her love interest that she was intimidated by her own mother? And that she didn't have a place of her own. So, Mary explained to Jeff that since her roommate was battling severe depression and was uncomfortable with visitors, she would prefer to meet him for their dates.

The following weeks with Jeff were a mixed bag of peaks and valleys. The social events with his law partners tapped into a potpourri of her insecurities. Having been critical of herself for so long, she recognized, with Jeff's help, that once she stopped judging how she dressed, where she sat, and what she said, Mary had fun. These times were interspersed with a visit before her statue, praying the "Hail Mary."

She was exhausting her list of people—both real and imaginary—as a cover for Jeff. Sophie became increasingly suspicious and peppered her with more and more questions.

"Mary, it's been so long since we've had lunch together. It must be near a month."

"Yes, mother. You keep reminding me." Mary nodded Lee over so they could order and she would then be finished with her obligation. "How many times do I have to repeat the same thing over and over again? I'm working on a project at school with the kids ... a play for English class. And then the other teacher and I go out for dinner afterwards or end up at her place later."

"Hmph. You haven't been yourself since this play thing started. I feel as though I've been replaced."

"And you expect me to get married? What do you suppose will happen then?"

"Whoever that might be will be a member of our family."

When Lee filled her empty water glass, she left a pitcher on the table. As Mary stared at it, Dorothy, in the Wizard of Oz, came to mind and how she used water to dissolve her nemesis into a cloud of hissing steam. Pinching her lips into a thin line and slithering them to one side, Mary was delighted when she remembered that she'd have to resort to one of her more enjoyable fantasies. She have to set fire to her mother first.

NINETEEN

After having lunch downtown, Jeff suggested they get a breath of fresh air near the lake at Grant Park, even though gray skies portended rain. Their usual gabfest was punctuated by awkward silences that pierced right through Mary—bubbling up insecurities she had worked so hard to tame. Analyzing her every action, every word, Mary was clueless.

As they lingered along the lakeside, Jeff stopped. "Ah, we need to talk."

"Oh, Jeff, I'm sorry. What is it?"

Guiding her to a nearby bench, he gestured for her to sit. With one foot on the space next to her, he placed his elbow on his bended knee and leaned in.

"Case in point—you just apologized, and I haven't explained myself. Mary, you are an amazing person. But you apologize about everything. Frankly, it's frustrating, you act as though your ideas or opinions don't matter. Differences are what make a relationship more exciting! You never disagree with me. Whatever I want to do is Ok with you. It's as if I'm dating myself. Pleasing me makes it impossible to get mad at you! And when I do, I crucify myself for being a selfish bastard. Turn that mirror around! Who are *you*, Mary? Conflict is good! I'm an attorney, for God's sake!"

Totally stunned and bewildered by what she was hearing, Mary scooted back on the bench, mulling over what to say. What advice would Addie give other than *fuck you*?

Damn it! I'm not Addie. Tired of her insane and repetitive rituals which she used to be forgiven for the same sin week after week, Mary decided to take a leap. "Jeff, I'm embarrassed. I am fond of you, and I don't want to say or do the wrong thing. I'm sure you've been with a lot of women. Well, you have the distinct pleasure of being the one man I've dated more than a few times, and I'm amazed you keep seeing me."

Jeff kissed her. "Mary! That attitude has to change! I'm curious to experience who *you* are. So, from now on, I'll tweak that nose of yours anytime I think you're not speaking your own mind. A fun way to break that habit."

That word "pleasing" disturbed her the most. How could she have any positive feelings toward herself when she was a clone of whomever she happened to be with? She learned to be invisible as a way to feel safe. A powerful realization of a budding freedom took shape within her, and it began to untether her from who she thought she *must* be to a person she had yet to discover. That awareness caused a shivering uncertainty, an awareness that she was tumbling uncontrollably down an abyss, grasping for a mysterious piece of herself out of her reach until she felt Jeff close to her. She was confident that, for now, he would ground her.

As they continued to spend more and more time together, much to her own amazement, she was beginning to experience a new mindset about sex. It happened when they were sky high in a cherry red striped hot air balloon sailing over Grant Park. The June day was beautiful, with the sun's rays warm enough to form beads of perspiration on her upper lip.

In spite of the blast of the burners and the aimless baying of barking dogs below, Mary nuzzled against Jeff in the gondola, and without warning, the scent of him triggered an urge to rip his clothes off and take him down right then.

That desire was squashed when she thought about her compulsion to profess her transgressions. Since impure thoughts were on the list of venial sins which she had memorized in second grade, she cringed at having to disclose her gondola fantasy to a priest. So, if she did the deed, how would she get to where she's imagined Jeff naked. Since her soul had never been tarnished with a mortal sin, she couldn't fathom what penance would befall her for the act itself.

When she broached her concerns with Addie, she received a loud whoop that mutated into convulsive laughter. "You are a carbon copy of your mother. I have news for you, my dear sister, the best part of life is committing sins, especially the carnal ones."

The Red Door Tavern became their favorite retreat. Since it was late afternoon, the bar was oozing with pongs of smoke and beer intermingled with the scent of Pine-Sol.

Mary wormed her hand into Jeff's and stroked his fingers while caressing his leg with her bare foot.

"Does this mean you want to marry me?"

"Who's supposed to ask who?" And then without warning, she became intensely aware of a rhythmic throbbing between her legs. "I want you." Highly aroused, she had the urge to lie down amidst the peanut shells and cigarette butts and let him plough through her. "Now or never," she said boldly.

As they sprinted toward his car, stopping abruptly, Jeff clasped her face in his hands and gently bit her pillowy lips. "One more block."

Once inside his car, he whispered, "No pressure, Mary. I want this to be the right time for you."

"What do I have to do? Rape you?" She excitedly drew him toward her. "But I have a confession to make. I'm a virgin. But a lot of Catholic girls are. At least that's what they say!"

"I figured that out. Hold on," he proclaimed, breathing like a hard-run horse. "I don't care about your past experiences; however, I want this to be special for you. Not in the front seat of a car." She clung to him, crisscrossing her legs over his back.

"Not any front seat. At least you have a Cadillac." Her lips pressed down, loose and eager onto his. She could taste tobacco and olives which titillated her in a strange way. The tingling sensations rippling between her legs transported her into an orbit of anticipation similar to the end of the school year. Their bodies collided as they hastily tore their clothes off. Being awkward with where to place her arms, Mary tucked them around his neck when Jeff whispered that she needed to relax. He entered her with care, yet she cried out at the pain and pleasure of it but then arched her hips to meet his thrusts.

"You Ok?" Jeff was breathing rapidly in unison with her.

"Yes ... yes, yes, yes! Don't stop!"

Breathless, they wilted in each other's arms.

"How come you get to do all the work?"

"That's a one-time special for a virgin. Just wait!"

"My place?" Jeff printed on the steamy front window.

The ambient streetlights illuminated the car enough for her to admire her lover's beautiful face: his cheekbones stuck out like ridges, a small freckle bordered the side of his nose and resembled a speck of nutmeg, and those piercing blue eyes reminded her of wet glass. She rested her cheek against his. *We're magical to each another because we're new together. I want this newness to last forever.*

"Hey!" He pointed to the smudged letters.

Mary drew a smiley face which was a duplicate of her own. Her mother's face was nowhere to be seen.

Wrapping Mary in his arms, Jeff carried her to his bed and slipped her dress off. "Good idea that you left your lacey underwear in the car."

"Losing my virginity taught me that time is of the essence!" They worked in tandem, tugging at their clothes. "See! Pretty quick, huh?"

Mary breathed him in ... his familiar cologne ... his salty skin ... she breathed in every inch of him. He tickled the backs of her thighs, and glided his finger up the ridges of her spine. He kisses her and kisses her, and kisses her, his hands roving, rousing. He nibbles the ridge of her chin, and with his finger began tracing a line to her shoulder, and then back up her neck. She shivered. No man had ever known her in this way; he taught her the power of her own body. When his lips found hers once more, she began to kiss him with a passion that she knew would drive him wild.

Rays of morning sun leaked through the damask curtains. Jeff tip-toed into the bedroom and without warning, leapt on top of her, but she was quick too, jamming her elbows close to her ribs, protecting her ticklish zones.

"C'mon! I want to hear that laugh of yours! The one that sounds like an opera singer with hiccups." Soon his relentless attack was paying off. She began giggling uncontrollably, and as he kissed her neck, he warned not to get too frisky because breakfast would be ready in a few minutes. The smell of bacon intermingled with coffee circulated around them.

"That's a great early morning tease!" Mary bounced up, snatched a shirt from Jeff's closet, and danced her way into the kitchen.

"Sit, my princess, I'll be serving you this morning."

Unexpectedly, Rod Stewart's gravelly voice belted out, *"Do Ya Think I'm Sexy?"*

"Oh! I can't believe you're playing that song!" Mary exclaimed, spreading her arms akimbo, revealing herself to Jeff. "Yes, you do! Yes, you do!"

Jeff nudged Mary's head with his chin as he placed a plate of golden yolks staring up at her, crisp bacon and a cup of steaming coffee on the table. Famished, she devoured his morning banquet and declared, "Delicious!"

As she continued to quell the rumblings in her stomach, she began to sway to the rhythm of the music.

"Hey, what are you staring at? Do I have food hanging from my chin? Or in my teeth?" She shielded her entire face with her napkin.

"No, I'm admiring how beautiful you are. Funny story. When you asked me out for a date, I labeled you as an easy woman. I'm old-fashioned and ten years older. You grew up in the middle of the sexual revolution and when you asked for the check, I was certain of it. Those were my assumptions and lo and behold, I was way off base. Your lovemaking was surprisingly ... ahhh ... Hey. What's this?" He dabbed at a tear dribbling down her cheek.

"My sister persuaded me to make that call. Well, she and Winston Churchill and my grandmother in a less direct way."

Jeff crinkled his forehead.

"Long story for another day."

"Thank you, Mr. Churchill and dear sister. I assumed you were already spoken for."

Playfully swatting his arm, Mary giggled.

As they kissed, their tongues danced together. She moved closer to him, and they swayed in rhythm to the sexual energy between them when, without warning, Jeff paused and began pacing about. Mary became unnerved.

"I'm in love with you. After the horrific divorce I endured, I swore, I'd never marry again and then you had to come along."

Mary stood unblinking as the collision of her past—dateless and unloveable—with this very moment—he loves me—left her unable to sort out the breathtaking surge of emotions that coursed within her. As the old loops of doubts and questions began to dampen her excitement, she leaned into him and almost toppled both of them over in the midst of her shrieks of laughter.

"What are you doing?"

"I'm radiant!" Mary's arms soared up.

"Yes, I know. Now I need to know if you love me!"

"You dummy. Can't you see it in my face? Hear it in my voice?" She smashed her nose against his, crossed her eyes, and then nibbled on one earlobe, switching to the other.

It's time to make myself completely visible.

Mary spilled her lies out on into the ether and disclosed that she lived at home with her parents and that her depressed roommate was fictional.

"Hmmm. I thought Catholics didn't lie!" He caressed her fingers and began chuckling. "I suspected that roommate of yours needed more medication! Mary, I haven't cared this much about any other woman. You are an incredibly special person."

"I am, aren't I? You're one lucky guy!"

"That's my girl!"

They half-walked, half-stumbled to the bedroom, bouncing on the mattress, eager to experience themselves as true lovers.

The lighting was bright enough for Mary to see Jeff clutching a martini at a table in the middle of the room. Maroon tablecloths topped by smaller ivory linen coverings, with red napkins resting close to the silverware added a touch of elegance to the ambiance. Since it was early in the evening, a few of the waitstaff were clustered together in various sections of the restaurant.

Jeff fiddled with his tie and took a hearty gulp of his martini when he spotted Mary leading her family toward him. Standing, he pulled out a chair for her.

Whispering in his ear, she warned him, "This will be a tough night. We are no longer a secret."

Jeff thanked the Gurin family for accepting his invitation. Unbeknownst to him, Irina was there because despite her mother's objections, Mary insisted that her babcia attend. The handshakes that passed among them were interspersed with the usual "Nice to meet you" greetings. Before he could welcome Sophie, she hurried to the table as if he emitted a most repulsive odor. When they were seated, the clatter of silverware rolling out of napkins cut into the smoldering friction.

"Well, Mr. Bauman ..."

"It's Jeff Bowman, Mrs. Gurin. Please call me Jeff."

Reaching for a roll, Sophie slapped a pat of butter on top as if she was punishing it. "Mary hasn't been truthful about how long the two of you have been dating. Perhaps you could shed a little light on that." Sophie's voice was brittle and each word rumbled as if it would explode.

"Oh God, Sophie, why don't you shut the fuck up?" Addie scowled.

Irina knew better than to say one word, so she closed her eyes and prayed her rosary.

Frank cleared his throat as he shot his youngest daughter a death stare. "Jeff, I hear you're a criminal defense attorney which I imagine to be fascinating work."

"I can't imagine who would have any desire to enter that profession ... those defense strategies are totally fabricated. And they charge those exorbitant fees ... for what? Those people are criminals and guilty." Sophie took a dainty bite of her bread. "Ah, it's Jeff, right? Mary informed us you're divorced. Why did your marriage fail?"

Mary blushed. "Mother, please."

"Sophie, that is fucking rude. Why would you ever ask that?"

"Addie, watch your language." Frank shook his head.

Irina kept praying.

"Well, Mrs. Gurin I don't consider it as a failure—"

"How could you not? What about the child?"

"Oh my God! Sophie, you are fucking obnoxious."

"Since your daughter attends Mary's school, I assume you're Catholic. Well, I guess not anymore. Mary is a staunch Catholic. Our entire family is."

"I'm fucking not!" Addie corrected her.

The remainder of the dinner wasn't any better. Sophie continued to pepper Jeff with more personal questions in between courses, and no matter how hard Mary tried to intervene, her mother became more aggressive. In an effort to derail Sophie from center stage, Addie began speaking over her mother as Irma throwing a few snorts here and there.

The discordant outbursts drowned out the piped-in crooners. A few nearby diners cast disapproving gawps in their direction; others squirmed at their tables. Even their server deserted them.

When Mary heard Sophie opening fire on Jeff with a question about his ex-wife, she had an urge to murder her. Not just set her on fire or blind her but murder her with her own two hands.

Jeff interlaced his fingers with Mary's under the table. Within seconds she hoisted their clasped hands in the air waving them like a trophy.

"Mother, you are ..."

As if a Molotov Cocktail had been thrust up her spine, Sophie sprang up and stormed off.

"Well, Jeff, you experienced Mary's mother at peak performance."

Frank kicked Addie under the table. "Jeff, Sophie wasn't feeling that well before we left. I'm sorry our evening ended so abruptly. Thank you for dinner, and I hope we get to see you again. Help your grandmother, Addie and let's go. Mary, see you at home."

Shuffling the sterling silver salt and pepper shakers back and forth, Mary wondered if she could throw them far enough to crack open the back of Sophie's head. Amidst tears and myriad apologies, Mary was assured by Jeff not to worry and that, as a matter of fact, Sophie taught him what a defendant has to endure ... in a murder case. "Your mother would shame my courtroom colleagues." He spread her lips into a smile with his thumbs.

"I hate my mother." This was the first test of her newly discovered self, and she gave herself a D. In less time than a blink, her guilt started to gnaw at the anger burning inside of her.

"Come on, Mary. We have to find humor in this situation. I'm pretty sure we entertained the staff and nearby guests. Based on the outrage plastered on their faces, I'm sure if your sister threw out another 'fuck,' the maître d' might have bodily escorted her from the restaurant." Jeff deposited a sloppy kiss on her mouth. "I love you with my whole heart!"

That worked.

"Let's go to the Red Door for a nightcap."

"I'll meet you later after I deal with my mother."

"Sophie! You are a bitch. Why in God's name would you treat Mary's boyfriend so rudely? You were as cold as a snowman's dick!"

"I go to bed." Irina muttered.

"Addie, please don't speak to your mother that way. Apologize," Frank demanded.

"No. She doesn't have to Frank. Her apologies are meaningless," Sophie said mockingly.

This was the ritual the three of them would engage in whenever Addie's insolence was displayed before her father.

The key in the front door clicked the lock open. With stooped shoulders, Mary peered into the darkened living room to see Sophie anchored on the couch, Frank was hidden from view as he slouched in his green wingback chair and Addie propped herself against the wall, picking at a cuticle.

"Babcia went to bed," Frank commented knowing that would allow Mary to speak openly.

Surprised that her mother wasn't holed up in her bedroom, Mary braced herself for a confrontation. Her new found self was trembling, but she was determined to speak her mind now.

"Am I the crazy one here? Aren't we going to talk about Sophie's hellish manners, or do we once again stick it in the pit of 'let's pretend nothing happened!'"

"Addie, this is between Mother and me."

Frank placed his arm on Addie's shoulder guiding her out the front door. "Let's go for a ride."

Hoping that this conversation would end peacefully, Mary plodded over to where her mother was and sank into the cushion beside her. Sophie blinked rapidly as though her eyelids were out of control. Mary glared at that Mother's Day gift of long ago and as she did, the nascent freedom she experienced with Jeff began closing up. The pleaser who was her mother's protector began shoving her independence aside.

In the few times Sophie would permit physical contact between them, a breath of melancholic chill would sweep through Mary. And today wasn't any better.

"Mary, I love you." Sophie's attention was fixated on her wedding ring.

"And I love you." Mary began nipping at the tiny balls of fuzz on her mother's sweater. This was the moment Mary knew she was now standing at the edge of a steep cliff, and if she spoke her truth, she was uncertain if she could fly. Hesitating, she fought to keep that tiny opening within her from sealing up completely. "But in order to be loved by you, I have to *be* you … have the same opinions, beliefs, and values. If I try to express myself, you withdraw or act out like you did tonight. I want to be seen for who I am and not for who you want me to be. Jeff doesn't judge me if I differ from him, Mother. As a matter of fact, he encourages me to be my own self." Mary hesitated and then folded her mother into her arms only to be flustered. *Oh, my God. So this is how it feels to hug a cadaver.* She shuddered.

"Mother, we can be close and not see eye-to-eye all of the time. I'm saying this to you, but I'm scared, too." Mary glided her fingers over the stitched threads of the sofa cushion. It was difficult for her to admit that as a daughter, she felt safe agreeing with her mother, parroting her opinions and thoughts. It was an innocuous way to live her life, but by doing so, that profound hollowness inside of her prospered. Who was *she*? Who was Mary apart from her mother?

"I don't know what you mean, Mary. I longed to have a more loving relationship with you than what I had with your grandmother. I've worked hard trying to make sure ours would be so much better."

As she studied her mother's taut face, Mary wondered if this woman beside her had the same fears and doubts about herself. Sensing these ripples of grief roll between them, Mary realized that it was the grief of separateness that frightened her so. *Does my mother feel this, too?*

That moment evaporated, and the turmoil of the evening resurfaced.

"If you love me that much, why … why did you treat Jeff the way you did? I'm so disappointed and downhearted …"

The blue veins across Sophie's forehead began pulsating. "Can you imagine how I feel? To find out you've been lying to me for months … months. Ha! When you told me you were spending the night at your friend's house, you were having *sex* with *that* man! How could you lose your precious virginity with *that* man?" Those words spurted out like the blade of a box cutter.

Mary recognized she was being manipulated. Or was she? Teetering on that cliff, she thought of Addie.

"Doesn't it matter that I've never been happier in my life?"

"Well, of course! But remember that I gave birth to you, and that wasn't easy. My happiness matters, too!" Sophie blurted out. "But oh! Mothers aren't supposed to be happy. We're supposed to sacrifice our lives for our children."

Fumbling for tissues in her purse, Mary imagined shoving the whole packet down her mother's throat, but that vision dissolved before her Mother-guilt could park itself. She was too exhausted. "Oh, that's right!" Mary grumbled. "I'm supposed to sacrifice my life for *your* happiness."

Sophie blurted out, "Fuck you" and slammed the door as she retreated to her usual hideout.

Mary realized this would be a very deep freeze indeed.

Mary and Jeff patronized the Red Door on such a regular basis that, as soon as any of the bartenders greeted them, they would point in the direction of the missing half. This night Jeff was at the bar, sipping a martini with two empty martini glasses stationed in front of him along with an untouched glass of red wine waiting for her. When he heard her voice, he stood up and swept her off the ground.

"Are you sure you weren't adopted?" He winked, touching her fingers.

"Adopted?" Mary laughed.

"Your family is an odd bunch, but, in a perverse way, I enjoyed meeting them. As I was waiting for you, I entertained myself, coming up with characters they reminded me of. Your mother and sister remind me of Joan Crawford and Lizzie Borden—your grandmother, Mother Teresa. Your dad is a nice guy. He'd be interesting to have drink with. God, he should be canonized for having to deal with your mother."

His observations stung, but Mary remained emotionless. "No, my love, I'm not adopted," she exhaled. My grandmother says very little if my mother is around—fireworks. And my dad is great, but marriage can suck the spirit out of a person."

"Depends on who you marry."

Mary began juggling the salt shaker.

"What's wrong?" Jeff asked.

"Please say nothing until I'm finished. Promise?" she insisted as she began fidgeting with her car keys.

"I need a drink." He ordered another round from the bartender. "Mary, I love you deeply."

She pinched his lips together and shushed him.

"Sorry, don't forget lawyers are notorious for yammering non-stop."

"We have a problem. My mother and I have a complicated relationship that I don't fully understand. I feel responsible for her … in spite of her tough veneer, she is the opposite on the inside—easily breakable. I don't remember much, but when I was about seven or eight years old she had a complete breakdown and attacked my dad. The story my sister and I were told was that she suffered from exhaustion, and then the next thing we heard, she was off to Poland to help an aunt whom we never knew existed.

"My grandmother took care of Addie and me. The three of us would go to Mass in the mornings and sit with the withered old ladies clinging to their rosaries mumbling Hail Marys as if in a trance. We made an altar to the Blessed Virgin on my dresser and I still have it. Kneeling down before the shrine, my grandmother pleaded with me to take care of my mother no matter what.

"She left for about a year. Addie and I would cry ourselves to sleep, not sure what we did to make her leave us. My sister was devastated, so I tried to be there for her. If it weren't for my dad and my grandmother, I can't imagine where the two of us would be right now."

"My God. That's one helluva responsibility for a kid. The well-being of your whole family rested on your shoulders." Jeff linked his fingers with Mary's.

"And then without warning, my mother reappeared. At first, we were furious with her. But when I saw her, I felt this need to protect her. But what confused me was how she had changed. She was frequently antagonistic toward my dad and my grandmother. I've never admitted this out loud, not even to Addie, but I believe she's mentally ill. I can't tell you what sets her off, but it's as if an invisible thief seizes her very soul.

"The worst thing is that the family behaves as if that whole period of time never existed. To this day, her absence is a taboo topic."

"May I speak now?"

"Yes," Mary decreed despairingly.

"That was a long time ago! So what? So, what, Mary? How is your mother an obstacle to our relationship? You began by professing your love for me, and now I'm telling you that my love for you is as passionate."

The crowd in the bar began thinning, and the reeking smell of smoke and whiskey slipped out with them.

"Jeff, I truly believe if I go against her in this matter, she would make our lives a living hell. She might take her own life."

"Last call for alcohol!" the bartender shouted drowning out Blondie's "Heart of Glass."

"Mary, you're an adult woman entitled to a life of your own choosing. We'd have each other no matter what she does," Jeff insisted, signaling the bartender for that final martini.

Mary raised her hand and started to interrupt him, but Jeff held it down.

"You'll let your mother control your life? Am I right about that? She's more important to you than our future together?"

How could Mary ever explain the fear that roiled in her stomach any time her mother was unhappy or upset? The obscenity her mother spewed at her swept Mary into the painful realization how little her mother appreciated her. That thread is a chain. "My mother would be the beginning of our problems. The other is our diverse backgrounds. Can you imagine our families getting together? Revisit the fiasco you experienced with my family. My mother parading around like a drill sergeant interrogating your relatives and my father trying to make up for her rudeness. My babcia praying the rosary. The first string of obscenities from my sister would send your family into an apoplectic seizure. And you know I'm right about that." Mary peered up at his face. His skin was gray with exhaustion but his eyes ... his irises had a thread of red in them.

"You're right but, you see, I don't *care*! That's the difference between us! As long as we're together, I wouldn't give a damn if I ever saw my family again." He pounded his fist on the bar.

"Please listen to me right now. You're a *son*! Mothers don't expect as much from them, so they get to live their own lives." Mary picked up a pack of Jeff's cigarettes and without realizing it, began crushing them.

"Let's forget my mother. What's wrong with *me* that I would succumb to her control? I thought I could confront her tonight and leave that house a free woman. Not so. I've been ashamed to say this out loud Jeff, I have violent fantasies about harming her. That's not normal. Maybe they'll turn into reality. You deserve someone who's a whole person. That's not me!"

Before the bartender set his drink down, Jeff snatched it and swigged his martini in less than a second. Holding the toothpick with three green olives jammed onto it, he plucked one off at a time, as he peered at Mary. Her eyes were drained of any color, stripped of their usual warmth.

"Mary, I'm frightened. You're retreating not only from me, but from your own life as well. I want to shake you. It's not hopeless."

Mary knew better. She wasn't able to jump off that cliff.

Here she was now, these many months later, sitting in the parking lot in front of her grandmother's nursing home. *Jeff seems ages ago, and I've been miserable ever since. I loved him. I still love him. How could I so easily give up on myself? What in God's name is wrong with me? I can live my own life. Maybe my mother will discover that she can, too.*

A security guard shone a flashlight in her face as he rapped on her window. "You Ok, miss? You been sitting here quite a while."

"Oh, yes, I am. Thank you. I'm here to help my grandmother pack."

As she bounded up to the front door, she wondered what Jeff was doing that night.

TWENTY

"*I hate Sophie!*" Addie declared as she drove to meet Mags. Continuing her soliloquy, she ranted, "Why did I go to the café today? Why do I keep asking the same old question? It never ends well. What will change? Oh fuck, who cares?" And then the reason for her appearance provided a bit of comfort: Babcia was coming home.

Rain triggered an outbreak of frustration for Addie since her jet-black VW's windshield wipers didn't work. The dark clouds that threatened showers earlier, burst open sending buckets of water from the heavens. With great effort, she rolled her window down, stuck her hand out and swished the wiper back and forth.

Popping her clutch, she lurched forward and nearly clobbered Mags, who was standing in front of their apartment.

"My God Addie! Will you be careful?"

"Sorry! Get in the car."

"Well, Jesus, I about lost a foot!" Mags whined.

They were quite a pair. Though they both thrived on attention, they understood when one or the other required center stage without saying a word. In elementary school, Addie would describe the two of them as "twins on the inside."

They couldn't have been more opposite on the outside. Mags was petite with frizzy honey-blonde hair which she incessantly complained about, until big and fuzzy styles became popular. Mags was a fan of heavy makeup … kohl eyeliner highlighting her mahogany brown eyes, orangey coral blush, and dark shades of lipstick while Addie loathed face paint of any kind.

If Addie would rant about her parents, Mags would grumble about hers. "Hey, at least you have parents. So, shut up. I was a bouncing ball between mine. The people at the courthouse would gawk at me ... those 'poor thing' and 'isn't she pitiful' faces made me furious. And then it dawned on me. Their custody battles weren't about me. I happened to be the object they competed for, but I never thought I was much of a prize."

Addie and Maggie traveled separate paths at times, but they wound their way back to their best friend status because of the secrets they held sacred ... and the nature of one which led them to Cincinnati was the glue that would hold them together to the end of time.

"Let's get a beer at Murphy's," Addie suggested as she switched the radio on to the voice of Donna Summer belting out "Last Dance."

Addie joined in when Mags stuck her fingers in her ears.

"You're ruining the song! *Stop!*"

"You're no fun! At least my crazy family loves to sing!"

It was drizzling, so Addie's hand was doing its job on the wipers as the rain soaked the left arm of her jacket.

"Why don't you get those fixed?" Mags picked at her frizz in an attempt to make a bigger afro.

"It doesn't rain that much, and besides, I figure there must be a short in here." Thumping the dashboard with her fist in several places, Addie admitted, "I did that once and the problem was solved."

A parking spot on Division Street in a *No Parking* Zone brought a smile to Addie's face. "I can't stay long. I have errands to run, and I promised Mary I'd have dinner at home tonight since she volunteered to drop the bomb about my grandmother on Sophie. I'll bring back leftovers."

Tiny, the doorman whose physique belied his nickname, greeted them with his customary, "Welcome, ladies!"

They knew Murphy's wouldn't be too crowded this time of day, but as usual the volume on the jukebox never deviated, so Madonna's voice blaring, *"Open Your Heart"* made it difficult to talk. The typical bar pongs permeated the place: stale beer and smoke, intermingled with tiny whiffs of what Mags dubbed a pea green stench. Smoking weed was enjoyed in back alleyways, apartments, or automobiles, but it didn't matter because traces of that stinky green clung to people's bodies.

Tugging two stools out from under the bar's window ledge, they deposited their purses on the sill as Addie ordered two beers.

Mags shelled a few peanuts, chomped them down and tossed the shells onto the floor when a hefty dollop of beer foam stuck to the tip of Addie's nose caught her attention.

"Wipe!"

"When I was a kid, I wore my food all over me!" Addie declared mopping the suds with her sleeve.

"Yuck!"

"It's still wet, for chrissakes!" Addie blurted.

"How about a napkin?"

"And what are you two up to?" Mags' boyfriend, Tom, asked as he kissed her. He wasn't that handsome, yet there was a mysterious attractiveness about him. Addie figured it was his bushy eyebrows that looked like anorexic wooly worms resting above his water blue eyes. He was sexy in an odd sort of way.

Upon Mags' and Tom's insistence Addie was the third wheel on their dates. People on the street referred to them as Frick, Frack and Fruck which tickled Addie to no end. "Me Fruck," she would introduce herself to no one in particular which was followed up with a wink and "Fruck me!"

This opened a new vocabulary to Addie...at least for a time since her attention span was short-lived. Purchasing a spiral bound notebook, she began jotting down bizarre words. A few of her other lexis included kerfuckle for kerfuffle, cafuckony for cacophony, and discomfuckulate for discombobulate and poppycock which she could happily leave as is. Anytime she heard or read an atypical word, she recorded it immediately transforming it to include Sophie's most hated obscenity.

When Tom invited Addie to join them for dinner at Gino's, Mags gave her the "look" that said, "not tonight." She watched them hand-in-hand, making goo-goo eyes at each other as they passed her waving from outside the window. *Hmm, that's what love is,* she mused. She doubted whether she'd experience that kind of stupid ogling from a guy. Blaming her "early childhood abandonment," or as her psychiatrist explained it, "You take satisfaction in the idea of being damaged goods" which pissed her off.

Other psycho-babble descriptors thrown at her—"fear of intimacy," "low self-esteem," and "perfectionism," fortified her mindset. Addie agreed with a number of these labels but was uncertain how to erase them other than to crack open her mother's secret.

Self-pity showed up in her emotional repertoire at the time her mother disappeared. Back then she didn't know how to label the hot, thick air that stirred inside her, but she became intimate with it as an adult and, at times, had an urge to strangle the shit out of it. From Addie's perspective, there was a certain stink to self-pity. Kind of like dirty socks, and today it stunk pretty badly.

As kids, both Mary and Addie would pester their babcia, wanting to know if their mommy loved them and though Irina repeatedly re-assured them that she did, *"Jestes kochany,"* as she would hand them some freshly baked pastry, they weren't quite convinced.

Addie's friends had mothers. Mothers who made their lunches, picked them up from school, helped them with their homework, and read to them. *Where is my mother? Why am I different from the other kids?*

Any time she needed an explanation why her mother left, her grandmother responded with that spiel about the invisible thread. Addie came up with the idea of dubbing her grandmother's stories as Babcia-isms but this 'ism' unnerved her. She decided her mother was threadless ... or, maybe, she herself was.

Last year, she stopped seeing one psychiatrist when the good doctor informed her it was time to stop blaming her mother for her problems— time to take control of her life. That suggestion placed that shrink on her "dump" list. As a matter of fact, as she stormed out of the office, slamming the door, she shouted to the forlorn people in the waiting room, "That's bullshit."

I'd be normal if Sophie wasn't my mother. These thoughts were relentless, and once the cycle began, it would spin endlessly taking up her mental space. Addie had a love/hate relationship with her victimhood and wasn't able to reconcile the two. When her depression sank to a certain level of anguish, she would feel a perverse satisfaction in it. Other times when life wasn't too oppressive, she would become irritated by it.

I'm smellin' it! Stop with the negativity. So what? So what? For chrissakes! You're an adult now, so shut the fuck up and get a life. These self-recriminations gave her migraines and subsided, but never long enough.

Then she saw him. Joe. The idiot she'd slept with in college. He declared his love for her immediately after sex. The word "love" tripped an indescribable wire in her without fail.

"You can't be serious!" She roared with laughter. Unable to stop herself, Addie rolled all over his bed.

Joe punched his "beloved" in the face, called her a bitch, and demanded she leave. Her fingers wiggled her nose to make sure it wasn't broken. Her pride clamped down on her fury because Addie couldn't tolerate being bested by anyone.

Unable to comprehend what happened, Addie, with a throbbing head and a metallic taste flooding her mouth, wiped her face on one of his shirts, and threw her clothes on. As she was leaving, she snatched a decorative landscape brick near his front door. "You egomaniacal asshole. Can't take rejection, eh?" She hurled it through the living room window and sobbed on the way home, asking the question that plagued her relentlessly: *What's wrong with me? Why do I do crazy shit like that?*

"Hey! How about another beer?" the bartender bellowed.

Jolted from her ruminations, she became aware that the happy hour herd was beginning to crowd out the afternoon regulars. A few guys tried to put the make on Addie, but her smirk conveyed her two favorite words. Sipping her beer, she swayed to the rhythm of the deafening music until she realized how late it was.

Oh crap! It's 7:30. It's Saturday … I promised Mary I'd be home for the big announcement! She will be so pissed and rightfully so!

The bar was wall-to-wall with people smashed together, yelling to be heard above the music. Addie pushed past clumps of bodies and raced to her car.

Sneering as she snatched the waterlogged parking ticket from her windshield, she placed it under the wiper of the car behind her. Addie sang out, "Who the fuck cares?"

Addie inhaled sharply when she realized the house was empty. In an effort to assuage her guilt, she began singing, *Here Comes the Sun*, rifling through the foil covered plates and bowls that occupied the kitchen counters until she discovered a *babka*. The least of her favorites, but she needed to absorb the alcohol swimming through her veins, so she sliced a hunk off and devoured it.

"Hmm. I do have a big *usta*, as Babcia would say," she proclaimed out loud. "Now, now. Be kinder to yourself. That's what you snort to your pint-sized viewers." The muscles in her face tightened, her nostrils flared, and she spoke through her nose sounding as if they were stuffed with tissue. Just like Irma.

Hearing heavy footsteps coming up the stairs from the basement, Addie quipped. "Oh. Hi, Dad. How was dinner?"

"How's my girl? I caught a late afternoon movie at the Gateway—*The Shining*. It was weird. Is your grandmother coming back?" Frank whipped out a scotch bottle and poured himself a drink.

"Yes! I'm offended you think I'd lie to you!" Addie teased, using her pig voice and ending with a snort.

"No, it's not that, you goof! I'll grab a few pierogis and eat in my cave unless you're staying."

"I feel terrible. I was supposed to be here to help Mary deal with the aftershocks of her announcement about Babcia returning to the household."

As he traipsed back down into his cave, Frank replied, "I didn't hear any sonic booms, but I'm sure there had to be a few."

With her self-reproach swirling about, a tidbit of Addie was relieved that she'd missed the show while at the same time wishing, for Mary's sake, that it was an uneventful discussion. However, knowing Sophie, that would not be the case.

Digging through the condiments and the Tupperware containers in the fridge, she hoped that her dad hadn't taken the last of the leftovers, but she was disappointed. A link of *kielbasa*, covered with plastic, was resting on a plate by itself. What was *kielbasa* without rye bread? Suddenly, she heard the front door open. "Mary? Is that you?"

Footsteps were too heavy to be her sister's.

Saturday night bingo at the church kept Sophie occupied at least until ten or eleven if the 'bingo-ers' were on a hot streak. But then ... oh, no! Maybe she didn't go—

"Adelajda. I see you are raiding my refrigerator without my permission."

Dropping the kielbasa on the floor, she banged her head on the freezer door.

Shit! She couldn't remember the last time she'd been alone with Sophie. Silence was like a poison. In that quietness, their animosity for each other was voiceless but real.

"Since I am a member of this family, I didn't know I needed permission. But, if that's a new rule, I'll abide by it."

"I take it you're aware of the situation with your grandmother?"

"Of course. Mary and I are thrilled she's coming home. Our grandmother never belonged in that dump of a facility. Oh, and by the way, I'm sure you'll be delighted to have me back home again, so I'll be able to help Mary." As that declaration rolled out, her jaw stiffened because now she'd never be able to leave, and she wasn't up for a fight tonight.

"Your grandmother is not who you girls believe she is. There is more to her than meets the eye."

It took an unforeseeable trigger to detonate this feral circuit in Addie's brain, and it was unpredictable, even to her. When it was off, she was more chilled out and able to behave herself. However, when it was switched on, it was on.

"Don't you ever, ever, say that again! She took care of us when you walked out after that horrible night. What mother does that? Dumps her kids, and right after they'd been traumatized by such violence?

"And then, when she needed *you*, you tossed her aside? Isn't that interesting? How you throw people aside? To a disgusting place for old people where no one gives a shit. And how often did you visit her? Huh? Not once! That broke her heart. Her own daughter doesn't come to see her once. I can't wait until you're old because this daughter will do the same to you.

"Oh my God! Where do you go when you can't handle the truth?"

Addie cocked her head, and was amazed at how much Sophie reminded her of a store front mannequin but those models appeared more life-like— at least their plastic lips were sculpted to smile.

How does she do that? Drain the life from her eyes? And where does it go?

As she pondered this, Addie happened to glimpse Sophie's weathered hands, a Babia-ism came to mind.

"Adelajda, though people not come into world with *obolaly* heart ... uh, how you say?" Irina pounded her fist into her palm.

"Angry heart?"

"No. *Obolaly* ... uh ... make mark, purple mark."

"Bruised?"

"Ya! Bruised. It take no time for it to happen. And guess what? People we love make most biggest bruise on our hearts. Forgive, then heart lightens."

Being a precocious kid, she figured out people needed to guard their hearts. She envisioned a bluish-red purple and orange splotch with red speckles and jagged edges right smack dab in the middle of her own heart. That's how she saw it as a child.

Her first bruise happened in the middle of the night when she woke up after the raging fight between her parents fearful she'd never see her mother again. From then on, that tender spot became larger. But it was the hatred that spilled from her mother's entire being on that drunken night when Mary took care of her ... that bruise chained her heart to a cage.

Her attention returned to her mother's stony face, and for a brief moment, it felt as though a soft breeze fluttered within her—*Maybe Sophie has a bruise*—but Addie's heart clung to what protected it, and so before that notion took hold, a voice within shouted, *Sophie's a bitch!*

Just then Sophie trembled, and the color returned to her cheeks.

"Are you still here?" Sophie blinked.

"Not for long." Addie bent down and picked up the link of kielbasa, blew on it, and then slammed the door as she left.

TWENTY-ONE

This particular Saturday morning, Mary sprung out of bed at 8:00 a.m. Today was the day she and Addie would bring Babcia home ... where she belonged. Mary forewarned her mother that Addie would relinquish her former bedroom so that their grandmother can be on the first floor.

"Why down here?"

"Mother. The stairs."

"I take it we won't be having lunch today?"

"Impossible. Please keep in mind that since Babcia will be living here, it would be rude if we didn't include her. That will make our lunches more fun!" Trying to keep the sarcasm out of her voice, she grinned at the same time her mother frowned.

"Well, can't you and I go, without her once in a while?"

"I'm sure Babcia would love to have mother daughter time with you." Sophie winced.

Kissing her mother on the cheek which was more of an 'air' kiss, Mary darted off feeling the stiffness in her chest loosen. *Mother will be fine. She has to get used to the adult version of me.* As she scurried toward her car, she waved at Sophie. A signal to reassure her that although they were on opposing sides of her grandmother's new living arrangements, all was well between them.

When they jostled through the door, they were squealing like three adolescents. Their excitement reverberated in every nook and cranny of the otherwise stoic house. Addie carried in two battered suitcases while her sister steered her grandmother into the living room.

Mary offered her tea but Irina crimped her nose as if she smelled a decaying animal. "No brandy?"

"At this time of the day?" Mary asked incredulously.

"Ach. No more rules. If I say brandy, I should have brandy. It's medicine ... good for heart," Irina declared as she patted her chest.

Mary shook her head in disapproval.

"I have rules for you! First, give me pity face again, I leave. Staff give those stupid faces. They treat us like we stupid ... like we children. Well, I get it. If we wear diaper, we like children, but we not stupid. So, no more of that. Rule number two: If no brandy any time I want it, I leave. I not sure where I go, but I go! Rule number three: No guilt if you go out. You go and leave me ... no problem ... as long as you follow rule number two."

Addie and Mary burst into peals of laughter.

"Ach. One more ... nobody look at old people. Any time young ones see old person, they get scared. They see their future. Be nice to old folks."

"You? Invisible? Oh, please. Who are you hanging out with?"

"It truth. You look at me ... as if I alive. Other times, I feel like ghost. I so happy to be home. Adelajda, get brandy from suitcase with broken lock."

Addie obeyed.

"Where I sleep now?"

Mary pointed to where her grandmother's room would be and explained that Addie would take over the other one upstairs. Before giving her a tumbler of her well-hidden elixir, Addie took a sip and started coughing.

"Whew! That will take a few more swallows to get used to."

"Ya!" Irina blinked as she sipped. No matter how hard she tried, her wink included her other eye as well.

"*Na zdrowie!* Cheer in English!" She scanned the room. "Sophie? You here?"

"She runs errands on Saturdays, but I'm sure she'll be back soon," Mary said.

The three women knew a lie just entered the ether.

A flame-red shape plastered to her soon-to-be bedroom door caught Irina's attention.

"What that thing? Why it say ... 'STOP.' Do I ask permission to go in?"

"Of course not. Don't you remember how it became a decoration for my door?"

Irina shook her head ever so slightly as if she was committing a sanctioned lie.

Addie reminded her that when she was a teenager, Sophie and Mary would go in and out of her room at their whim, pretending they were dropping off folded laundry as a ruse to clean it. Raising an eyebrow, she squinted at Babcia, making her aware that she was equally guilty. Despite her wishes that they "stay the hell out of my bedroom" more than once, Addie's pleas were ignored.

"Now wait a minute ... you were famous for leaving food in there and mother complained about bugs."

"Ya. Me, too."

"Oh bull-oney." Addie smirked.

"I was out with friends and after a football game, I saw this pitiful 'STOP' sign dangling from its post. Two of my friends wiggled it down and carried it home for me where I proceeded to stick tons and tons of Velcro and tubes of Krazy glue on my door and, Voila! It's been there ever since!"

"So, it work?"

"Don't you remember? Sophie wasn't too happy with it out in the open, but as you can see, it hasn't budged an inch. Didn't work with her, Mary, not so much so ... and you!"

"Well, I not remember, but I like sign. Rule number five: You knock first. If no answer, I not dead. People think old people quiet, they dead. And what if we dead? Dead is dead."

Mary and Addie clasped their grandmother's fleshy arms as they helped her up and escorted her to her new living quarters. As the three of them clustered before the door, Babcia traced the letters with her fingers.

"*Doskonały* ... perfect!"

After they helped her unpack, they strutted arm-in-arm, with their grandmother between them, to their favorite place in the house. As Mary was foraging for food, Addie collected dishes and silverware while Irina rummaged through cabinets for the necessary pots and pans.

In the midst of her search, Irina would frequently glance at the back or the front doors. Any noise stopped her midmotion as she craned her neck to identify where it originated.

Where was Sophie? For the past week, she'd fantasized how their initial encounter would play out. Because she broke her sworn promise, Irina was not certain what to expect from her daughter and her imagination couldn't move past the first "hell-o." Would she even say hell-o? Maybe Sophie would avoid her mother as much as before her banishment. Her daughter ... how she missed what they once had together. *Maybe she forgot me, but, how could any daughter ever forget her mother? Or hate her? How? Why?* These questions gnawed at her.

Sophie's arrival disrupted her ruminations.

Addie nosedived into Sophie's hostility. "Well, we are celebrating the homecoming of our prodigal grandmother."

Sophie glowered. "I see."

Irina's voice cracked with emotion. "I so happy to see you."

"Mother." Sophie gave Irina a stiff embrace as if she had a contagious disease. "I'm tired. Good night."

"Babcia, I'm sorry Mother is so ..."

"No. No. Your matka need rest. We talk tomorrow."

Hope springs eternal but when it's pinned on a hopeless situation, it's filled with disappointment, but for Irina, as a mother, it weighed her down with despair.

"Sophie is a b—" Addie bit her tongue before the word slipped out. "Who treats their mother that way?" As soon as she heard herself, Addie wanted to swallow her tongue.

"Ah, that's the pot calling the kettle black, dear sister."

"Well, Sophie isn't a real mother, so zip it!"

Irina waved a soup spoon in Addie's face. "Your matka good woman. Don't never forget, Adelajda and Marysia. Be kind and pray for her."

TWENTY-TWO

Good woman? How could her grandmother say that? *What did Sophie mean when she complained that Babcia isn't who we believe she is?* Dismissing the rumblings that annoyed her, she knocked on the 'STOP' sign.

"Babcia? Are you Ok?"

"I not dead. Give me few minutes for clothes."

Mary tapped her on the shoulder.

"Is she in there?"

"She informed me she wasn't dead."

"It's awfully quiet in there." Mary flattened her ear against the 'P.'

Once again, Addie tapped on her grandmother's door. "You alive?" Addie enjoyed teasing the old lady.

"Ya! What I say? Stop with the dead talk. You girls come in."

She was clipping on large gold earrings that added the finishing touch to her outfits when she attended Sunday mass or when there was a special occasion. The bulk of these pinkish pearl discs stretched her earlobes so that they reminded Addie of wilted flower petals. When she was a child, she thought the few age spots that speckled her babcia's face were placed there by God since those oddly shaped blemishes seemed to have been painted on by Him. Now as she noted them, they appeared to be dancing mainly when her grandmother laughed.

Irina's timeless hairnet clung to her snow-white curls. And, of course, her outfit was uniquely hers. Splotches of pale pink flowers were scattered here and there on a long-sleeved silk blouse. Her skirt was covered with tiny blue checks that nearly touched her ankles. But this potpourri of shapes and colors simply added to her charm.

"Mother and dad left for a Bible study group. Interesting, huh? How about if the three of us make dinner tonight?"

"Help me up," Babcia clamored.

The dining room table was empty except for a few glass candle holders. Addie placed the Spode dinner plates and silverware onto the mahogany top but a twinge in her stomach compelled her to whip out the flowered placemats and matching linen napkins. As she admired her work, she shuddered.

Oh, my God! Am I becoming my mother? But before that question could land, she chuckled out loud. *Ridiculous. They're just placemats.*

"Addie. Come help with Babcia. I'll bring the food in."

As they settled themselves at the table, they congratulated each other on their teamwork: a feast that included *golumpki* stuffed with beef, pork and rice, mashed potatoes, sautéed mushrooms, and pickled beets. This time, however, Irina, while balancing herself against the counter sipping her brandy, bossed the girls about and shared her old country cooking methods.

As they were passing platters and bowls of food, the doorbell rang. Addie stuffed a forkful of potatoes in before she dashed off and returned with Mags who had stopped by to drop off more of Addie's belongings. As always, Babcia insisted she join them for dinner. Declining at first, Mags was no match for Irina especially when it came to food.

Addie brought another place setting in, and as she passed more of their cookery to Mags, the four women prattled on about Mary's students, the latest ratings for Irma, and Mags' boyfriend, Tom.

"I'll be getting a proposal soon. We're debating about where we would have our wedding."

"Have it in Grant Park. It's such a magnificent place alongside Lake Michigan," Mary suggested.

"Where did you get married, Irina?" Mags stabbed a *pierogi* with her fork.

"Get brandy, "Babcia ordered.

Working in tandem, Mary retrieved her grandmother's elixir while Addie rummaged for glasses.

"On boat ... we married by captain." Irina brightened as she thought about that moment.

"Too bad I get sick ... water sick. Waves big. No sex until we on dry ground."

Addie and Mags cackled.

"Babcia!" Mary scolded her.

"What? Nobody believe old people talk about sex. You forget this body not always so saggy. I would do sex now ... but it desert down there. Ok, Marysia, I stop sex talk.

"Adelajda, go get pictures from old days in basement. Your matka and me stick them in cedar closet long time ago."

"Stop talking until I get back!" Addie heard the story many times over, but she never grew tired of it. As she sprinted down to her dad's foxhole, a whiff of his pipe tobacco wafted past her nose, a rich and robust scent with touches of both sweetness and spice that she found pleasant. Sophie would complain about the smoke rippling about the living room and discouraged him from smoking in her presence.

Addie rarely visited this area of the house, so when she flicked the light switch on, she was amazed to see it was pretty much the same, except the sewing machine was missing, replaced by a caramel-colored La-Z-Boy and a dusty shelf loaded with a hodgepodge of books. A desk under the glass block window was stacked with papers, along with framed photos of her and Mary in high school, the entire family including Babcia at Mary's graduation from college, and another of her mom and dad vacationing on a beach. It seemed as though they were posing for a sunscreen commercial.

Since the door to the cedar closet was stuck, she had to use both hands and a surge of extra muscle power to pry it open. It was dark and the pungent scent of cedar overpowered her. A lonely bulb dangled from the ceiling. She pushed up on her toes to tighten it, and the tiny storage room lit up. A number of long forgotten winter coats were bundled in bunches along with an array of woolen dresses that had lost their fashion appeal. Foraging through shelves, Addie found a semi-battered cardboard box with tons of old photos and a couple of musty albums spilling over its edges.

"Addie? What's taking you so long?"

"Relax! I found them, and I'm on my way up."

While Addie was gathering her family's past, Mary and Mags cleared the plates and platters off to the side to make room for the treasures Addie rooted out.

"Here you go! Here!" Mags exclaimed.

Mary started to dredge up batches of long forgotten photos while Addie was wilting under the weight of the box she held in mid-air.

The girls laughed at the black bathing suits women wore back then along with black shirtwaists with blossoming sleeves covering everything from their necks to their knees all the way down to their wrist.

"Babcia, you were lucky not to have to worry about your flab or cellulite," Addie declared.

Squinting at the colorless shadows, Irina probed her memory bank trying to decide who many of these people were. In a tattered brown box, lots of pictures of Sophie were sorted into batches according to milestones, revealing her young life as she'd experienced it.

Leafing through photos of Sophie as an infant, Mags cooed, "A Gerber baby!"

"Get a load of those chubby cheeks. Looks like she's storing *pierogis* in both of them," Mary roared with laughter as she held up the picture and puffed her cheeks out.

Seeing Sophie as a child was off-putting since Addie never thought of her as a child or as a girl, just as a heartless mother. In her First Holy Communion photo, along with a crystal tiara and veil, Sophie wore all white: a lacy organza dress, stockings, and patent leather shoes while holding a prayer book and a pearl beaded rosary intertwined between her fingers.

Mary giggled. "Here are Mother's graduation pictures from college. Check that hairdo out. I'd swear that was a helmet plastered to her head! Don't you think mother resembles Bette Davis?"

"Are there any pictures of the three of us after Scotty beamed her back home?"

"Addie, let's not ruin this with your ..."

"Gosh! It's getting late. Thanks, ladies, for a fun time!" Mags kissed Irina.

Addie insisted she stay. As Mags started for the door, she reminded her soon-to-be former roommate that Tom would be spending the night.

"Won't you be glad when I'm out of your hair!" Addie gave her a peck on her cheek, setting a date for later in the week to get the rest of her things.

Mary kept shuffling photos until she came across her parents' wedding pictures. Her mother's gown was simple as was her bouquet. Her dad was beaming, wearing a dark suit with a boutonniere brightening up the lapel. "Too bad these aren't in color," Mary fretted. "It's so blah."

"Adelajda, your matka has wedding picture in bedroom. Go get it," Irina commanded. "I pay for picture in color ... cost lots, but for my daughter. She make beautiful bride." Holding a photo of herself between Frank and Sophie, Irina stared at it as if trying to grasp how the years wore away at the joy of those three people and left them where they were today.

Since her dad was the sole visitor allowed in that room ever since Sophie came back home, Addie shrugged her shoulders. "Uh. Maybe it's better if we wait for dad—"

"Adelajda. You girls must see your matka in color as bride. You go!"

As Addie stood before the closed door, her heart thumped and her clammy hands stuck to the knob. The room was dim and smelled like melted beeswax from the votive on her mother's dresser.

Facing the other way to make sure Sophie wouldn't sneak up on her, Addie scanned the room until a glint from the silver frame caught her attention. She snatched it up so urgently she lost her balance and landed at the edge of the bed, dropping the frame on the carpet.

Alarmed, she crouched down on her knees and examined it for any damage. "Thank you, God," she prayed aloud, bracing herself against the bed frame. A tiny pyramid shaped object that was jutting out from behind her dad's bureau intrigued her. One of her babcia's isms crashed into her as she stood a few feet from the dresser. *Curiosity leads to hell. Oh, I'll just see what it is.*

Tugging the exposed corner out, she was intrigued when a large envelope stuffed with a thick wad of papers slipped to the floor. She held it to the light trying to discern what its contents were. It was taped closed and large letters were scrawled on the front: *Sophie* Gurin *1965-1966 Personal and Confidential.*

Those were the years Sophie disappeared. Addie's thoughts turned in on themselves. *If this leads to hell* ...

"Addie! What are you doing?"

Clasping the picture and envelope, Addie slunk out of the room when Sophie's voice paralyzed her. "What are you doing?" With every step she took toward her thieving daughter, Addie took one in the opposite direction.

While shoving the envelope behind her back, Addie's other hand was so clammy, the frame slipped and toppled to the floor. Not again ... "Babcia insisted that I get your wedding picture. We've been sorting through old photos." She swooped down, pounced on the picture, and handed it to Sophie. As she swiveled around, she surreptitiously swapped the envelope to her front side.

"What are you hiding, Adelajda?" Sophie spat.

"Don't get excited, Sophie," Frank implored, as he touched her shoulder. "It's just your wedding picture. Addie, be careful with it," Frank instructed as he arranged himself between the two women.

"What's the ruckus?" Mary stuck her head out from the kitchen.

Addie slithered toward the front door.

"Adelajda, you come here this minute," Sophie demanded.

"C'mon," Frank interjected, I'd love to see those old photos myself. Addie, let's go." Frank winked and motioned for her to follow him.

"So, this is hell," Addie moaned as she lagged behind Sophie.

After greeting Irina, Frank pulled out a seat for Sophie who was fuming and then signaled for Addie to come all the way in. Irina was confused by the commotion but the tension that followed everyone in, warned her to be silent.

The hush was like a cavernous space needing to be filled with noise, arguments ... anything.

Addie maneuvered herself between her grandmother and Mary, hiding the envelope behind her back.

When Sophie spotted Addie's plunder, she shot up and thundered, "Give me that! My God ... how dare you steal from me? Those are my private notes. God damn it! Give them to me!" Sophie screamed glowering at Addie.

"No!" she burst out. "Your secrets are in here, and we deserve to know what you're hiding, Sophie!" Scanning the exit routes, Addie realized she would have to sprint past Sophie to get to the front door. The other exit wasn't close enough so her dad could easily block her escape.

"Addie. Those are your mother's. Give them to her," Frank broke through the prickliness that loomed over them.

"What is that? Where is picture?" Irina's head swiveled from the envelope to Addie.

"They're mine now!"

Holding her by the shoulders, shaking her, Frank blurted out, "Addie, I love you. But secrets are a part of life. Secrets are a way to protect people. I'm certain you either do or will have secrets to contend with on your own." Frank squinted at her, pleadingly.

She swept her dad aside and rooted herself in front of Sophie. "No, Sophie. Look at me! I won't let you weasel out of this. Why did you leave us? Why?"

Addie was startled at a faint light in her mother's eyes. Sophie started to reach for her. Unnerved, Addie jerked back and toppled onto her knee, overwhelmed with a mishmash of questions. But now, she had a crushing urge to crawl under her bed.

A Babcia-ism cruised past her. "Prayer powerful. Ya. But careful what you pray for. You might not like answer." And what if she didn't?

Ignorance permitted her to create her own narratives about her family—about herself. Storylines that fit snugly into her mindset helped her make sense out of what was senseless. Her obsession unexpectedly terrified her. What if the secret was more than she could deal with? Before Addie stormed out, she threw the envelope on the table.

TWENTY-THREE

So as not to intrude, Frank tapped on their bedroom door before he entered. Sophie was swaddled in a coverlet, hunched up on the loveseat, clutching her secrets. These past years had been randomly filled with reading, watching TV, napping, and working late hours, none of which eased the immense desolation he lived with and, he suspected, for Sophie as well. He followed her lead on the pace of their relationship, hoping that his love would heal what she was hiding.

Those secrets she burdened him with all these years felt like a malignancy spreading throughout his body. Whenever he colluded in her scheme: falsifying letters and phone messages from her to the girls, concocting fictitious responses to their questions and legitimizing her absence, chipped away at what was most precious to him—his relationship with his daughters.

He tottered on a razor's edge between wanting to expose Sophie and this powerful urge to protect her; however, when her face glazed with fear skimmed passed him, he was convinced he needed to shield her: on their wedding night, when he walked away from her at the hospital, or the time Addie rejected her when she came home. He could never betray her. But, what good did it do? She didn't get any better. He wasn't able to help her ... to love her enough. That envelope destroyed their marriage, their family, their girls in particular.

"Sophie, can you talk about what you've been holding on to these past years?"

"No."

"What are you waiting for?"

"Nothing, Frank. I'm waiting for nothing."

"I'll sleep in the basement tonight." As he closed the door, he knew he was unable to resurrect any modicum of hope for the two of them. In the morning he would meet with Father Ted to discuss an annulment.

TWENTY-FOUR

After she cowardly kowtowed to her unforeseen fear, Addie aimlessly drove about the north side wailing. When she caught her reflection in the mirror, her eyes were puffy and streaked with bright red spider-leg veins looking as if a firecracker had blasted her face. Bile migrated up her throat threatening to spew forth—as her head started to spin, she knew that the girl in *The Exorcist* must have invaded her body.

Why did I run? So flustered with her thoughts, she sped past a red light and swerved, nearly side-swiping a parked car on her way to, well, but then she realized that her old boyfriend, Scott, lived a block down the street. Parking the car, she stormed up the flight of steps leading to his apartment.

Before he had fully opened the door, Addie rushed in, tore her clothes off as well as his, and as she was aggressively kissing him, threw him against a wall, where they rolled off and plummeted to the floor. Scott gashed his cheek on the edge of the coffee table. As he tried to get up to staunch the blood, Addie wouldn't stop fondling and kissing him. After their second round of sex, he pushed Addie away. "Jesus Christ, Addie! You're too much for me!" As he stumbled toward his bedroom, Addie taunted him.

"Oh! I'm too much for you? Is that right? You wanna see too much, asshole?"

Rage shortened her breath. Hurling whatever objects were lying around the living room against the wall, Addie launched an ash tray through his TV screen. Scott leapt on her back and pinned her down when they both crashed to the floor.

"Do I have to call the police?"

That word took her back to that night of long ago. Her body relaxed as she apologized.

"I'll pay for what I destroyed. I'll write my address down so you can mail me a bill."

These destructive episodes were becoming a pattern which frightened her. The words, "I love you," from Joe set her off, and then Scott screeched that she was too much for him.

There was this voice in her head that sounded like a violin with a broken string reminding her that she was a weirdo. But her moods and outbursts were Sophie's fault—or were they? Maybe her dad was right about secrets being a way of protecting people. Addie shuddered when she recalled her mother reaching out to her when she refused to hand over that envelope. *What normal daughter reacts that way to the woman who gave birth to her?*

"*Addie. Will you please pick up? Addie. I know you're there. Pick up! C'mon, you were supposed to go back to your apartment and collect a few things. It's been two days. I'm worried about you, sister. Please call.*"

"*Addie! Pick up! C'mon now. I know you're there. Mags told me that you're holed up in your old room. It's been three days since I talked with you. Babcia is upset. Please come home!*"

"*Adelajda? ... how this work? She can hear me?*"

"*Just say what you want to say. You're talking to a recorder. It'll record your voice.*"

"*Adelajda ... it's Babcia. Where are you? I miss you. When you come home? I so worry. Do I hang up now?*"

The pillows and covers Addie stuffed over her head didn't muffle the voice messages as she hoped they might. But she didn't care. Nature was the one call she'd respond to. Neither her obvious need of a shower nor the growls in her tummy motivated her to budge. The darkness was comforting to her because in an odd way, she found its spaciousness freeing. It felt like the color white—a nothingness she needed to cling to since she betrayed herself. A Babcia-ism wavered in the atmosphere. "Prayer powerful. Ya. But be careful what you pray for. You might not get answer you want."

Mags banged on her door so furiously that she wasn't able to hear Addie insist that she go the hell away. Barging in, Mags ducked as Addie attempted to throw a shoe at her, but it scantly left her hand.

"Addie. You're scaring me. If you don't get up, I'm dialing 911."

"I'll get up, I promise."

"Well, I'm leaving for work. I'll be back here by six. If you're not out of bed by then, I mean it, you'll be hearing police sirens."

As much as she threatened herself to get up, her body knew she wasn't serious.

Those fucking psychiatrists haven't helped me. I'm done with shrinks. I'm still miserable. What the hell was I paying them for? I fired three of them. The first to go advised me to stop blaming Sophie for my craziness. The next recommended that I sign up for an anger management class. Like I want to be with a bunch of pissed off people. The last one kept hounding me with the same question. 'How would your life change if you knew the secret?' That question scared the crap out of me. What if it didn't change? Then what?

That's why she ran out when she was on the brink of uncovering the answer to what plagued her since she was a child. She'd have to figure out who she was without hiding behind her mother's secret. Her stomach lurched at the thought.

What she yearned for right now was to be cared for, and it was Babcia who fit that bill. Replaying her grandmother's message again, she kissed the answering machine and blurted, "I love you."

An unpleasant odor overwhelmed her. *Whew! I smell like Irma.* Needles of hot water jabbed at her flesh, filling her with a modicum of renewed energy. She scrounged around for clean clothes and was relieved when she came upon a pair of slacks and a blouse that looked as if they slept together. Foraging through the fridge, she was delighted to find a pint of caramel ice cream swirled with dark chocolate ribbons. She wolfed her comfort food down so quickly that she felt the sharp pain of brain freeze stabbing her forehead. As she sat cross-legged on the floor chewing on a chunk of caramel, Mags burst in.

"Well, hell-o. And thank you for saving me from embarrassing you."

"I've been discombobulated ... oops ... discomfuckulated."

Addie handed Mags a spoon, who laughed. "You dumb ass! Addie, find another psychiatrist."

Rolling her bloodshot eyes upwards as if searching for her forehead, Addie grinned.

"Don't give me that 'fuck off' face!"

"Sure," Addie agreed, without any intention of doing so. She was tired of firing them.

TWENTY-FIVE

After checking in with Mary, Addie learned that her sister and Sophie were doing their lunch thing the next day, so she'd be able to settle in without any interference from them.

"I'm back," she shouted as she lugged in a few boxes. The yeasty odor of *placzek* pumped up her spirits and took Addie back to the times when, as a kid, her babcia would draw her into her drooping breasts and squeeze her until she thought she would suffocate.

"My paczki! Why you scare us so?" Irina sniffled as she hugged Adelajda fiercely squashing her insides together.

"God, I love you!" Addie pinched her cheek.

"Come. Sit. *Placzek* still warm."

Addie bit into a slice of the bread slathered with apricot jam. Even the flavorful taste of her babcia's baking wasn't able to distract her from questioning her cowardice. The answer to her misery was right in her hands, and she tossed it away as if it were dirty laundry. That, in and of itself, proved she was a nut case.

"What wrong with you? You got crinkles on forehead. You skin pasty. You puny." Picking up the crumbs that surrounded her coffee cup with her fingertips, Irina leaned over and kissed her granddaughter.

"Adelajda, when I was child, I want to know things I had no business to know, my papa point," Irina held up her crooked index finger, "and say ... don't call wolf out of woods ... *nie wywołuj wilka z lasu* ... better you leave your matka be. Here, have more slice."

Babcia was the only person who could speak to Addie that way without a few expletives smacking the old lady in the face. "Thanks, but I have to

168

unpack." Her grandmother's wolf story ricocheted, giving her a Babcia-ism hangover.

Emptying out the pockets of her favorite blazer, she came across an old appointment card from a Dr. Newmiller. Addie thought she was fairly smart until she pointed out that hostility has the power to form a steely emotional bond between two people, explaining that Addie kept it fired up because, in an oblique way, it sustained her connection to her mother. It was like a toxic glue cementing their relationship together.

"Love and hate are two sides of the same coin. What do you suppose would happen if you flipped it over and let yourself love her?"

"How can I love someone who abandoned me, my mother of all people? And after she came back, she was unbelievably cruel to me. You people are fucked up! Mothers aren't supposed to leave their kids or hate them," Addie replied bitterly as she stormed out of the office.

When that session darted about her head, Babcia's "ism" about the wolf idled in her head. Maybe she should let Sophie have her secret. But then again, that wolf had been toying with her for way too long.

TWENTY-SIX

As she was parking in her usual illegal space on Division Street, Addie tried to imagine why Mags needed to meet with her at Murphy's on a Sunday afternoon.

A new greeter flirted with her as he opened the door. "Good afternoon, sweetheart!" He sounded like a wannabe DJ.

"Go blow." Dashing past him, she scanned the bar until she saw Mags crouched on a barstool sipping a martini. Martinis portended trouble. Those speared olives served as red flags signaling that a major problem was looming over them.

Ordering one for herself as she made her way toward Mags, Addie couldn't imagine what would prompt this get-together.

Dropping her purse on a barstool and propping herself up on one next to Mags, Addie lit a cigarette and waited until her friend was ready to share the disaster that was troubling her. The last time they indulged in olives and gin was when Mags failed the Law School Admission Test. Her dad was livid. Addie lectured her about not having a Plan B.

"Mags, remember whenever you have a major decision to make ... let's call it Plan A ... you also have to come up with a Plan B. It's a back-up and is essential in being able to deal with the disappointment of not getting Plan A."

It didn't take long before they came up with a Plan B, where Mags would become a paralegal, thus having a better chance of being accepted into law school later on.

"Hey, whatever it is that you're in the dumps about, have you got a Plan B?"

"Addie, this is nothing I planned on.

"Here you go." The bartender carefully placed the nearly overflowing drink in her hand.

"Bring us two more in a few minutes," she ordered, sipping the gin, careful not to waste a drop.

"No. Not for me," Mags lamented, fiddling with her speared olive. "I'm pregnant!"

With that declaration, her thick lashes clumped together with tears and as they dripped down, smudges of black streaked her face. Addie was confused. Placing her drink on a nearby ledge, she practically toppled Mags over as she congratulated her. Mags burst out bawling ... bawling so loud that the people nearest to them shuffled closer to the bar.

"My God! What are you upset about? Tom loves you. We should be planning a wedding."

"I found this in my mailbox this morning along with five hundred dollars cash." Mags began gasping, unable to catch her breath.

Addie was beginning to realize this wasn't going to have a happy ending.

Dearest Mags,

I've been having a terrible time the last few days. Your "condition" is sinking in, and I've been unable to sleep or eat. I'm not mature enough to be a husband, let alone a dad. You're no more ready for those responsibilities than I am. I feel terrible, but it's best for you to have an abortion. I found a doctor on the south side who performs abortions ... I called and this should be more than enough to cover the cost of the procedure.

I'm sorry.

Tom

"What? Here's another perfect example of how love works. He's an asshole. How far are you?"

"About twelve weeks. Plan B—I've decided I'll have to have an abortion."

"You're not serious!" Addie clamped down on her shoulders. "Mags, you can't do that. You can't let him buy his way out of this."

"Addie. My parents would insist on the same thing. It would be a huge embarrassment to them."

The nuns in her high school religion classes preached incessantly on the topic. It became a predictable coming attraction to lectures on pre-marital sex. Assuming she'd never have to deal with an unwanted pregnancy, Addie didn't have any opinion about it. She was upset because Mags was making this decision to please other people. The two of them argued until the crowd inside the bar thickened. Their loud voices revealed way too much information to the nearby patrons, so they carried their argument to Addie's car.

Another ticket adorned her windshield, and Addie tore it to shreds.

"Why don't you think this through? What do *you* want, Mags?" In an effort to keep from ranting, she banged her fist on the dash. Out of the blue, the wipers began swishing.

Addie straightened up and stretched her neck to catch Mags' reaction, who gasped as if she had the wind knocked out of her. They crumpled into each other's arms, howling with laughter, and for a few minutes, those wipers gave them a time-out from their heated debate.

"Addie, please don't be mad. I don't know what the hell I want. I'm scared." Mags began blubbering.

"You are a *mother now* ... intended or not. You are a *mother*. Mothers don't get to decide whether to abort a baby or leave it. Mothers are crucial in the life of a child. If you keep this baby, I'll be with you. We can be co-mothers!"

Those remarks waltzed about the open air until they rested on the magic thread. "Mags, we can be what our mothers weren't."

"Well, I can't stay here. We'd have to move out-of-state and lie about it. Are you willing to do that?"

"Yes. Of course. This will be our secret."

"We'd have to do this now. I don't want to see Tom or my parents. If I tell them I'm going to school, they won't question me."

"No problem. I can be ready in a week. We have to figure out where we'd go."

"But what about your family, your job?"

"Not to worry. As my babcia would say, 'If goat not jump, she have miserable life.'"

Addie was well aware of the turmoil Mags endured with her parents and of their recent estrangement. It's funny. In spite of that, Mags didn't want to disappoint or hurt them. She confided to Addie that they would be more upset about the damage inflicted on their public persona than about their daughter's plight. Her mother was a member of the Chicago City Council, and her dad was a big shot judge who would bend the law to his advantage. Thanks to him, Addie's Division Street parking tickets were "fixed." But the judge couldn't fix this situation other than to insist that his daughter have an abortion. How else would either of her parents be able to explain their unmarried, big-bellied daughter to their friends and colleagues?

It didn't take long for the two of them to decide their Plan B would have to be Cincinnati or Indianapolis: far enough, but not too far, smaller than Chicago, but not too small. They tossed a coin. Cincinnati was the lucky winner.

TWENTY-SEVEN

Saying goodbye to her family was far more difficult than Addie expected it to be. She worried how Mary and Babcia would do without her. In spite of her myriad self-criticisms, loyalty was a quality Addie valued most about herself and more so when it came to the two women she loved most.

Unable to sleep for days, Addie felt as though her brain was engaged in a ping pong match trying to decide whether to stay in Chicago for Mary and her grandmother or to leave and support Mags.

She decided to ask.

"Whats'a matter? Don't she know birth control?"

Addie shrugged her shoulders.

"My paczki. You friend in trouble. I have Mary and my brandy! Not to worry. You go."

On the day of her departure, Addie promised she would call on Sundays.

Her grandmother patted Addie's chest. "You have good heart."

Her dad pressed a wad of cash in her hand.

"Well ... Addie ..." Sophie moved stiffly toward her as if her joints were locked up.

As her mother came within reach of her, Addie's neck flushed, which pissed her off because Sophie suffered from the same condition, but she thought the blotches of her mother' s embarrassment were less conspicuous than her own.

"My name is Adelajda. I prefer that, Sophie." Addie kept her attention focused on her grandmother. A cold tingling vibration inching up her chest was unsettling. Her baffling emotions were doing somersaults, and then she recalled the discussion she had with her last shrink. *There have been a few times my heart softened toward her. I guess that's love. But before I took my next breath it evaporated. As I think about it, that feeling scared the crap out of me. And then boom! I get royally pissed at her. I guess I am afraid to let myself love her. It's like jumping into a field of landmines.*

"Ok, my girl." Frank held her close to him. "Please give your mother a hug goodbye."

Addie backed away and about toppled over her suitcase.

"For me, Addie. Please." His breath tickled her ear.

"Dad, that's a big ask."

"I'll owe you."

Loading things into her car as if in slow motion, she was tortured by her dad's request. Touching Sophie weirded her out, and her usual dismissive gesture of affection would not be acceptable. It had to be a real for her dad's sake.

As she was about ready to take off, she observed her family standing in a row as if they were at a gravesite: Babcia, sniveling while waving her hanky, was squashed between Mary and her dad who were choking back their tears, and then there was Sophie who stood a distance from them with arms crossed.

Moisture settled on her forehead as Addie strode toward Sophie and clasped her shoulders, but was shocked when Sophie moved within inches of her. Addie wasn't able to remember the last time she was close enough to catch a whiff of that Chanel Sophie constantly wore.

"I do love you, Adelajda," Sophie confessed as her voice wobbled with emotion.

Mystified that her mother's eyes were glazed with tears, Addie hurried away. She never felt so empty yet so full of emotions that were foreign to her. None of her therapists explained how it was possible to feel both at the same time.

TWENTY-EIGHT

It took but a few days for Mary to feel the void of her sister's absence. She opened the door to Addie's room and absorbed the smells it exhaled: a blend of ivory soap, nicotine, and Shalimar, an expensive fragrance. Mary was captivated with the ads that touted it as an "exotic Oriental scent" and surprised Addie with it on her last birthday.

"Have you met me?" Addie grimaced as she accepted the package.

"I was hoping I could transform you into a girlie girl."

Addie chortled. "I'm quite sure God has bigger miracles to fry."

Surprised that the scent was so strong, since it was wrapped in its original box, Mary chuckled. "Addie, Addie ..." she mumbled. On her way to last night's leftovers, Mary heard pitched voices coming from her parents' bedroom but she wasn't able to make out the conversation. She slowed up and pressed her ear to the door until she heard the knob rattle.

"Dad."

Flinching when he caught her at the edge of his sight, Frank nabbed his hanky and feigned coughing.

"Are you Ok, Dad?" Mary stopped and changed directions.

"Yes. I'm fine. Where is your grandmother?"

"I drove her to church. Why?"

"No reason. Why don't you go in and see how your mother is doing?"

"Mary? You can come in," Sophie called out.

A sharp fruity scent strayed from a bowl of potpourri sitting on her mother's dresser. Nestled on the love seat, Sophie closed her book and asked her daughter to sit next to her.

"Your father wants an annulment."

For years Mary felt the hollowness between her parents, but her mother's declaration left her speechless. *I prayed this wouldn't happen. You're to blame for this. You've driven him to this with the way you treat him.*

Addie would taunt her sister about her elevated status with their mother, a reminder that she was Sophie's favorite; that, in fact, Mary was a replacement for their dad. That was the time Mary told Addie to fuck off!

"Why does he want that?"

"You'll have to ask him." Red specks began climbing up Sophie's neck.

Mary started toward the door, then stopped. This situation with Babcia, Addie, the envelope, the secrets, she was sick of it. The family she loved was disintegrating. Mary hauled her mother into the living room. "Sit down!"

"Mary! What are you doing?"

"Dad! Where are you? Dad?" Mary yelled as she paced in front of her mother.

"What do you want?"

"Come in here and sit next to your wife," Mary demanded. "It's whatever is in that fucking envelope that's terrorized this family for years. Where is it, Mother?"

As if a battery went dead inside of Sophie, her body sagged and the light from her eyes dimmed.

"Dad, do you know where it is?"

"No, I do not. It's your mother's and it's hers to share, not yours to take."

"Damn it! It might be hers, but whatever is inside has destroyed your marriage. You enable her. It's not just hers, it belongs to this family." Addie's anger roiled in Mary's veins.

"Where did she go after she was in the hospital for that BS exhaustion story you and Babcia lied to us about? When she was expelled after her slip of the tongue, I assume she betrayed Mother. You lied, blaming her drinking. And we don't have any relative in Poznan. Addie and I suspected that for a long time, but I, too, enabled her. I didn't want to know. I was afraid to know. We were afraid except for Addie. The rest of us pretended. We kept her sick. Is that what a family's love is supposed to do?"

Sophie's vacant face stirred emotions in him he could no longer ignore. "You're right. It's time. I can't deal with this anymore. It's lodged behind my bureau. I came across it accidentally several years ago but never opened it. You might as well go get it."

It didn't take long for Mary to find the envelope. She realized that whatever its contents, she was risking destroying her mother. Her chin trembled. *How ironic. Ever since I was a child, I did what I could to protect her, and now I'll be the one to make her unleash the mysteries we've lived with. I understand why Addie didn't want this. In what way will it —* she held the envelope out in front of her — *make a difference? How will we change because of it?*

Her mother and dad hadn't budged. As she tore the strips of tape off, she became lightheaded. Loose papers, notes, and index cards begrudgingly tumbled out as the envelope slipped from her grasp. *Dear God. Please let me be doing the right thing here.*

Mary spied her mother and sensed that Sophie was trying to hold herself together as she pushed down on the twitching muscles in her face.

"Mother?" Mary stared at the scattered papers at her feet.

Like an unexpected crack of thunder, Sophie bolted up. "Give me that!" As she reached for the papers, she tripped and landed on top of Mary, teetering the chair. "Give it to me!" Her eyes screamed in fear. Scrambling on the floor, she became still for a moment rubbing her forehead. As Frank tried to help her up, she bashed him in his chest with her fist.

"Sophie, please. I love you. It's time for you to let me love you, to let your family love you. Read it out loud, Mary." Wrapping his arms tightly around her, Frank had difficulty holding her down.

"No! You can't do that to me, Mary!" Sophie begged.

Mary moved furtively to a section of the room where she would be invisible to her mother. Her voice was thin as if she had to squeeze it past the lump in her throat.

He's telling me I'm his special person. He's hurting me and I want to scream for help. But that makes him mad, so I stop. What is it about me that he thinks he can do this? He's pulling my braid, ramming my head down on the bed. His hot breath on my neck terrifies me. My stomach is churning. He pulls me closer to him. He tells me to be good, to be quiet. I feel this pressure in my chest. I'm crying,

"It hurts. He smells like grass and gasoline. My cries are muted, and it's so hot. I cling to that yellow bedspread that stinks of sour milk. I stare at the

blue flowers. Something is sticking inside me, but I don't understand where.
It burns like fire and takes my breath away. I can't breathe. He rams a cover
over my face. It feels as though I'm dying. I try to be still and disappear.

Then he abruptly stops. The door opens, and I hear ... "Hey, Dad ...?"
Now I can see Mr. Gurin's face clearly as he yells at Frank to get the hell out.

The last sentence trembled in the air ... and clung to the dead silence
that embraced each question mark.

As Mary tried to comprehend what she read, the words circled over
and over again and then tightened around her neck like a noose.

Sophie broke free from Frank and dropped to the floor, crawling
toward Mary, scraping the carpet with her fingernails.

Frank let loose a gut-wrenching wail, *"No!* No ... oh my God ... *no!"* as
he rocked back and forth banging his head against the wall. Clutching his
throat, he gagged and choked down the vomit that threatened to escape.

Sophie sprang up, wrenched his head back, and began to scratch his
face over and over. "You knew! You saw him raping me! Is that why you
married me? Out of guilt? And my mother? Did the two of you ever talk
about that? And what about your mother? Why didn't any of you help me?"

"I swear to God ... I had no idea what he was hiding. You have to
believe me!" Wrenching himself from Sophie's grip, Frank staggered back.

"You must have known there was a child beneath him. Even if you
didn't know it was me, how come you didn't tell your mother?"

Sinking to the ground, curling up into a fetal position, Frank moaned,
balling his hands into fists as he pounded his legs.

Sophie fell to her knees, condemning him. "Remember not long ago
you berated me for having secrets. When is a secret a lie? That's what you
badgered me with. How dare you, since you carried the evilest secret of
all—or was it a lie?"

Her fingers coiled so tightly in her palms that her knuckles shone.

Fighting for more oxygen, Frank groaned. "Sophie, my mother admitted
to me after my dad died that he was a pedophile and his perversions weren't
limited to girls. There was more she wanted to tell me but ended that
confession with three words: 'Pray for me.' Her despondency about the
denial she lived with as a way to protect our family from the sins of her
husband drove her to take her own life. Another secret that's plagued me."

Hoisting herself up and looming over him, Sophie screeched, "I'm glad she's dead. She knew! She knew what he was doing to me! She deserves to burn in hell along with him. I was a child, Frank ... was your father's reputation more important than a child's innocence? Was that it?" Sophie threw a ceramic bowl filled with candy at him but missed leaving shattered remnants at Mary's feet.

"My God Sophie! Please stop and think about it. In a way, you and I were doing the same thing—trying to protect our families but I had no idea about my father. I didn't remember walking into his room until Mary read your journal. I never suspected that you or anyone else was abused by him. I swear to God, and I don't believe your mother did either."

Sexual abuse? A child? In her entire life, Mary had never known such perversion existed. Her insides curdled when an image of a man hovering over a naked child swept past her. As Mary visualized that little girl being her own mother, the contents of her stomach were minutes away from spilling onto the floor until she clenched her throat.

Finally, her mother's strange behavior began to make sense. But why wouldn't Sophie confide in her daughters when they were older? Was it her way of protecting them? But then again, the perpetrator was their grandfather. She couldn't believe her dad knew but where was her grandmother in this? A million questions plagued her, but at the same time a flood of relief washed over her as the jagged fragments of her childhood came together.

Seeing both of her parents in such agony shattered many of Mary's fears about living her own life, more so with her mother. Sophie had no choice and needed to cling to her because there wasn't another soul she could feel safe with. Mary realized that her mother's fears about the world became her own.

Other than Frank and Sophie's convulsive gasping for breath, Mary felt that the silent space in between was filled with its own horrifying grief.

The anguish that blanketed them was so thick, Mary wanted to cut it to shreds. Frank remained sprawled out on the floor and other than the rising and falling of his chest, could have been taken for a days' old cadaver.

Sophie curled in on herself and teetered from side to side in slow motion. Each of them was locked in a separate pain, stuck in a barren place of uncertainty, without means of escape, searching to find the right words to say, what they "should" say.

Mary questioned how anyone would be able to have a normal life and recover from such violence without professional help. God love Addie. Her motive for seeking therapy may have been self-serving, but she was on the right track. They all needed therapy.

Sophie exhaled. "I wrote the rest of those in the hospital. That's where I was those many months. I didn't want you girls to know that such evil existed. I believed I was complicit in an inexplainable way. That's why I made your grandmother and dad promise that they would never tell you the truth about how sick I was."

"Mother, what do you want me to do with this?"

"Find a safe place where no one can find it, not even me."

"I am so sorry you experienced those horrific things. My heart breaks for you and for that child you once were." No longer able to contain her sorrow, Mary sat next to her mother and wept.

"Mary, whenever I was haunted by a memory or a flashback, I tried to trick myself into believing it didn't happen. That I made it up but they were too powerful to be denied." Sophie blinked. "Do you believe me? I was terrified that people would think I made it up."

"Of course, I do!"

Groaning as he straightened himself up, Frank breathed heavily. "Sophie, for me to say I'm sorry is like placing a Band-Aid over a bullet hole. But I am. Sophie, what do we do now?"

"Nothing. It's what I have to do. I'll make an appointment with Dr. Meizner. I have to go back."

"Mother, do you realize that you didn't leave? You stayed here with us. You tolerated the pain." Mary craned her neck and peered up into Sophie's face.

"I did. Didn't I?" Mary's observation startled her as if the wind had been knocked out of her.

"Dad, I know this is awful for you, too, but what Addie says about secrets is true ... now that we don't have any more, maybe we can let ourselves be loved by one another."

Babcia came to Mary's mind. The mother of that tortured little girl. Mr. Gurin—her savior. His wife complicit in abusing her daughter at the time she believed they were helping her survive after her husband's fatal accident. Mary was grateful that her dad's parents were dead and more grateful that they were never a part of her life. These people who bore the label of grandfather and grandmother were wicked. A swell of outrage overtook her grief as she recognized that the acts of sexual violence against her mother and the secrecy that surrounded them were acts of abuse against the entire family.

"I drown in self-contempt any time I re-live a memory. When I was being abused, I asked God to make it stop and it didn't stop. I believed I was a bad person. What disturbs me is that I didn't fight back. I let it happen. How can I ever let anyone love me?" The life in Sophie began dwindling.

"Mother! Stay with me. Mother!" Mary pleaded. "Please don't leave. I love you. You were a child, just a child. You're safe now."

Sophie remained unresponsive for a while but then her muscles loosened. She brought Mary's hand to her cheek and caressed it. "Thank you for reminding me. It's difficult for me to accept that." Her voice was as quiet as a drop of water.

Mary was certain that the guilt which she suffered from her violent fantasies would be uprooted and replaced with the love and kindness that normal daughters experience. However, it did leave behind what she never wanted to experience: grief over the loss of what could have been.

PART III

Addie and Mags

Cincinnati

TWENTY-NINE

When they sighted their destination on I-74, they were surprised at the hills leaning against the sky. Since Addie wasn't paying attention, prattling on about how dissimilar the two cities were, they veered off course and ended up in Mt. Adams. The panoramic views of downtown Cincinnati with its bridges, church steeples, and river valley were fantastic for two Chi-town girls who were accustomed to scoping out scenery from the L train barreling above the Loop. Nothing could compare to Lake Michigan, but in spite of its murky color, the Ohio River was charming in its own way.

They explored Hyde Park Square, a quaint area with shops and restaurants which they serendipitously came upon because once again, Addie was not paying attention to Mags' navigational instructions. Delighted when they found a *2 Bedroom For Rent* sign close to the shopping district, they were more excited after they inspected it until they discovered that it wasn't available until the next day. Rather than get a hotel, they decided to be adventurous and curl up in the VW.

"Whose dumb idea was this?" Addie asked.

Moaning and groaning as they extricated themselves from the car, they headed off to McDonald's for coffee before they met their landlord with the key to their new home, a two-story brownish brick building with a central entrance way providing access to the two apartments on either side. These transplanted Chicagoans were now within a stone's throw of the square.

Buying beds was assigned to Mags while Addie perused available jobs in the classified section of the papers. They met for lunch at a diner known as Goldline Chili, unaware that they had stumbled upon the town's iconic eating place known the "world over," as described by their waitress. As they searched for a vacant booth, the pungent smell of onions was powerful enough that Addie began humming her babcia's onion song.

"Well, we'll have beds by Friday! And a sofa along with a TV. Got them under our budget!" They high-fived. "We're all set."

"The royalties I made for the last series of Irma the Pig voiceovers should last us for a good while. In the meantime, I'll apply for waitress jobs. Remember Hamilton's? That dump of a bar paid for a chunk of my college expenses."

Mags kept on making a list of other household items they needed.

"If I find the right place, we'll be rolling in the dough especially with my charming personality. I'm sure you can find a job near the apartment. There were a few law offices in the business district of the square." Since Addie's VW was their only mode of transportation, a coin flip made that another quick decision. Mags could walk.

Gaping at the hot dogs piled high with chili, cheese, and shredded onions placed before them, they agreed these were no comparison to good old Chicago Vienna Jumbo hot dogs slathered in veggies, relish, and mustard. After a bite or two, Addie became homesick and lost her appetite.

"Addie? Hey? Aren't you finished?" Mags hungrily eyed the two chili dogs overflowing with their renowned toppings.

"You can have them."

As they waited for their check, Mags continued to bug Addie about her added baby weight. "Do I look fat?"

"Don't rationalize that you're eating for two, piggy." Irma snorted. But the powerful smell of those onions brought to mind another childhood lyric. Addie bolted up, and began singing in Irma's voice. "Fatty, Fatty, two by four, can't get through the kitchen door. Fatty, Fatty, two by four, can't get through any door ..."

"You bitch!" Mags yelped as servers and diners alike stared icily at them.

The manager gave Addie the bill and escorted them out.

"These Cincinnati people are way too serious!" Addie declared.

THIRTY

Within the week, Addie was hired as a waitress at Chester's Roadhouse, an upscale restaurant on the east side of town, while Mags landed a job as a legal secretary at a nearby law firm in Hyde Park. They celebrated their good fortune with a cheap bottle of champagne.

It didn't take long for Addie to start schmoozing the manager, Mark Lansing. He reminded her of a taller Tom Cruise blended with Harrison Ford and that crooked nose of his. His dusky eyes were set too close together, but when he laughed, which was rare, they brightened. While he interviewed her for the job, his attention danced from the neatly stack of papers on his desk to his watch to his phone when suddenly he bolted up. "Have you ever worked as a server?"

"Well, yes ... in college. But my real experience comes from the love of eating out!" No response from her interviewer. "Ah, that was a joke." *Oh my God, way too serious.*

Escorting her to the door, he shook her hand. "Welcome to Chester's."

In a bit of a daze, Addie traipsed down the stairs from his office and into the parking lot, noodling over that interview which was unlike any other she experienced. At first, she was pissed because he never looked at her, asked her one relevant question, and dismissed her. Even though she was hired, Addie was put off by his indifferent attitude toward her. Something she was determined to change.

Scheduled for lunches and based on her job at Hamilton's, she knew tips that time of day would be less than the evening shift. Plan B propelled her into high gear where she catered to her guests with exceptional attentiveness, captivating them with her wit and charm. Even though her daytime gratuities were significantly higher than the other servers', she knew she could double them at night.

What would she have to do to convince Mark to schedule her for dinners? She decided to enlist her customers in her mission by asking them to sing her praises to the manager, and they were delighted to do so. Her patience thinned out when nothing changed. Meeting with Mark was her last option.

"I don't get it. I'm doing a fabulous job, customers love me, and you won't schedule me for dinners," Addie complained in a honeyed voice.

"I have a wait list for that shift."

"Does your mouth ever curve up? You know like this?" The corners of Addie's lips almost touched her ears.

Mark straightened his tie in the midst of an awkward lull which stretched thinner and thinner, like a rubber band waiting to snap. Addie inhaled every ounce of the holding pattern between them and enjoyed it.

"I ... ahhh ... d-do," he stuttered.

"Staff want to know if you have any teeth in there." She pointed to her own.

"Not funny."

"Mark, you're a nice guy. A bit of a workaholic. Loosen up a bit. The staff would relate to you better. C'mon, you can spread these out!" She contorted her mouth into a smirk exposing way too much of her pink gums as well as a few fillings. The corner of his mouth lifted which was quickly followed by the other side. Her employer revealed a charming and guileless grin that exposed crooked teeth, but in spite of their unevenness, they didn't detract from his attractive face.

"Next time I'll bring my camera and tape the photos in the break room. The staff will need evidence! Say, how about if you and I go out for a drink? That is, if you can free yourself from work! But then again, I'm sure you're the kind of boss who doesn't socialize with employees."

"Ah, well, uh ... I ... I kind of do."

Not a good liar, Addie surmised.

"But bars aren't my thing. I have some land over the river in Rabbit Hash."

"Are you kidding me? Rabbit Hash ..." She snickered. "Is that where the Beverly Hillbillies came from?"

Mark glimpsed down at his watch. "Oh, and you're still on lunches."

As she left his office, Addie fretted. Once again, her big yap had foiled her plans. There were people she could joke with, and then there were those who didn't get her. Once again, she regretted not having a filter. And she was beginning to understand the people in this city were far too intense. So, she did her damnedest to come up with a creative way to make amends.

Waiting for him at the foot of the stairs, Addie blocked his passage to the bar. "I'm pretty sure I offended you. I'm sorry. I am. I never heard such an unusual name for a town. If you forgive me, I'd like to see that neck of the woods, if that was an invitation." Moving aside, she touched his arm and for a brief moment, Addie detected a tingling sensation permeate her insides.

His demeanor was serious which belied his flirtatious gaze. "I'm sorry I was abrupt with you. I'm from Kentucky, and we are often referred to as 'hillbillies' on this side of the river. And it's far from a compliment." As he continued to speak, a slight lilt glazed each word with a masculine sweetness to it. It was quite captivating.

"Oops, my hillbilly twang slipped out. It does any time I talk about home."

"Sounds pretty sexy to me!" Her quirky grin exposed only one of her dimples as she batted her eyelids at him.

"How about if you join me on Sunday for a short road trip to Rabbit Hash, if you're off, that is."

Addie wagged her head.

"Oh, and I won't be able to schedule you for dinners, but you'll do well as a bartender. Steve can train you."

Even though this wasn't Addie's first choice, she considered it a win in two ways: higher tips than lunches and possibly higher than dinners, and more importantly, she was able to bend her manager to her will ... almost.

"I would love to join you on Sunday, if I'm off."

"We'll see."

While Mark advanced toward the bar area to check on liquor supplies, Addie checked out his ass. *This will be most interesting.*

THIRTY-ONE

As Mark drove up in front of her apartment that Sunday, he honked his horn and grinned as she rushed out the door carrying a large wicker basket covered with a brightly colored napkin. When he opened the car door for her, Addie sniffed the musky scent of spice mingling with the clean smell of soap and wondered if the chili she brought would cause an explosion of undesirable odors.

Hello!" She peeled back the paisley cloth. "In here we have two bottles of red wine, plastic plates with napkins that don't match, cups, silverware, and pickles, ham, and swiss on rye bread. I hear from an unnamed source that you're a fan of Goldline chili. Voila! Here's a super-sized tub of it!"

Her intention was to make this simple and bring that chili in a bag. Instead, she found herself driven by more of a desire to make an impression. After all, he was her boss. Unable to deceive herself about her motive, she laughed as she shopped for the picnic paraphernalia and added more to her list of food other than his favorite. There was this mystifying aura about him she was drawn to—gentle, kind, sincere. *Not a good idea to dip the pen in the office inkwell. Shut up. Attraction doesn't mean love. I've mastered the ability to remain buttoned-up.*

It was a perfect day—bright blue sky, thick puffs of clouds—the sun made its appearance, after being on strike the entire week. Scrounging in her oversized purse, Addie let out a whoop while she waved her sunglasses at Mark.

As they sped down I-75, they began singing, *"Here Comes the Sun"* as the lyrics cut loose from the radio. They yodeled like two cats in heat and giggled throughout their yowling.

Mark shared more of his Kentucky background, which wasn't that far off from her Polish upbringing. College was not an option for him, as it wasn't for her or Mary: it was a given. Her grandmother delivered the same sermon to them as she did to Sophie: "Don't be dummy like me! Go to college!"

Addie remained vague on the topic of her family except for her grandmother's expulsion from the nursing home which was sure to bring a hearty chuckle from Mark, and it did.

He exited the expressway, and for the next eight or nine miles, they were comfortably silent, listening to more of the Beatles until Addie inquired how much longer.

"Getting bored?"

"No. I'm impatient to see this magical place."

"How about a smoke?"

Pressing the hot cylinders of the car lighter against the end of the cigarette, she took a few long draws, and placed it between Mark's lips. He touched her hand, and she knew that her vow about the inkwell would be defiled without a trace of guilt.

When they exited from Highway 18, the winding and narrow roads that lay before them mystified her. Barns, farmhouses, and trailers with various odds and ends crowding front lawns—a hodgepodge of shabby furniture to corroded washers, rusted swing sets with missing swings, and tires on the loose. She had never seen such poverty before.

Mark reduced his speed as he announced they were approaching their infamous destination. The branches of the many trees on both sides of the road stretched above the car, providing a shady entrance to the one-store town.

Addie felt as if they'd slipped into a time warp—the twentieth century morphed into the nineteenth. The pot-holed asphalt narrowed further. And this rickety building listed dangerously close to a row of trees: The General Store, a historic eyesore with character. Addie tapped Mark's shoulder, asking him to slow down as she tried to soak up the hodgepodge of rusted-out cars, lopsided ice machines and scattered empty coke bottles, contrasting with the lush greenery. The store resembled a Hollywood location from a John Wayne western, with the exception of the four motorcycles lodged in front of it.

Two scraggly, grey-haired, bearded men, teetering in tandem on weathered rocking chairs, were having an energetic but private discussion, obvious by their closeness and furtive glances. Dressed in overalls and well-worn boots, they waved at Mark when he opened his window. "Howdy."

"Wow, you weren't kidding about how unusual these folks were compared to city folk. I see the overalls but no hayseeds."

Alongside a bearded motorcycle owner was a decrepit dog lounging quite contentedly on what was probably the biker's leather jacket thrown haphazardly at his feet. Taking a sip from a beer can, the biker gave them a perfunctory wave and a nod of his head.

"Do you know these people?"

"Yes and no. They recognize my car from the trips I make up yonder," Mark boasted, mischievously. "That's the hillbilly way."

Mark pulled over and retrieved his camera from the glove box, insisting Addie pose in front of the General Store. The mangy mutt rolled over with a groan as Addie hopped over him. Shifting her weight to one side and placing her hand on her hip, she giggled.

"This is how models do it!"

"Ok, say 'Cheese!'" Encouraging Addie to pretend she was on a photo shoot, he snapped myriad pictures using the natural props at hand. After receiving permission from its owner, she straddled the motorcycle, wearing the leather jacket that smelled of wood smoke.

"I can't wait to send that to my grandmother. She will love it!"

About three or four miles later, they came upon Mark's pride and joy snuggling up to the riverbank. Mark puffed his chest out, pointing to a parcel of mostly barren land with trees and patches of weeds here and there, announcing that this was his. The entire five acres of it.

"Ah! See! You *do* smile! And it is quite sexy at that!" It was more than his smile. As he stood admiring his very own scrap of earth, his shoes were dancing.

Mark blushed.

Other than her dad, she had never experienced such a kind and sincere man. *This guy can't be for real.*

Addie made her way to the gargantuan catalpa tree that cast a shadow over much of the ground surrounding it. Craning her neck, she crooked her head up toward the top branches, which appeared to be tickling the sky.

The smell of grass, hay, and what she guessed was country air invigorated her into a gallop toward Mark, who was gazing at ripples of muddy water in the Ohio River. She took a running leap onto his shoulders knocking them face down on the damp ground.

Addie deposited a kiss on his cheek and then bolted for the basket of food. Mark was chuckling as he opened the trunk to get a few picnic blankets. Addie peeked in and was curious about the other stuff that was jammed in there.

"Oh. My pop-up tent. If the weather is reasonable, I camp out here." Mark closed the trunk, and as he trudged through the grass, he started to stamp the ground to see where it was driest.

"I've never slept outdoors in a real tent. When we were kids, my sister and I set up an old tarpaulin in our backyard. We never made it through the entire night. Too many bugs!" Addie shivered.

"Well, we could make plans to do that here." Since he was pre-occupied shaking out a blanket, Addie could grin and high five herself without being seen.

Persistently trampling the soil, Mark eventually stopped and gave the ground a few more thumps. He shook the cover out and placed it on the area that met his approval. Addie knelt with her basket and grumbled how hard the ground was. She dug out the packaged food and wine, giving Mark a spoon and a plastic cup.

They left the car door open, which amplified the voices of the Beatles' singing "Hey Jude" as the melody streamed toward the riverbank.

Addie sighed deeply when "Imagine" billowed out. Singing along with John, she clasped her knees together and rested her chin on them. "That one gets to me: *Imagine all the people living life in peace.* Imagine if the people we loved were able to do that."

"Seems as though your family ..."

"Nope, my family is fine." Addie was annoyed with herself for rambling on.

"Snort!" Whiplash, another subject. Whimpers interrupted her at the same time she was imitating Irma.

"Oh my. What's that?" Addie sprang up and beelined toward the distressful yelps.

Mark caught up with her. "Hold on, Addie. We don't know what kind of animal is in there." She edged into the squeals until she saw a dog of miscellaneous origins trapped by a clump of broken branches and creepers.

"Addie, stop."

Squatting down on her haunches, she patted the dog's muzzle so as not to frighten him and began untangling the vines that held him hostage.

"Hey, fella. Well, let me get you out of here, and we'll see if you are a fella. How did you get yourself into this mess?" The branches and twigs snapped whenever the animal tried to get up, and when he did, he cried in agony.

"Addie, that dog might bite you. It's in pain. And country animals aren't vaccinated," Mark cautioned, standing behind her.

"Hey, buddy, let me help you." Getting down on her knees, she crawled closer and saw that the fur on his leg was caked with crimson beads.

In trying to break free, the dog tightened the vines that imprisoned him, slicing a gash in his leg.

"Rumor has it that country boys don't leave home without a pocket knife." She thrust her hand out from the foliage.

"Of course."

Taking hold of it, she ordered him to back off and give her more room. Her voice was stiff and edgy like a serrated knife.

"Here, let me help."

"No, he's wedged in there. Easier if I do it."

Careful not to make the injury worse, Addie tried to comfort the pooch by explaining what she was doing. Once released, the animal limped out and wagged its tail, licking Addie's face.

His injury was worse than she first thought. "We have to take him to a vet. I saw an animal hospital on the way here." Gazing into his matted up furry face, she was mesmerized by his oversized eyes, black like pools of oil.

"Mark, we have to take him to a vet. That gash on his leg needs stitches."

"Addie, it's Sunday. They'll be closed."

"Well, let's go back into town and find the number to an emergency pet hospital." This was a command. Addie bent down and promised her four-legged patient that he would be well taken care of as she led him to the car. The dog's fur was knotted with mud, full of ticks, and burrs, and his muzzle was green from eating deer shit.

"Addie. Wait. Are you familiar with ticks?" Mark stopped in his tracks.

"I'm a city girl. Tick! Dick! I don't care. Let's go, Mark." *Why doesn't he want to help this animal? Maybe he's not such a good guy after all.*

"C'mon, fella." Addie threw open the car door. Maneuvering him into the back seat as she wedged herself next to him, she assured their wounded passenger all would be well.

Mark packed up and fed the interloper a hunk of ham.

After spending three hours at the doggie ER, they zipped down I-75 on their way to Addie's. The vet "fumigated" Winston before he treated his injury all of which took much longer than they thought. Muddy mats of fur and ticks were transformed into a snowy white coat speckled here and there with smoky gray patches and a lopsided chocolate brown patch that covered his left ear.

"I hate dog names. They're stupid and insulting. Dogs are like people to me which means they should have people names. Famous people, at that. And this dog kept fighting and never gave in. So ..." Remembering her favorite quote, Addie modulated her voice into a Cockney drawl. "I baptize you, Winston. Winston Churchill." She peered over the front seat and grumbled as she toppled back and scanned the car mats trying to find her soft drink cup, hoping to find melted ice resting at the bottom of it. And as luck would have it, a few drops of water clung to the sides. The deed was done.

As she patted her dog who was resting on her lap, all forty pounds of him, Addie's eyes blazed as though they were being lighted from within. Whenever she helped an animal or a person in need, she would feel this warm glow circling her heart. It felt like the color green—a sea foam green—and had this indescribable peacefulness to it. In first grade religion class, Sister Bibiann would sermonize about God and how His greatest gift to the world was this spirit of goodness which flowed from the human soul. Addie was certain that's what this sensation was. Maybe if she weren't so pissed off most of the time, she'd feel it more often.

THIRTY-TWO

As promised, Addie checked in on Sundays at two o'clock. After filling her dad in about the state of her finances, she spoke next to her grandmother who filled her in on her church lady friends, their health problems, as well as her own aches and pains. The sisters would gab nonstop about the latest happenings in their lives leapfrogging from topic to topic but Addie spent quite a bit of time providing details about her manager and the dog they found.

"Well, as soon as we got back to my apartment, I let Winston out with his leg bandaged in gauze. As I was fastening this doggie head cone on him, the landlord, who is a nosy old bag, ran out. "No pets allowed. Read your lease!" I couldn't believe it! I started to go off on her which was doing me no good. Then Mark, using his Kentucky charm, tried to convince her the dog would not be a problem. She insisted that if that was the case, then he should take him. It was kind of funny. He didn't want to. But I was upset. He agreed. And now, I have visitation rights. This guy's unreal."

"He might be a keeper ... this boss of yours ..."

"Nice guy, but I'm not interested." Addie had great difficulty being truthful with herself when it came to any potential love interest.

After sharing an update on Mags, Addie was interrupted by a brief description of Mary's run-in with Jeff.

"Churchill lives! What about Sophie?"

"It doesn't matter about Sophie. He proposed!"

"Oh, Mary!" Addie blurted.

"I've never been so happy! But I have more to tell you, but not over the phone."

"That had an ominous ring to it. Bad news later. I'm more interested in my future brother-in-law! And how that came about."

"Long story and I have to go. It's all good!"

THIRTY-THREE

Chicago

Addie's dating advice was simple. The First Commandment: keep men guessing. *They're hunters and thrive on the chase. Whenever their dicks are left hanging, they chase harder. So run faster!*

Despite her sister's words of wisdom, Mary decided to be the "hunter." Addie remarked months ago that she saw Jeff at Murphy's a few times on Friday nights with a group of guys which prompted Mary to frequent the downtown bar, hoping she would run into him. She regretted breaking it off with Jeff but had to because she believed that if she opposed her mother in any way, the two of them would somehow fall apart without each other. Mary uncovered a smidgen of Ridley Scott within herself on the day she read her mother's secret out loud and although she wouldn't have to fend off aliens, she would need to stay grounded in her newfound determination. Hunting down Jeff was her first challenge.

Mary invited a friend to join her at Murphy's, but she backed out at the last minute. Apprehensive about implementing this scheme without an ally, especially on a Friday night, she decided to drive by. As her car crawled passed the bar, the usual assortment of people was clumped together itching to start partying. There, looming above the sea of heads, was her quarry. After rounding the block several times debating whether to go in, she sighted her sister's usual *No Parking* space. She believed it was a sign.

As soon as she was carded, she saw Jeff at the far end of the bar. Mary ordered a vodka martini and "excused" her way through hordes of bodies, slowing her pace as she forged ahead closer to her target.

Sitting knee-to-knee with an attractive woman, Jeff was riveted by her conversation. With the martini stoking her self-confidence, Mary pushed herself closer and gave him a bump with her derriere.

"Oh! Pardon me!" She took a swig of her drink, praying she did the right thing.

"No problem." Unaffected by the disturbance, Jeff leaned in closer to the woman Mary assumed was his date. There was not an iota of space between their bodies.

Shoot. What would Addie do? Never give up!

She repeated her planned interruption, but this time, Mary's scheme about knocked Jeff over.

"Hey!" As he was about to speak, his face split into a broad grin. "Oh my God! Mary!" His reached out to embrace her but paused as if he wasn't sure it was a good idea.

"Oh! Jeff. What a surprise!" This piece of fiction was coated with guilt. She leaned into him and patted his back as if to reassure him all was well between them.

Moving aside, he introduced her to Lilly, whose face was as stiff and cold as a frozen fish. Mary held her hand out but was ignored. Jeff plunged through the chill and asked Mary if he could get her a drink.

His bar companion fumbled in her purse and retrieved a cigarette making obvious gestures for Jeff to light it. His attention was transfixed on Mary who began counting the peanut shells littering the ground. Squeezing Jeff's shoulder, Lilly wagged a pack of matches in his face.

"Oops. Sorry." After doing his gentlemanly duty, he lessened the distance between him and Mary.

Scooting off the barstool, Lilly pitched her cigarette to the floor and smashed it with her spiked heel. "The party, dear, we have to go."

"Why don't you go on ahead? Mary's an old friend. I'll get there as soon as I can," he replied, as he sipped his drink and scrutinized Mary from top to bottom as if he couldn't believe his good fortune.

"You can't expect me to go without you!"

"Oh, no. Jeff. Please go," Mary interjected, praying he wouldn't take her up on it.

"Lil, normally I would never do this. You know that, and I wouldn't if you didn't know those people. I shouldn't be long."

Perusing the tavern, he waved at his law partner. "Hey! Stan! Can you take Lilly to the party? I'll be late."

Sipping their drinks, they both knew he wouldn't be late at all.

Mary's legs were intertwined with his while her head rested on his shoulder. As he slept, she focused on the pace of his breath rising and falling. A faint scent of nicotine blended with mint wafted past her nose. She remembered that he was self-conscious of his "ashtray breath," as he referred to it, so he was obsessive about masking it with evergreen candy.

The bedroom was the same since she was last here except for the duvet, which was a patchwork paisley. Ashtrays were overflowing on the nightstand along with recent photos of Katie. In one, she was hanging upside down, doing a cheer, and in another, she was propped up against a pimply-faced boy's arm, wearing a snazzy prom dress. As with the majority of her students, once they graduated, they faded into their futures as Katie did. At least until now.

Jeff stirred and kissed her on her forehead. "Good morning."

"Good morning. Uh, I'm not quite sure how this happened." *Be mysterious.*

"You weren't that drunk, were you?"

Mary muffled a yawn as she covered her nakedness with a blanket. "No, but the martinis did loosen my inhibitions. I am surprised we bumped into each other." She gave him a good whack with her hip.

Glancing at his watch, he kissed her and as he hurried to the bathroom, declared he was late for a client meeting. Mary admired Jeff's lanky physique most of all the flab jiggling on his hips and those long, skinny legs.

As she dressed, she debated whether or not she should leave or wait for him. Insecurities began to percolate.

"Mary! How about coffee? I'd appreciate it."

Humph! What am I? Sex partner and coffee maker ... what about a little conversation? What's the rush to get out of here?

Striding back to the bed, she found her shoes and slipped them on. For a minute, she was going to leave, but then decided to play it out and see if he was who she thought he was. She moseyed into the kitchen and rummaged through the cabinets for coffee cups, noticing that dishes, silverware, and pans were in disarray and located in the oddest places from when she was here last. Mary's curiosity nipped at her. How many other women did his bidding after sex? What was the deal with that woman at the bar?

With a towel wrapped around his waist, he glided right up to her and studied her face as if meeting her for the first time.

"What's wrong?" She began fussing with her hair.

"Not a thing. But I need you to pinch me," he grinned, pointing to his arm. "I have been waiting to be with you again, to hold you, to simply have you milling about my house."

Tilting her head and with eyebrows knitted together, Mary blinked a few times, unable to accept what she was hearing. This man whom she'd lost sleep over and stupidly gave up, refused to give up on her!

"Are you that astonished by my confession?" Jeff boosted Mary up and placed her on the countertop. "Hey, Mary Gurin. My life has been dull and boring since you withdrew yourself from it. I tried so hard to forget you. I was miserable. Can't you see how baggy my clothes are? I love you. Love you enough to propose marriage, if you'll have me." He peeked down at his towel and grinned.

"What?" Was he that arrogant to presume she pined for him? Why did he assume she wasn't in a relationship?

"I need to get dressed, but I can't wait! I'm not crazy! Yes! I mean it. I've been with women. Lots of them since my divorce. But our relationship was exceptional. We're a good fit Mary!" He rolled back and forth on the balls of his bare feet.

"Well. I've been with lots of men since you. As a matter of fact, I've been dating a gentleman who's crazy about me," Mary smirked, as she straightened her shoulders, and scooted off the counter, pushing Jeff away. "People see me as a good girl. Well, I'm not! I can sleep around, too!" She shouted with hands on her hips.

He headed for his bedroom.

Oh my gosh! Why is he leaving? She wanted to chase after him, but her legs felt like wood. "Are you done with me? Do I mean that little to you?"

Jeff loped toward her, picked her up, and carried her to the bedroom. "Actions speak louder than words." His towel and her clothes took to the air, flying above them as they toppled into bed.

His breath sent chills throughout her body. Mary pulled him close and wrestled him down into the sheets. It didn't take long before their bodies were moving in a natural rhythm.

"What is it about smoking a cigarette after sex? I see that hasn't changed." The smell of sulphur filled the air as Mary struck a match.

"Habit, I guess," he replied, tendrils of smoke meandering above his head. "So, who's this guy?" Jeff sprawled on top of her.

Mary caved. "True Confessions. I have been a virgin since we broke-up. But I want you to know it wasn't for any lack of opportunities. Now, who is this hot-tempered Lilly?"

"Ah. I am glad you're jealous! We work together, and a few of those after-hour depositions crossed professional boundaries. By the way, I talked to her earlier and apologized for being a no show. That is not normal behavior for me. See what you make me do?"

He scooped her up. The heat of his body intensified her awareness of the void she had been living with. There wasn't any sadness attached to it but more of an appreciation for it. How would she ever have known such wholeness without it?

"I have to ask you a question. Why did you accept our break up so easily?"

"Mary," Jeff rolled back over. "I knew this situation with your mother would cause more problems for you. And don't forget, I was brutally interrogated by her. Whenever that night came to mind, I stopped myself from contacting you. The last time we met, I could see being in the middle was terribly painful for you."

Sitting up and leaning on her elbow, she tickled Jeff's ear lobe. God, how she loved him. "Ok. It won't be a problem anymore, I promise."

"Was she miraculously transformed by a saint's relic or a Catholic pilgrimage?"

"Ha. Ha. You're funny. It isn't about her. It's never been about her. It's about me. I've come to a new understanding about the two of us and our relationship. I'll tell you all about it but not now."

Mary turned and looked him squarely in the eye. "I have to ask why you walked away from me in the kitchen."

"I had to contact my client and cancel that appointment. I wasn't leaving this house until I convinced you that I love you!" Checking the clock on his nightstand, Jeff pleaded, "God, Mary. I do have to go. A no show for a date is rude, while a no-show for a partners' meeting is disastrous!"

"Another habit that hasn't changed. You're constantly running late!" Patting him on the rear, she laughed. "Go! Get ready! Go!" She shooed him toward the bathroom. Mary danced and twirled until she was so dizzy she bumped into the nightstand and tripped into the warmth of the bed and pinched herself.

As she straightened the bed, it dawned on her that so many things were the same between Jeff and her and yet so very different. The difference revolved around her thorny emotions. She never dreamt that knowing and witnessing Sophie's internal hell would free her. The beliefs of her eight-year-old-self held her captive all these years. The magical thinking of that child believed that her mommy's happiness depended upon her and that if she was a good enough daughter, the two of them would be safe.

When she shared this with her mother a few days ago, Sophie smiled and announced, "You're fired! I have to heal those damaged pieces within myself. I'm moving in the right direction in therapy. Go live your life so I can live mine."

The secret ... what about Addie? She needed to know. Nausea joggled Mary's insides as she pictured divulging the abuse to her. That veneer Addie shielded herself with was as flimsy as a butterfly's wing. Shame and guilt would gnaw at her for the cruel and horrible things she spewed at their mother.

Before she left, Mary wrote Jeff a letter.

My dearest,

I can never express in writing how much you mean to me. You are the one person I completely trust. I'm glad you let me go, because I wasn't ready for any relationship at that time.

There's a story that's near and dear to my heart about a caterpillar who was afraid to learn what her true destiny was. With great courage, she risked stepping into the unknown, only to discover that she could fly.

I have a bit of unfinished business to take care of before I can fly.

So, my love, I'm asking you to give me a bit of time, as there is a family matter that I have to attend to with my sister. You remember her? The "fuck" girl?

We've waited this long. A few more weeks won't matter. That's right! I never formally responded to your proposal! I expect a fabulous engagement celebration! I will be back in touch.

All my love,
Mary

THIRTY-FOUR

Cincinnati

After the trip to the bowels of Kentucky, Mark and Addie began spending more time together. Their first camp out with their pooch did not last but for a few hours. The "creepy crawlies," as Addie dubbed them, and the daunting barking of the coyotes, which terrorized Winston, caused them to pack up in the middle of the night and schlepp back to Mark's place.

Their first sexual hook-up was awkward and brief. It didn't help that there were three bodies bouncing into each other until Mark exiled Winston to the living room. Distressed, the unwanted visitor scratched at the door and whimpered incessantly. Mark commanded him to knock it off.

"Mark, be nice. Winston, please settle down." Addie's voice sounded like velvet.

With a final, desperate groan, Winston curled himself up in his basket.

It was obvious to her that Mark was a neophyte, but sex wasn't a deal breaker for Addie. Sex was purely that: a physical need, like relieving an itch or consuming food to increase her blood sugar levels. It never bothered Addie if she was a one-night stand or a sex partner for months. If the relationship wore itself out, Addie never gave it a second thought. She devised a way to categorize men according to type, which she based on her experiences. Once she labeled them, which was accomplished after the second drink, she would sit back and enjoy her own cleverness.

A "1" was charming, with movie star good looks, and someone who loved himself more than anyone else. A "2" was nice, but boring. A "3" was a perennial frat boy who was happy watching sports' teams as if they were porno movies, drinking, and hanging out with his buddies. This far in her dating life, there was an overabundance of 1s, which appealed to her since those guys gave themselves every bit of love they required.

But Mark was a bit of an outlier, so she wasn't sure what group he belonged in. Maybe it was time for a category 4: nice guy, laid back, definitely not boring, but kind. She was flummoxed when he saved Winston from being homeless again. *Who does that?*

Sprawled out beneath the covers of his bed, she scooted over and fluttered her eyelashes on his cheek. "That's a butterfly kiss." She leapt on top of him and was air born when without warning Mark bolted out of bed.

"Hey! What's wrong?" She kicked the covers to the floor and scooted up. Winston clawed at the door.

Returning to the foot of the bed, Mark brushed a lock of his hair back. "Sorry. I didn't mean for that to happen. Well, I'll bet you see me as sexually inexperienced. But, I've had sex with quite a few women, and based on the reviews I've received, I believe I'm quite 'good in bed,' as the saying goes."

Where the hell is he going with this?

"They were dates, nothing special. But it's not the same with you. I couldn't let loose." Mark lit a cigarette as he confessed. "It's a self-preservation thing. Once I let myself go there, I'll fall in love with you, and that's clearly not where your head is."

Snatching his cigarette, she teased. "Bet you can't do this." Filling her lungs with smoke, Addie blew three perfect smoke rings that trailed one behind the other.

He agreed to the challenge, and she was right: he exhaled an "O" and it floated out like a crooked exclamation point.

"See!" Addie giggled and took another drag.

"I'm the champ!"

"Did you hear me?"

Addie exhaled another perfect smoke ring.

"Well, Mark, I'm a complicated person. You're a good guy. Keep that self-preservation thing going. I have fun whenever we're together, but that's the way it is with me," she disclosed without emotion, as a ring of smoke levitated between them. Addie couldn't bring herself to tell him she had her own self-preservation thing going. But lately it was faltering which scared her. This time she didn't get hysterical when the "love" word loomed overhead.

He extinguished his cigarette, giving her a peck on the cheek. "I guess I'll risk it."

Addie closed her eyes and stopped herself from saying, *I wouldn't recommend that.*

THIRTY-FIVE

It was an oddly quiet Sunday afternoon at the restaurant. Staff buzzed about a Bengals game with the Steelers, which explained why there were a few customers scattered about the lounge. Football never appealed to Addie except that, if the Bengals won, her tips would be double what they typically were. Unfortunately, their victories were far and few between.

While Addie was mixing a Rob Roy for a customer at the far end of the bar, a strikingly pretty young woman sauntered in, hopped on a stool and ordered a single malt scotch straight up with ice on the side.

"Would you like to run a tab?"

"Sure, thanks," was the pensive response as the woman scanned the room.

A few more patrons jockeyed for the bar stools in the middle of the bar and ordered a bottle of wine. *Funny,* mused Addie, *when it's not busy, people need their personal space and get annoyed when their territory is invaded.* She didn't mind running from end-to-end of the bar since it provided her with the exercise she was too lazy to do on non-work days.

Kibbitzing with the Rob Roy person, she learned his wife left him and his divorce attorney was incompetent … more information than she cared to know. The wine group, whose raucous laughter erupted unpredictably and annoyed the Rob Roy guy, ordered another bottle. The lonesome Scotch lady flagged her down. Addie thought she should introduce her to the wine group since they were having such a fun time.

"Miss, is Mark Lansing working tonight?"

Addie stopped dead and as she was cutting up lemons, she barely missed slicing her pinky off.

It never occurred to her that Mark would date other women. But then again, why wouldn't he? Since she made it clear that she was in it for fun, why was she stabbing the oranges as if they were trying to attack her? She decided to ignore the question.

"Ahh, can you tell me if Mark Lansing is working tonight?" Scotch Lady had a similar twang to Mark's hillbilly drawl only hers was thicker. "He's the manager here."

"He's off tonight." *What will I do if he shows up?* Scolding herself, but rattled as to why, she kept on slicing the lemons and limes, although there was more than enough to last for a week. Never having seen this woman before, she taunted herself, trying to figure out who she might be. *I'll bet Mark has been involved with her this whole time. She's a hillbilly, too! More his type. What was that crap that he'd risk falling in love with me? Maybe he is a "1". Why do I care? Shut up.*

"Dee? Is that you?" Mark's smile showed more of his gums than usual. Striding toward Scotch Lady, he embraced her for what seemed a ridiculous amount of time.

"Your bartender told me you were off tonight," Scotch Lady nodded toward Addie.

"My schedule changes from day-to-day." Mark retrieved a bar stool and settled it close to hers.

While shaking the martinis, Addie peered over at the two of them and was flabbergasted at their chumminess. Questions about them began invading her head space. She lost her grip on the olive jar and cursed under her breath. Reining in her thoughts before they hurtled down into the pit of her anger, she delivered the requested drinks and tramped over to Mark.

He and Scotch Lady were having the time of their lives as he was bending over in laughter. *This isn't happening. I don't give a damn about Mark. Then, how come I'm so pissed off at the two of them?* She exhaled trying to expel the pressure in her chest. Under no circumstances would she reveal the burning heat rising up within her. *What does it matter if they have a thing going? Who gives a shit?*

"Hey, how about a glass of merlot for me?" Mark scooted closer to his companion. "You Ok, Addie? You seem tense."

"No. No." The first "no" shot out like a bullet. "No. Just tired." She yawned a fake yawn, giving Mark a mental third finger.

The color green—yellowish green—is often associated with jealousy but for Addie, it was red... blood red. Feeling the heat of splotches sprouting, she held up a bar towel, feigning a sneeze. She wished she could scrape her neck down to the bone because those spots revealed way too much to the world.

The bar began filling up, and the crowd was exceptionally boisterous since the Bengals beat the Steelers ... a real miracle. Clouds of blue smoke lingered about at the same time people were barking out drink orders left and right. The din of voices became rowdier as more fans spilled into the lounge area. Glaring at Mark to get up as she bobbed her head toward the crowd, Addie tried to appease her impatient customers with no success. This time, she waved at him to help but he was too engrossed with Scotch Lady to notice.

"Bartender! Set up a round here," thundered an unshaven drunk Bengals fan wearing a bright orange and black sweatshirt with a roaring tiger plastered on the front. His belly was so voluminous the mascot appeared to be on steroids.

"I wanna buy that girl over there a drink!" A big hulk of a guy with oily hair sticking out of a greasy ball cap was pointing to Scotch Lady as he shouldered his way through the throng and rammed his rather large paunch against the bar bellowing a Bengals cheer, "Who Dey! Who Dey!" He sounded as if he had a tuba in his throat.

Yelling above the ruckus, his lusty eyes gave Mark's companion the once over. "What will you have, pretty lady?"

Mark took hold of Dee's arm and guided her to his office. The hulk was annoyed and started to muscle his way through the ocean of black and orange hats and shirts to follow them.

Stretching over the bar, Addie heckled. "Well, guess you struck out, fat boy. How about buying me a drink?" A hot sense of recklessness took hold of Addie.

"That depends on what you're doing after work."

"I'm off at 2 o'clock."

What was she doing? Flirting was one thing, but making a date for sex with a drunk was way beyond her risk level. But a surreal, bluish gray visual of Mark and that woman, writhing on the floor with their bodies intertwined, spurred her on.

Having sex in the cluttered and dirty cab of a truck was new for her. Having sex with a pot-bellied whale was an equally novel experience. His greasy mop poked out in strings from his Bengals hat and reeked of what she guessed was Brylcreem and nicotine. Those disgusting odors along with his beer breath and dime store cologne failed to disguise the putrid stink of his body. It was as if she was watching a movie of herself.

She came back to life while he was pawing her breasts. Unzipping his pants, he snatched her hand and jammed it on his limp penis, and like a jackhammer, jerked it up and down, demanding she go, "Faster! Faster!" His breath was coming so rapidly, sprays of his spittle landed on her face.

"*No!*" Buttoning her blouse, she was disgusted with herself.

"Hey. What the fuck! What are you doing? That wasn't worth the ice in that drink I bought you."

"Oh yeah? Well, with that pathetic dick of yours, you should've bought me a whole lot more than one." She lunged for the door.

He snagged her by the hair, and slapped her with such rage, her forehead slammed into the dash. "Bitch!" He bashed her head again.

But before his meaty hand could make contact with her face, Addie squeezed his balls with such ferocity that her long nails served as spikes, cutting into his flesh.

Gripping his crotch, he howled in pain. Addie fumbled with the door locks, and as he hooked his fingers around her arm, she jerked away and leapt out of the cab.

"Oh no you don't, you whore. I'm gonna kill you, I swear!"

She plummeted onto a large cobblestone which she hurtled at the windshield, hoping she cracked it.

"You bitch! I don't believe you did that! You're gonna pay for this. You wait!"

When Addie heard him slamming his shoulder against the door, the pounding of her heart did double time. With help from her adrenaline, she beelined to the back of the building and tucked herself amidst the bushes and shrubbery that clung to the side of the restaurant.

She was never more grateful to Mary for bribing her to join the track team in high school. Holding her racing breath, she slid deeper into her lair. Her clothes were soaked with perspiration, more so than at any long-distance track meet she had ever run. The ripe smell of sweat assaulted her nose, as she flicked a bug from her arm.

She heard the wheezing of his breathing as well as his feet crushing gravel as he searched for her. He mumbled in a frazzled voice, "I will find you, bitch. If not today, there's always tomorrow." Then a queer stillness muffled the rumble of traffic on Montgomery Road.

Why did I do that? What's wrong with me? Addie wept. As she continued to berate herself, the remarks of a shrink she fired infiltrated her aching head. "You are self-destructive." At the time, she blew him off, but her viewpoint was beginning to change. If a person believes they're worthless, why wouldn't they be self-destructive?

The hollowness within her tasted like the color blue ... frostbite blue ... oppressive and raw.

It wasn't until sunlight warmed her swollen face, that she awakened.

Mags was distressed at the display of cuts and scrapes that spattered Addie's body. "I fell in the parking lot at Chester's. Would you let Mark know I won't be in for a few days? And don't say anything about the fall. He doesn't know about it."

While she was dabbing iodine on the remnants of her recklessness, she met her own eyes in the bathroom mirror. She felt an urge to smash her face with her bare hands. Her all-too-familiar companion began dragging her down into an abyss of gloom. Her bed lured her into its arms where she hunkered down, burying herself in her feather stuffed pierzyna. From now on, she decided to put a muzzle on her reactions and be as invisible as possible until Mag's baby came. The *Invisible Woman* and in that way, she would be safe from her own craziness.

Throwing her covers to the ground, she reluctantly acknowledged ... *I guess I'm more like Sophie than I ever imagined.* Dropping back into her pillows, she slapped her forehead. "Oh my God, no!

THIRTY-SIX

A week passed, and her purplish, orange, and yellow smudges were less visible with the make-up Mags dabbed on her face.

"Your complexion is so pretty with foundation."

"Shut-up!"

Being bored, they joined the Chester's crowd for happy hour but hovered close to the door in case Addie needed to make a quick getaway. So as not to be trapped behind the bar, she decided to camouflage herself as a patron in case that baboon showed up. Not likely though. During her frenzied escape, she saw that his license plates were from Illinois.

Wearing a black suit, a light gold shirt, and a paisley tie, Mark was greeting dinner guests and escorting them to the dining room. He winked at Addie but the Invisible Woman didn't acknowledge him and kept on yakking about nothing with Mags.

In spite of the smells of grilled meat and smoke, a faint scent of calla lilies drifted about. Addie boasted that it was her brilliant idea to scatter a few vases of these trumpet-shaped flowers along with a spray of roses and orchids on the bar. The combination of white, gold, and magenta added a much-needed touch of color to the softly lit room. Complimenting her, Mags shouldered through a group of couples and ordered a red wine for Addie and a Coke for herself.

"Addie. Hey. Winston misses you," Mark said with an intentional hillbilly drawl.

That was a sorrow she wasn't able to dodge. She relinquished her shared time so she wouldn't have to answer any questions about her battered face.

Whenever his leash draped over her bedroom door jostled, she'd give it a kiss.

"Give him a dog bone for me. I'll pick him up at the usual time."

"Addie. Sorry to hear about your accident. I would've called or come over, but I know how you are so—"

"You know nothing about me!" Addie thrust these words out like spikes. She was hoping to piss Mark off so he'd go away. And her wish came true.

I am so discomfuckulated. I want him. I don't want him. I'm afraid to want him. What do I do with him if I get him?

One of the regulars was flirting with Mags, who was enjoying the attention, since it was a rare occurrence. In fact, non-existent. No matter how hard she tried to offset the physical changes she was undergoing, her efforts were in vain. It wasn't as if Mags wanted any relationship. All she needed was a tad bit of assurance that she was desirable, at least from the neck up. Before they left for their long-awaited night out, Mags arranged her coat in such a way that her protruding belly was well hidden.

Addie was surprised that her friend who continued to wear an overabundance of face paint and dye her kinky hair the color of a fire-engine, could attract a man. As time went on, Mags began to resemble a fat Kewpie doll who needed a do-over. With more and more frequency, Mags would study her bulge in front of a mirror and ask Addie if she was fat, never wanting an honest answer. Addie complied. *That's what good friends are for.*

"Mags, I'm off to the john. I'll be right back." Greeting people she knew as well as those she didn't, Addie came head-on with Mark and that woman.

Jealousy sprouted as if a typhoon was shearing her insides.

"Addie. I'd want you to meet someone who's dear to me: this is Dee."

Seeing her up close, Addie realized this woman wasn't quite as pretty as she thought. Shorter than average, a bit pudgy, with a Farrah Fawcett mop of blonde frizzles, she couldn't be Mark's type. What the hell did she know about his type?

"Addie, I've heard so much about you. I'm happy to meet you. I'm married to Mark's older brother, Adam."

It was as if a grenade had been tossed in her face. That blood red envy drained from her veins and pooled at her feet. This mishmash of emotions that she was experiencing for Mark—anger, hate, jealousy, love—signaled big trouble. She wanted to peel back her skin and set fire to every fucking one of them.

The muscles on Addie's face crimped into a bogus smile until she noticed Mags wobbling towards her pointing toward the exit. In spite of her make-up, Mags' face was the color of dough. Addie rushed to her side and steered her to the door.

As they were leaving, Mark asked, "Is there anything I can do?"

"No. We're fine," Addie bristled with a tremor in her voice.

THIRTY-SEVEN

The moon hardly penetrated the clouds as Mary and her grandmother ventured onto the expressway. The six-hour drive from Chicago to Cincinnati was tedious. Irina catnapped on the way except for the three bathroom stops, during which times Mary would peruse her Ohio map. Once back on the road, the boredom of the flatlands of Indiana roused her unease about her

Addie's panicked and cryptic call. *A car accident? Maybe she's been hurt. Or is she sick? Or is it Mags? Stop.* She was alarmed that the speedometer was inching toward the 90 mark.

Her unsettling thoughts probed for a more comforting place to land. Jeff proposing to her did the trick. Flipping the radio on, the song, *We Are Family,* roused a desire to join in despite her lack of talent.

"Paczki! My head!"

It was a rare occurrence when her grandmother annoyed her but these times seemed to be increasing.

When they arrived, the three of them clung to one another without moving. Drawing back, Mary scrutinized Addie from top to bottom reassuring herself that she was Ok at least physically.

"Forever remember ... *rodzina nie jest czymś ważnym. Jest wszystkim.* How did I do?" Mary hoped for the usual laugh from Addie, but she was stoic.

"You murder Polish," Babcia chided.

"I'm grateful you both are here. How about a glass of wine?"

"Marysia, get my brandy. Wine on Sunday at altar."

Whatever the crisis, Mary knew that her sister had to be desperate to ask for help. A funereal silence surrounded them for the longest time. Since boredom was setting in, Mary made her way into the kitchen and began scraping dried food off plates, but the pungent odor of trash became a more immediate task.

As she started to bundle it up, Addie laid into her. "Mary, sit! You've been on the road for a long time. C'mon, let's have another glass of wine."

Addie remained impassive as she started from the beginning with the contractions at Chester's, the mad rush to the hospital, and the long wait as Mags went through hell in the delivery room.

"It was stillborn, and it was a girl. Mags had a placental abruption, where the placenta separates from the uterus. She took a hard fall on her way to work the day before, and Dr. Keller believes that's what caused it. I should've driven her, but she insisted I take the car."

"What a nightmare. Why didn't you let me know sooner?"

"I thought she was Ok but when Mags wasn't getting any better, I freaked out. What I was doing wasn't enough, Mags needed more than I was giving her."

"Addie, this will take time. Don't be so hard on yourself."

Dawdling in front of Mags' bedroom door, Addie hesitated to disturb her.

The loud bursts of snoring emanating from their grandmother sent Addie over the edge. "Babcia! For God's sake, if you have to sleep, go to my room!"

Strident footsteps echoed in the hallway followed by repeated pounding on the door.

"Hey! Addie? It's Mark. Open up. Please."

She gathered up a few ashtrays overflowing with crushed cigarettes and disappeared into the kitchen, humming as if she'd heard nothing.

"Who is it?" Irina wiped the drool from her chin with her lacy handkerchief.

"Addie! Why won't you return my calls?"

Getting hold of Addie's shoulders from behind, Mary steered her into the living room.

"Let go of me, Mary. Mind your own goddamn business!" A flash of that stinking truck driver pawing at her twisted her stomach into a knot. How could she ever face Mark?

Mary elbowed her sister aside, and as she opened the bolt, Addie shoved her back so vigorously they both crumpled to the floor, zigzagging to avoid fists and kicks. Mark muscled the door open.

"Girls! Girls! Stop! You upset me!" Irina fretted.

Addie blasted her grandmother. "Shut up, old lady, and drink your damn brandy."

Bending down to separate them, Mark was drawn into the melee. Addie yanked at his hair leaving a tuft of it in her palm. As she was about to grab another hunk, Mary clouted her, except Mark's face intercepted the blow.

"Get out of here!" Addie kicked Mark in the shoulder.

Unexpectedly, cascades of alcohol drenched their bodies bringing an end to the chaos. "You like dogs fight, I get you wet to stop ... so I use brandy. No more left."

As the three pugilists attempted to untangle themselves, their grunts and moans were followed by restrained laughter. Mark reached out to help Addie and Mary pick themselves up.

Irina offered them a few towels to dry off.

Touching Mark's shoulder, Mary introduced herself and her grandmother, announcing that they were off to find a liquor store to replace her babcia's medicine. "Addie, deal with this."

Addie wanted to pop her sister right in the face. With Mags' depression as well as her own, she didn't need this. She just wanted to stick a pillow over her head.

THIRTY-EIGHT

Addie parked herself on the couch twisting a lock of hair around a few fingers. "How's Winston?"

"Fine. He misses you."

Silence stretched between them like a dark, cloudless winter sky.

Mark asked if she wanted him to leave when he heard an inaudible sniffle, then another, and then a torrent of convulsive wailing. Striding toward the blubbering, he sank down next to Addie and held her in his arms.

"Oh, Addie. I took care of that guy. Nothing to worry about."

"What guy? What are you talking about?" Keeping her eyes focused on her fingers, Addie was taken aback. How could he possibly know?

Taking a brandy-soaked towel from the floor, he dabbed at her cheeks.

"What did you mean? What did you take care of?"

"... the incident in the parking lot with that truck driver. Uh, I don't remember his name."

Addie picked up another towel and mopped her face. *Oh my God! What must he think of me?* Sister Joan, her sophomore biology teacher, pontificated about boys and how they lose respect for girls with loose morals. *Why do I have to be reminded of those stupid lectures now?*

Springing to her feet, Addie hightailed it toward the front door.

"Will you relax? My God." Mark gently pushed her back into the sofa. "You constantly have your dukes up. This gruff guy limped into the bar the day Mags called in sick for you and demanded to see the bitch bartender, bellowing that he intended to sue the restaurant for his medical bills and his shattered windshield. The barkeep who subbed for you escorted him to my office to shut him up.

"He recounted a sexual encounter he had with a sleazy ... his description ...bartender the night before and demanded reimbursement for damages. Since you're the only female who works behind the bar, it wasn't hard to figure out who he meant."

Addie racked her brain trying to figure out how to get the hell out of there, but Mark was within tackling distance. *How do I explain this?*

"We dickered about a fair settlement and then I wrote him a check as he signed an agreement that he was paid in full. What he claimed about the damages to his truck had your name written all over it. The sex stuff ... no doubt he made that up. What happened?"

Addie picked up the dishcloth on her lap and covered her tell-all neck with it, slowly moving it up to cover her eyes. What explanation could justify what she'd done? Anytime an orange tiger plastered against a fat gut caught her attention, she cringed. How could she ever tell Mark the truth? He would dump her and rightly so.

When she was able to stop snookering herself, she knew Mark meant more to her than she was willing to admit, but he deserved so much better. After all, she made up a whole new dating category solely for him.

"Why do you care?"

"I do, Ok?

"Well, you shouldn't!" she snarled, taking a long drag from her cigarette. Staring at the smoke circling the space between them, Addie tried to scrape her thoughts together. *All he needs to know is some of what I did but not why I did it.*

"Go away!"

"Not until you hear me out." Mark nabbed a bottle of wine from the fridge and installed himself next to Addie, who curled herself up like a ball of yarn.

"When I graduated from college, my brother, Adam, who had a bad case of wanderlust, begged me to travel with him. With his Eurail pass, he schlepped through most of the countries in Europe. He invited me to go to South Africa with him, but I was dating this girl pretty seriously and wasn't interested, so he bribed me with a free trip. Funny how that relationship ended right before he was leaving, so I agreed to go."

Offering Addie a cigarette, which she ignored, Mark lit up one for himself. Spirals of smoke streamed about his face.

"On my first day there, I noticed how happy people were. They strolled on the sidewalks or on the streets, in the stores, and would greet each other with a single word and a smile: *Sawubona*. I must have heard it a hundred times. '*Sawubona*.' I asked Adam what it meant.

"It's a Zulu greeting and means 'I see you … the real you … you are important to me, and I value you.'"

Addie yawned while she fidgeted with her fingernails. He smashed his cigarette in the ashtray so hard the embers singed his fingers.

"I have to tell you that any time we were together both in and out of work, I experienced pieces of you—not just the fun and exciting parts—but the softer side, your sensitivity, your love of four-legged creatures, your kindness to your friend, Mags. Unbeknownst to you, I've seen you turn over your tips quite a few times to some of the staff who needed extra cash.

"These fragments would sneak out once in a while since they're a natural part of who you are, Addie. This tough, fuck-the-world person is some character you created to push people away.

"Your problem is you don't like yourself. But what you dislike isn't you at all. It's that 'bitch' side you present to everyone. You need to connect with who you are and not define yourself by what other people have done to you. We've all been hurt." Angling himself next to her, Mark kissed her nose and whispered, "*Sawubona*. I see you, Addie, I see through that façade you hide behind. Stop being so damn stingy with those loving parts of yourself." He lifted her face to his. "I see you. I wish you were able to see who I see."

Mark stood up to leave. "I'm certain you have a good reason for not being honest with me right now, but I'm sure you will. Let Steve know when you want back on the schedule."

Mags sat next to Addie, whose face was streaked with dried up brandy and tears. After digging around in her shoulder bag for a smoke, Addie suddenly hurled it across the room. "I can never find anything in that piece of shit."

"Why don't you buy a new one?" Mags handed her one of her smokes.

"I didn't mean to eavesdrop, but I heard that conversation. Addie, you promised me you'd find another psychiatrist. Now, don't get huffy with me. I'm not sure I want to hear about that truck driver. And a truck driver?" Mags slapped her forehead. "You must have been majorly pissed at Mark."

"Well, let me explain ..."

"Don't interrupt me. We grew up together, so I've experienced your craziness. Anytime a man or anybody, for that matter, hurts you or doesn't measure up, you do the stupidest things. You act like a two-year-old, leaving people shell shocked wondering what just happened.

"I see you, too, Addie. The way you dress, your language, your whole demeanor says, 'Watch out!' What people don't realize is that what you actually mean is, 'Watch out! I'm fragile.'"

"Hey smarty pants! It's not that I'm fragile. It's that I can't trust people."

"Oh, it's the world's fault you're an emotional cripple."

"Aren't you funny? I hate people. Just this minute I formed the IHP Club. You can be my co-president. You get that honor because of how Tom dumped you ..."

"Oh, Addie."

"Oops. There goes my mouth again."

"I don't hate Tom. I don't hate anyone. You can be a real pain in the ass, but I don't hate you."

Addie kissed Mags on the cheek.

"How about a walk? I haven't been out since ..." Mags hesitated.

"How are you doing? You haven't wanted to talk much since ..."

"I want to go outside, please. No talk. You have been great just letting me be ... no talk just walk."

"That's what I need, too. Whew! I stink of brandy! Give me about twenty minutes to shower and change."

As she was undressing, Addie grappled with the idea that she was good and kind, as Sister Bibiann's lecture about God's gift of goodness replayed itself ... *that* she could accept. But Mags and the fragile crap, maybe not so much. If anger consumes every bit of her emotional space, there is no room to be fragile. Saying "fragile" out loud prompted a shaky laugh, which morphed into a "fuck them," followed by sniffles, and a stuffed nose.

Fragile. Addie knew that was bullshit, but her adrenaline cranked up as she recalled what Mark thought about her. Her skin was clammy and stunk of her anger. Addie hopped in the shower and while she was lathering up, she felt woozy. Her breath became uneven. Resting against the cold tiles, she shuddered, imagining what would happen if Mark saw all of her. Not what she lets him see. But that other part ... the raging destructive part. She can tell him that she's fucked up, but he's never seen how much. That skirmish earlier was barely a preview.

The cloud of breath blurring her reflection in the mirror above her dresser didn't prevent her from recognizing how fragile she was. Those lines etched around her mouth spoke of her anger—anger she wasn't ready to let go of yet. Who would she be without it?

"*Sawubona*," she murmured to the reflection before her. "But I'm not crazy about what I see."

THIRTY-NINE

The apartment had been tidied up ... at least the living room. When she and Addie were kids, the state of Addie's bedroom reflected her moods with incredible accuracy. It was either a disaster or squeaky clean. The place wasn't squeaky clean, but it was in much better shape than when she and Babcia left Addie in a muddle with that Mark fellow.

There was a note on the door: *Mags and I went to Eden Park. Will pick up dinner.*

Mary watched Babcia as she toppled into the cushions, and let out a full-throated grunt. Questioning her decision to bring her along didn't last long since Mary wanted to be there to support her grandmother when Sophie confronted her.

"Paczki ..."

Before her babcia made her request, Mary removed a large bottle of brandy out of the bag and retrieved a glass, pouring a tiny amount into it.

"If I need eyewash, I go to eye doctor."

"You drink too much!"

"Rule number two." She held up two fingers.

Oh, what the heck. Mary doled out more.

It wasn't long before she heard Babcia breathing noisily. She found a quilt in Addie's room and covered her grandmother with it.

Resting on Addie's bed, Mary agonized about the conversation she needed to have with her sister and her grandmother. The more she pictured revealing her mother's secret, the more her imagination fired up these possible reactions: Babcia, at first would deny it and then babble in Polish asking how in God's name Mr. Gurin, her savior, could do such a thing?

As for Addie, despite her outrage, she would be flooded with guilt and shame which concerned Mary. Would she hurt herself?

They were scheduled to leave in three days if Mary was to be back at work. *Will my mother be disappointed because I didn't let her deal with it? And my dad? He wanted the family to be together.* As she plodded back into Addie's bedroom, she shrouded herself with her sister's pierzyna. It felt as though an electrical storm was passing over her entire body.

FORTY

When Addie returned to work, many of her customers offered to buy her a drink on the condition that she would never cast them aside again. Mary accompanied her while Mags volunteered to hang out with Irina.

"What an interesting place, Addie." Mary was drawn toward the center of the dining area where a multi-colored container holding a sturdy leafy tree that was stretching to touch the skylight was shading nearby tables. The lighting was dim, and a slight savory aroma reminded her she hadn't eaten all day. A few guests were having dinner in cozy booths that were lined up with others on either side of the dining room. The voice of Frank Sinatra crooning "Chicago," billowed above the chatter of the guests.

Mary settled herself in at the bar, relishing the fragrance of flowers and ordered a merlot. Addie snickered.

"Why don't you try a chard or a pinot grigio?"

"Hey, bossy pants, I want a merlot!" Mary snickered.

Addie avoided Mark, making it obvious to staff and regulars that their relationship had deteriorated and was now a few degrees above freezing. The chef, who was obsessed with being the keeper of staff gossip, asked her about the two of them. She thrust her third finger in his face.

As Addie served guests, Mary fiddled with her bar napkin, creasing the corners until it shredded. Before she'd left Chicago, she had contacted Jeff to explain Addie's mysterious plea for help as well as the grisly details of the family secret.

"Hey, when are you leaving?" Addie asked.

"Sunday morning. Say, can you and I have time together before then?" Now she was committed.

Salting the rim of a margarita glass, Addie mumbled, "Sure."

"How about tomorrow?" Mary needed to wait at least a day for the aftershocks.

"Sure. Let's go to a favorite place of mine for breakfast, but I can't stay too long 'cause I promised a server I'd sub for her lunchtime schedule on Saturday."

The bar was filling up with people waiting for tables, and as usual, Addie was inundated with drink orders. Mary waved at her and mouthed the words, "See you later."

As she drove back to the apartment, Mary mulled over whether a public place was a good idea for their meeting, but then again, she hoped Addie would be less inclined to go haywire. Another rationalization, but it gave her the fortitude to go through with this.

How do I tell my sister that our mother was raped as a child? Should I give her the horrible description in Sophie's own handwriting? No. There's another way; an entry that doesn't mention our grandfather. I have to break it down into small pieces. There are so many layers to our mother's disappearance. The worst being that the pervert was our grandfather. How can Addie be mad at her anymore?

FORTY-ONE

On their way to the restaurant, the sisters gabbed about the classic late-night movie they watched, *Mildred Pierce*. Mary tried to change the subject since Addie was getting riled up about how the film idealized mothers and stereotyped daughters.

"Poor Mildred! Sacrificing her life for her bitch daughter," Addie carped.

"How much farther?" The pain in Mary's head felt as if one of her students had jabbed a pencil through her eyeball.

"Here we are. We won't have to wait long."

The delicious smells of coffee, fried eggs, and bacon encircled them as Addie steered her sister through the door gossiping about an old friend of theirs. Since she had breakfast there on the weekends, Addie informed Mary that she'd order for both of them. As she was rattling off her choices—two omelets with cheese and mushrooms, sausage, English muffins, hash browns, and OJ—Mary's stomach churned.

Addie prattled nonstop.

The noises coming from her sister were fuzzy, as though Mary's ears were stuffed with cotton. Addie sliced the fork into her omelet and swallowed a hearty hunk. "You shaid there was shome thing you wanted to tell me."

"Don't talk with your mouth full and take your time."

Addie pointed her fork at Mary's untouched plate. "Didn't you like the food?"

"I'm not hungry."

Mary coughed, hoping the words lodged in her throat would unravel.

"Here we go. Addie. Please promise me that you won't flip out." Mary waved the waitress down to fill her glass with more water.

"Wow. This must be a biggie. I know you know that my flip-outs have a mind of their own, but I promise I will control myself so as not to embarrass you." With exaggerated motions, Addie straightened up and folded her hands.

"I read the secrets in that envelope you found."

The stillness was eerily unnatural, as if the words Mary spoke devoured the noise around them. Addie barked out a broken laugh. Her eyebrows dipped together as if her brain was laboring to make a new connection.

Mary placed a handwritten paper on the table, easing it toward her.

Addie pinched the bridge of her nose. She zeroed in on her mother's scribbles, and she tore it in half.

"Stop! What is wrong with you?"

"This is it, isn't it? I'm scared, and I don't know why." She rested her head on the table.

Mary squeezed in next to her. "It'll be Ok. Remember Babcia's story about the goat having a miserable life if she didn't jump? It's time to jump, Addie."

Straightening up and fitting the ripped halves together, she stared at them for several minutes before reading. When she reached a certain part, she covered her mouth with her hand.

... He flips me over, and I cling to that yellow bedspread that stinks of sour milk. I stare at the blue flowers. I can't breathe. He rams a cover over my face. It feels as though I'm dying. I try to be still and disappear. I can't breathe. I feel like I must be dying

Those words—"*muted blue flowers ... yellow coverlet*—stood out from the page.

"That's why she collapsed at the store that day." A vivid image of that bedspread sprang up on the undersides of her eyelids.

"Are you ready for more?"

Addie blinked as if she wasn't sure who was sitting across from her.

"Yes."

"The man who abused her was our dad's father ... our grandfather. Dad swears he never suspected his own father was a pedophile, even though he accidentally barged in on them, and I'm not sure about Babcia.

"I happened to hear them arguing one morning, and it unraveled from there. When dad asked mother for an annulment, I lost it! So, I brought the two of them together, and after the hysteria passed, I found the envelope and read this journal entry to them. Addie, I didn't know what to do. Dad was wailing, hammering himself with his fists. The last time I saw Mother in such a rage was the night—"

Addie pled, "No more."

Rushing past Mary and stumbling outside, she vomited on the curb. Gazing back at her sister for a moment, Addie bounded down the street, as pedestrians stepped aside for her. As houses whizzed by, she willed herself to run faster and faster.

My God! I never ever imagined a child ... What kind of freak would do that? My own fucking grandfather! Where was Babcia? My God. Sophie! My mother! How has she been able to live with this horror?

FORTY-TWO

Addie fled to Ault Park, where she climbed the concrete walkway leading to the pavilion. It wasn't crowded this late in the morning. Anxiety had been a familiar companion to her, but this episode was intolerable. It felt as though her insides were being crushed by an ever-tightening vice. Her legs wobbled, so she supported herself against the pillared flagstone railing and trembled as she fixed her gaze at the leafless trees that were scattered about. They seemed to be as desolate as she felt.

Addie's memory catapulted her back to a night she had submerged in her consciousness ... the screaming ... the chaos ... the terror. Her mother's disappearance. That's why she was in the hospital.

Sliding down to the ground, she massaged her temples, but even though she pressed her back against the damp and chilly slab, she felt heat rise from her skin.

"My mother's secret ... oh my God. My fucking grandfather! Why didn't she fight! Goddammit, I would've fought. I would've told on that bastard! Why didn't she?" Addie hammered her fist on her knee. But as her mother's description of the abuse played itself out in her mind, sorrow flooded her heart. A sorrow that was massive, because it wasn't Addie's alone. Recalling her mother in that Holy Communion picture, made her weep.

For so long, she believed that her mother intentionally and selfishly deserted them. All that whining about how it was Sophie's fault that she was screwed up, when in fact, Sophie was wounded, the one with a bruised heart.

Her brain resisted this new reality because the old ones were so comfortable right where they were. Being angry at Sophie was so much easier than reflecting on the pain of the horrific violence she must have endured as a child. And where was her babcia when this was going on? Sophie's ominous warning ... "your grandmother isn't who you think she is" ... cut into Addie. What did she mean by that? Surely, she didn't know ... or did she?

As the chill of the cement began to penetrate her clothing, she shivered uncontrollably.

Delving in her purse, she searched for cigarettes and matches. When she felt the cellophane wrapping, she rooted one out so roughly, it broke in half spilling tobacco everywhere. "Fuck." Digging in again, she found another, lit it, sucking the nicotine deeply into her lungs.

The answer to her lifelong quest fucked her up more. This is far from what she expected. But then, what *had* she expected? Clearly not the confusion she felt about Babcia—the person she loved with her entire heart.

Mary and Irina were huddled together engrossed in a TV show. Brandy and red wine were sitting before them, along with bowls of popcorn and mixed nuts.

"Addie! I was worried about you. Someone from Chester's called to see if you were Ok since you were a no-show. After this morning I—"

"Adelajda! You wet! Go change clothes. You want food?" Babcia rose and shuffled toward her granddaughter to check her temperature.

"I'm not hungry." Addie quivered scraping wet strands of hair from her face.

That question about her grandmother was so unsettling that she was pissed at herself for considering it. *But she was a mother.*

"Go change. You're dripping."

Mags was sitting cross-legged on the floor reading the newspaper. On her way to her bedroom, Addie stopped, tapped Mags on the shoulder, and nodded her head in the direction of the door.

"Say no more."

"I appreciate it." Addie's adrenaline was hard at work as she wrestled with what she didn't want to know.

Mary whispered. "Addie, Babcia doesn't have an inkling about what happened to mother. I was asked not to tell either of you—"

"Fuck! No more secrets!" Addie's outburst startled both of them.

"Please. Dad wanted to discuss this as a family. Mother is trying to figure out how to deal with Babcia on her own. But, it's not fair that we're privy to what's been painful for our whole family. Let's be gentle with her. She's old. We have to ease her into this since she let Mother go there."

"Mary, I just found out my grandfather raped my mother when she was a child and that my own dad was aware of it. Where was Babcia? I need more time to get my mind wrapped around that bit of news."

FORTY-THREE

Addie plodded to the shower and propped herself under the spray of hot water, curious if she could drown. How she wished she could swirl down the drain and evaporate into a mist of steam. Her thoughts were bending at the edges and on the verge of snapping. *Deal with this. If Sophie can live with ... with what happened to her, I can deal with this.*

She slipped into a t-shirt and jeans that hung on her like a hanger, and then she tied her freshly washed hair into a topknot that looked more like a fountain spraying strands of her locks to her shoulders. Maybe she should leave that wolf in the woods, but this was about her family. Giving up on them left her with nothing. Addie brooded over how their lives would have been different without those secrets to hide behind. A chill crawled up the back of her neck.

The aroma of roast pork, peas and pearl onions, and kapusta flooded her nose as she tramped into the living room. Babcia commanded her to eat as Addie settled herself close to Mary.

As she beheld her grandmother's weary face, she felt disoriented as if this woman was a stranger. What was she needing from her? What should she ask? Maybe Babcia wasn't aware of what was happening to Sophie? What if she says she was? What was perfectly clear earlier looped into a vortex of doubt again. The time for secrets was over.

"Babcia, we don't have any relative in Poznan, do we? And in fact, our mother was a few miles from our house, and in a hospital that entire time. Why did you lie to us? Why?" Addie dipped her head toward Mary, who reluctantly held up the envelope.

"Do you remember the day I found that?"

"Ya ... You not eat now? It get cold."

"The notes in it are journal entries our mother wrote while she was hospitalized," Mary mumbled.

"Babcia, I need to read this aloud so sit." Addie began reading the page Mary gave her.

"... *He pushes me down onto the bed covered with the yellow coverlet with the muted blue flowers on it. Sometimes I try to count the flowers when I want to escape the pain. He unzips his pants. Even though I know better than to resist him, my body won't cooperate. He grabs my flailing arms and pins them down. I cry some more.*

Irina tilted her head in confusion.

"Babcia, our mother was sexually abused." The words stuck in her throat like a fishbone.

"*Zatrzymać!* Stop!" Fighting for breath, she cried out. "That not your matka writing."

Mary assured her grandmother that it was.

The bellowing that voiced Irina's sorrow mimicked that of a moaning whale—forlorn and grief-stricken.

It was so painful, Addie battled with herself not to let it get in the way of the truth. "Tell me you didn't know about it. As her mother, I'm sure you would've protected her."

It took Irina a few minutes to gather herself. "*Mój Boze!* My God! All time she with me if I not work, after your *jaja* die."

"How long was that?" Addie demanded, ignoring her babcia's cries.

"Helen watch her few years."

How could a child endure such horrific acts of violence without any adult knowing? Why didn't Sophie tell her mother? Why didn't Babcia have any idea what was happening over there? And what about Helen, her other grandmother? This began to gnaw at Addie as she studied the wizened woman before her.

"Didn't you suspect anything?"

They were distracted by a neighbor jangling keys across the way. Standing up and with arms crossed, Addie began pacing before her grandmother. "Well, did you or didn't you?"

Babcia took the hanky she kept hidden in the sleeve of her sweater, and began to weep. "She did. She came two, maybe three time in beginning ..."

Irina flattened the embroidered cloth to her face as if it might shield her from her granddaughter's wrath.

Addie thundered, "I don't believe that. You would have protected her."

"Adelajda—"

"No!" Snatching an upholstered foot stool, she dropped down onto it. "Don't give me that pitiful face. Why did you keep sending her there? You are a *mother*! You should have protected her. That's what mothers are supposed to do, Goddammit!"

"Adelajda ... please, I know no sex with child ... never."

"But it was your daughter ... who were you protecting?" Addie's throat thickened as the question rushed out. "Who was it?"

"It had to be ... but ... he good to us. He gave Jaja job, and help me get job. He give money to live on ... Helen take care of Sophie—no charge."

Springing to her feet, Addie was within inches of Irina's face. "You didn't believe her because it would've made your life much more difficult? Did it ever occur to you that was all a bribe to cover up what was happening to your daughter?"

A piercing groan tore out from Irina. "Nie! Nie! No!"

Another bruise speared Addie's heart—the profound love she carried for her babcia shattered.

"I'm severing our thread like my mother did." The word 'mother' slipped out effortlessly. "And I never want to hear your 'family is everything' bullshit." The fury that was comfortably lodged and aimed at her mother deposited itself on to her grandmother.

Stomping out, Addie began jogging as soon as her feet hit the sidewalk. A side stitch stabbed her, and as she bent over gasping for air, another of her shrink's insights reverberated in her head.

"More times than not, people don't say or do things with malicious intentions."

Bullshit. That doesn't apply to Mothers. They're mothers. They're supposed to always do the right thing.

FORTY-FOUR

Before the sun rose, Mary and Babcia left for Chicago. Addie was nowhere to be seen ever since she stormed out in a rage the night before. Mags was clueless as to her whereabouts.

Waiting to get the signal from Mary that it was time to go, Irina was praying her rosary.

Mags asked if either of them wanted breakfast.

"We'll pick up a sandwich on the road."

As she placed the last bag in the trunk, Mary's mind was jammed up with these patchy impressions of her mother as a child crying for help from the one person she loved and trusted. Driving off, she heard Mags yelling for her to stop.

"Mary! Your grandmother! You were leaving without her!"

Apologizing, Mary reversed the car and settled Babcia into the front seat.

The drive was boring and since Irina never enjoyed American music, Mary didn't have any distractions to prevent her from dwelling on her grandmother's admission of guilt as well as her own unwillingness to accept it.

"Marysia. You mad at me, too?" A tear landed in a fleshy rivulet and crawled down Irina's face.

Mary bit her lip. "Well, yes. I was upset that you kept the most damaging secret. My mother told you!"

"Marysia, I know no sex with child, never in my life. I kill myself if I don't go to hell. Little Sophie say her peepee hurt, but she never let me see. I try, she scream, so I stop. She not let me dress or wash her. She have fit. I get mad. We fight. I ask Helen why Sophie say her peepee hurt. She say no, nothing wrong. I ask her to talk with Sophie. She tell me Sophie Ok. I want her to go to doctor. Since I work long hours, she say she take Sophie. She say he say Sophie Ok. Then Sophie stop complaining about peepee. I think she fine. But like Adelajda say, I no good mother. Mother should know."

"Is that how she described it? That her peepee hurt? And Dad's mother volunteered to take her to the doctor?" It took her a few minutes to grasp what her babcia was saying.

"Ya." Irina's face was blotchy and then she released an ear-splitting yowl. "*Zawiodłem jako Matka*. I fail as Matka."

Speeding up, Mary scanned road signs for the next exit and left the expressway as soon as she could. Tears glistened on her eyelashes as she kissed the old lady's pallid cheek. "Listen to me. This wasn't about not believing her. You didn't understand what she was trying to tell you, and you trusted Dad's mother. You tried ... you tried. You were a good mother."

As she sobbed, Irina's breath stuttered. "I love her, I die for her."

"I'm not mad at you. I forgive you for what you couldn't know because you trusted Helen."

"You forgive me? Ya? Were you mad at Sophie like Adelajda?"

"Yes. But not in the same way."

"I had to lie about hospital and fake relative, Marysia. Your matka hate me enough. And I make promise on Bible."

"I understand, I do. I'm sure you prayed whenever you lied to us."

One half of Irina's mouth hitched up revealing a red smear of lipstick on her upper denture. "Ya, I did. Marysia, you forgive, but what about your matka? And Adelajda? And your papa, too?"

"Don't you worry about them. They will. I'll make sure of that."

"Marysia, let's say thanksgiving prayer to Blessed Mary."

It wasn't long after, that Irina dozed off. Mary wasn't bored with the rust brown flatlands of Indiana on the drive home. The landscape was strangely different from just a few days ago but she couldn't put a finger on it. The weathered farmhouses and barns reminded her of a scene in the Wizard of Oz. She imagined that if she stopped, she'd catch Dorothy and Toto sitting on one of the circular haystacks scattered over the fields.

Glancing at her grandmother, Mary's heart overflowed with a profound affection for her that wasn't confined by a label filled with infinite expectations. All the lines and wrinkles on Irina's face held the story of a woman who was thrust into this world like everybody else and did the best she could.

How is it that mothers are expected to love their children unconditionally, but it isn't reciprocated? Perhaps it's about those damn expectations.

It was about three thirty in the afternoon before Addie showed her face. Mags was sprawled out intently reading a *Vogue* magazine and in between page turns asked Addie why she didn't say good-bye to her sister and grandmother. A grunt was her response.

Picking up glasses, bowls, and dried-up plates of food, Addie piled them into the sink with such vigor that a bowl cracked in half as it crashed against a greasy pan. The steel wool pad crackled as she scoured the sticky and crusty dishes from last night's feud.

"Hey, I was planning to take our kitchenware back home intact."

Curious to know what the mood was when her relatives left, she was too drained to ask, and if truth be told, didn't want to hear the answer.

"How about a pizza?" Mags asked.

Addie dialed LaRosa's and ordered their usual fare.

"I take it last night was pretty difficult." Mags drew smoke into her lungs.

"I have a lot to think about."

Addie's daunting predicament was how to act with Sophie and her grandmother when she saw them next. It was understandable why Sophie was so hateful toward her own mother—she didn't believe her, so the abuse continued. How could Sophie ever forgive her?

Like a silent movie reel playing before her, fragments of the cruelty Addie inflicted upon her mother, her insensitivity when Sophie attempted to close the space between them, rushed past. Addie's overwhelming dilemma was whether or not her mother would ever forgive her. Or if she could ever forgive herself. The familiar chasm of self-hate began to sweep Addie into its clutches. She needed to strangle its venomous whispers.

"Hey, come sit over here." Mags wiggled her feet hinting for Addie to massage her toes.

"Mags, I've been burning in the fires of my family's hell these past few days. We can talk about them another time. May I ask about the baby?"

"I'm not ready yet. Thanks for not pushing me. Maybe I'm rationalizing, but I wouldn't have made a good mom. I'm selfish like my mother was and is—more interested in herself than she ever was in me—ow! Too rough on those toes."

"You're not selfish. I'm selfish. I guess ever since your first OB appointment, I wondered what kind of a mother I'd be."

As she wandered through Hyde Park the night before, Addie puzzled over how Sophie would have been different if Babcia had stopped the abuse. Sophie was a fine mother, except Addie's blind spot enabled her to only see her mother through the eyes of an abandoned child.

What disturbed her was why Sophie despised her as much as she did. Scouring her memories, Addie knew that she was a pain to deal with, but what did that have to do with the abuse? Why was Mary her favorite? She swatted at the voices of her shrinks. *Hmmm. Maybe it was the way I treated her. I was a pain in the ass—but I was a kid. Shouldn't a mother be more patient and understanding?*

A knock on the door interrupted Addie's musings. Their usual pimply faced delivery boy, bundled up with a red LaRosa's jacket and hat, holding a large cardboard pizza box with a matching logo plastered on its topside. After paying him, Addie inhaled the delicious aroma of mozzarella cheese, pepperoni, and mushrooms.

"Ah. Nothing like pizza to lift one's spirits."

Their established division of labor sent Mags off to set the table while Addie, as house bartender, poured the drinks. To her dismay, the fridge was devoid of any wine, but upon shoving aside a pickle jar, a carton of eggs, and several bottles of diet Coke, Addie spied a few cans of ale hiding behind the OJ. Beer reminded her of Murphy's, where the brew on tap either smelled yeasty or like a burp. Hating to acknowledge how homesick she was, she popped open the can, took a whiff, and gulped it down. *Yes, Dorothy was right. No place like Murphy's.*

"Addie, c'mon, the pizza will get cold," Mags griped as she bit down on a slice, leaving a string of melted cheese clinging to her chin.

"Don't get your panties in a wad! Here's a beer, we're out of wine."

As she grabbed another slice, Mags rattled on. "Uh, isn't it time to go home?"

"No reason to stay, so far as I'm concerned. Anytime is good."

"Ah, Addie, I have news to share, and I'm sure you won't be happy about it." Standing up and entwining her fingers, Mags anchored her feet to the floor. "Tom is begging me to forgive him. We're getting back together."

"Are you fucking kidding me? How can you consider taking that asshole back?"

FORTY-FIVE

The two of them were unbending in their arguments about Tom.

"I love him."

"He's an asshole."

"He was scared—"

"Dump him. I would kill him and be quite happy to go to prison."

"That's your solution without fail! You're a professional dumper, Addie. I worry that you'll dump me if I don't measure up, and it will be 'bye-bye, see ya later.' I've lived with that since we were in grade school, and I've been careful to keep us friends by not pissing you off."

"That's not true! You've pissed me off many times!"

"Oh, shut up! I love you, Addie, but you do have a dark side. God forbid if someone you care about disappoints you or doesn't meet your expectations, you become a total bitch. After listening to your ranting about the gazillion therapists you saw, I realized that you act the fool any time you're scared, and you're scared whenever you're feeling insecure. I believe the word used by your shrinks is, 'fragile.' Therapy by proxy ... thank you for ranting about their shortcomings. Underneath your anger is this sadness. That's as much as I know considering you kept firing them. Maybe if you listened to what you didn't want to hear, you'd be cured by now!"

"What? That makes no sense."

"Open these!" Mags slid next to Addie and tweaked her ears. "I know you'll be pissed, but I'm not dumping Tom. I've forgiven him, and I'm sure you'll be delighted to learn that we intend to get therapy. Any recommendations?"

Addie was beginning to despise the F word: 'fragile.' *How can I be fragile? Angry people are far from fragile. They're tough and indomitable.*

The name of that shrink was lost to her like so many of them, but Mags was right about that sadness thing. *My bruised heart. I guess I am fragile. Mark was right. My fuck-the-world attitude keeps me from feeling it.*

Addie thrashed about in bed that night. Apart from having to deal with Sophie and her grandmother, Mags dumped this on her. It was difficult to understand why she would want that bastard back after he ditched her. How could things ever be the same between the two of them, in spite of the best counseling in the world?

Tossing and turning, Addie found herself knotted up in her covers. *What am I fighting?*

This shield she hid behind was becoming more of a burden. But without it, she was terrified that she'd be like a feather in the wind. Tossing that idea about, she wondered if forgiveness was more like the wind, since it took a helluva lot of energy to do. Would she ever be able to forgive her babcia? Never!

An uninvited memory flickered before her. The two of them were meandering home from church when her grandmother stopped and placed her finger under Addie's chin, tilting her head up.

"You hear priest sermon?"

Addie nodded her head.

"Ya. But you not know meaning. Forever remember ... truth hurt, but it set you free." Addie screwed up her face as if her babcia was babbling in Polish again. Babcia uttered one word: "Forgiveness."

Another F word. Fuck forgiveness. How can I forgive anyone who doesn't do what they're supposed to do?

The next day, while her morning coffee was percolating, Addie was struck with a few revelations that weren't accompanied by any of her therapists' voices. How could she be so infuriated with Mags when it was

Tom who deserved her vitriol? Until Addie learned of the abuse, she was pissed at Sophie for the longest time, but her grandmother had been the offender. How was it that the people she cared about became the culprits?

"Hey," Mags mumbled.

"Good morning. Hey. Getting an apology from me is like spotting a shamrock in a field covered with them. I'm sorry about how I reacted yesterday. I know I can be prefuckterous."

Mags gawked at Addie as if she announced she was joining the convent.

"Come on!" Addie howled, "Preposterous!"

"Well, I appreciate the apology. I'm glad you haven't thrown me out of your life!"

That was brutally harsh. Addie bit her lip.

"Addie! Don't' be so gloofuckmy!" Mags broke out into giggles.

"What?"

"Gloomy ... gloofuckmy. Get it?"

"Stick with regular English. That was terrible!"

After breakfast, they began debating how much longer they needed to stay in Cincinnati, as well as the details of their departure.

"I'm nervous about going back though. Aren't you?"

"Yup. We both will have a shit show of stuff to deal with. But, remember my grandmother's goat story? It's time to jump."

Addie shopped for her buddy ... two bowls, another leash and collar, dog food, and Milk Bones. A few chew toys that appealed to her were tossed into the cart. Uncertain as to how Sophie would react to having a dog in the house, Addie decided she would find another place to live if her mother wouldn't agree to her four-legged roommate. Whenever that dog nuzzled her with that cold snout or plunked his paw on her leg for attention, whatever low mood she was afflicted with dissolved. Saving his life made her responsible for him, "Like *The Little Prince*," she mumbled to the cool air which surrounded her.

That entire day as they began packing, Mags harped non-stop. "When do you plan on telling Mark that you're leaving? And what about that shared visitation agreement for Win ... ?"

"Please stop! As far as Winston goes, he's my dog and always will be. Secondly, bartenders have a reputation for being flighty. Managers expect them to be no-shows or leave on the same day they quit, and God knows what else."

Another of Addie's blathers intended to distract her from facing what she was "supposed" to do. How could she ever tell him the truth about what prompted her to hustle that truckdriver? These mental snapshots of confessing ended in the worst possible outcome: he would be repulsed by her which would add more layers to her own self-hate. Her capacity for surviving another loss was on the verge of collapse.

FORTY-SIX

Addie realized there was a limit to how much fruit she needed to cut and bottles of liquor to inventory so she begrudgingly waved Mark down asking if he was free after her shift was over that night. He agreed, confirming he would be in his office. Since their last encounter, they had been socially polite with each other.

The bar was quiet. Tony Bennett was crooning his signature San Francisco song. A server gestured for Addie to lower the music because guests in the dining room were complaining. She agreed, but to be obstinate, upped the volume as high as it would go. Tony began yelling about that love of his life. Waiting a few minutes, she reeled it back little by little.

"Oops!" She disingenuously apologized to the hostess, who was holding her ears.

A few of the regulars were sitting in their usual spots, staring into their cocktails or playing with the speared fruit drowning in their drinks. As a farewell to her customers, Addie poured double shots for her favorites, didn't charge a few others, and under poured for those who had been a pain in her ass.

As the night wore on, she heard herself yakking non-stop. Her laughter was way too loud. She was annoyed by a constant thrumming on the bar until she spied her fingers as the culprits drumming against a bottle of vodka. A patron noted that she gave him change for a fifty when he handed her a twenty.

Though she'd rehearsed for the past few days, she kept floundering for the perfect farewell script. Mags advised her to keep it simple and stick to the facts. From Addie's point of view that would mean two things: telling him she was quitting and making arrangements to collect her dog. In and out.

Climbing the stairs to Mark's office reminded her of the time her grandmother made her go to the rectory and confess to Father Ted that she drank altar wine after Sunday mass. Right now, she longed for a whole bottle of the stuff. Breathing in and out several times helped tame her anxiety. She tapped on the door surprised that it sounded louder than she intended.

When she walked in, Mark pointed to a brown vinyl armchair with lumpy cushions in front of his desk, which was crowded with papers, a few ash trays, and a radio with Sinatra professing his affection for "New York New York" which Mark switched off.

Most times Addie was unaffected by noiseless space but the dead atmosphere in this room was stifling. Mark offered her a smoke as he took one out for himself. Declining, she scoured the insides of her purse, withdrew a cigarette from her own pack, and lit it, trying to steady her hand while she kept staring at the burning ember.

Inhaling a lungful of smoke, he admitted, "Addie, I suspect you're leaving. My guess is within a day or two."

"Yes, today is my last day here." How did he know? "I'm sure you won't have any difficulty finding a replacement."

Mark grinned. "You're funny. I already found your successor. She starts tomorrow."

Her neck fired up flame red streaks. He didn't care that she was leaving! All that crap he rattled on about how wonderful she was. *Sawubona.* Her dejection morphed. *So, this is fragile. Fuckabona.* Her familiar weapon took charge of the situation without any effort from her. "Well, that's great. It was a real joy working here especially the added benefit of screwing my boss, who, by the way, was terrible in bed." She shot up so abruptly, she teetered forward. Mark asked her to please sit down.

Unbuttoning his jacket, he situated himself on the edge of his desk, and tried to regain his composure. "Addie, I didn't have any interest in having a personal relationship with you. In our interview, I thought you were weird. When you tried to manipulate me about your schedule, I came up with the idea that you'd be better suited as a bartender because the ones I've hired are a bit odd, ergo, I knew you'd be a perfect fit."

"Oh, yeah? Why did you ask me out, then?"

"I was curious to see if my initial impression was accurate. You exceeded my expectations!"

"Is that right? Well, you were worse than terrible in bed!" Addie's sarcasm was sharp as the edge of a shovel.

"Speaking of sex, Addie." Mark stood. "Tell me that trucker guy made it up, that you pissed him off, which you have a sterling reputation for, and he wanted revenge. I paid him from my own personal funds to get rid of him."

Addie gasped but tried to muffle it with a cough. Although she was taken aback by Mark's actions, she was finally able to grasp that he loved her. Revealing that ugly part of herself would be too painful for both of them. At least she could leave knowing that the one person who cared about her didn't think she was royally fucked up. Even if she lied.

"He made that up."

"I figured! But why did you do something so stupid as to vandalize his truck? What would possess you!" As he was about to continue his rant, he stopped in mid-sentence and flinched. "Oh, I'm acting like you." His shoulders drooped as he fell back into his seat.

Leave. All I want to do is leave this fucking town. As she stood and marched to the door, Addie was beginning to give way to her emotions. With her back to him, she said, "I'll pick Winston up before we leave in the morning."

"We need to work out an agreement regarding that situation. We're both attached to him and he to us. It's not fair that you yank him out of my life. I'm asking if I can keep him for a while, and we can figure out what to do later."

Without answering, Addie sprinted down the stairs and out the front door. Her trusty companion began to weaken. That familiar void looping haphazardly around her heart made her realize how fragile she was. Sorrow sliced through her like a thousand tiny cuts. *So, this is what my anger armored me against. I feel naked and alone.*

PART IV
The Family

Chicago

FORTY-SEVEN

The day after Sophie's secret cracked open Frank's world as he knew it, he drove aimlessly in unknown sections of Chicago until he found himself at St. Adalbert's cemetery making his way to his parents' grave sites. Staring at the stone markers, he scraped his throat raw screaming and cursing at the words etched on their tombstones: *Rest In the Peace of the Lord.*

"People like you belong in hell." Those monuments were a mockery to Sophie, his family, and whoever else was violated, so he decided to have them uprooted and destroyed.

Frank continued to be haunted by the abuse Sophie suffered from his family. It wasn't until an accounting error of his resulted in a client leaving the firm that a co-worker suggested he make an appointment with his family physician.

After he confessed that the extent of his depression included suicidal thoughts, Dr. Phillips, who knew that Frank's mother died by her own hand, wrote a prescription for an anti-depressant and asked the nurse to schedule Frank for a follow-up appointment in a month. He agreed to the time and date, but had no intention of keeping it because he would do this on his own.

As the days passed, an impulse to end his life began to overtake him. No matter how hard he tried to rub out the memory of his father looming over Sophie, it seemed to be permanently etched in his mind.

That day so many decades ago when he received his acceptance letter into college, Frank danced around his mother in the kitchen, asking her where his dad was.

"Somewhere upstairs, I think... in our room."

Taking two steps at a time, he burst through the closed door only to be met with a string of profanities that rebuked him mercilessly. Although Frank had been a recipient of his dad's explosive temper many times before, there wasn't any reason for this reaction. He never suspected his deeply religious father of abusing a child. Never.

As this scene continued to haunt him, Frank developed a plan: he bought a gun and chose the exact place where he would end his misery. It was to be in the shed behind his parents' house. Since it was for sale again, he drove there late one night and snuck through the backyard to see if the extra key was where he buried it long ago. Scooping through the dirt, he felt the cold and jagged final where; now but one detail was left—the when.

On what he planned to be the last day of his life with the pistol stuffed in his coat pocket, Frank chanced on Sophie as she was baking. Patches of flour speckled her apron, dusted her cheek, and made its way into her hair. How was Sophie able to continue living with what she had endured? A great tremor overtook him as torrents of grief streamed down his face. He drove to church. Kneeling for hours before the statue of the Blessed Virgin, Frank was tormented when he thought about deserting Sophie and the girls in that way. What a selfish and cowardly act, leaving them with another trauma to deal with. They didn't deserve that.

It was quiet. The last of the sun's rays filtered in through the open damask curtains. The house was empty but for the two of them.

"Where did you go?"

"A ride."

"Where's your pipe?"

"In the basement. I thought the smoke bothered you."

"Well, I don't mind the tobacco that smells like vanilla and something else." Sophie gathered up a black afghan she knitted and covered her face with it. Her first and last attempt at fiber arts to fill her time.

"Oh. I didn't know that."

Sophie had to ignore the heavy stone of grief that nestled near her heart. There was so much Frank didn't know about her. But how could he? The abuse shielded her from being a real person who could stay connected to her feelings and tolerate the more painful ones. What bothered her most of all is that he didn't know the simple things husbands know about their wives. Things she didn't know about herself.

"Frank, that flashback ..." her voice was small as if she had to squeeze the words out.

"... when you burst into the room keeps replaying itself. There's no possible way you would have seen me. This two-hundred-pound man was hovering over me in this darkened room. It became clear when I discussed it with Dr. Meizner."

"Soph, I've replayed it a million times, and God, I didn't know what he was doing. I'm grateful you're able to understand that. When did you start seeing Dr. Meizner again?"

"Since Mary spoke the words I never wanted to hear. I'm meeting with her three times a week. I shouldn't have left the hospital, but I wasn't able to deal with any of it. I ended up doing what I was fearful of ... tearing our family apart. There are so many uncharted emotions and memories I have to plow through. I can't stop blaming myself, but I'm getting closer to having compassion for that little girl I once was."

"How could you possibly blame yourself?"

This wasn't the time to wade through what was so confusing to her. There were myriad damaged layers she needed to dive through in that maze of abuse, and she was uncertain if releasing any bit of them would open caverns better left closed for now.

"Not now, Frank. I don't want to talk about that."

Frank broke into the quiet. "Sophie, is it possible to save our marriage?" He cleared his throat.

Sophie mumbled from under her flawed coverlet.

"I'm sorry, what are you saying?" Frank caught hold of her protective prop. "May I sit here, or is this too close for you?"

With her head turned away from him, she blurted. "I'm working through my shame and rage but I'm a mess."

Clasping his hand into hers, he relaxed when she didn't recoil from his touch.

"I despise those sinful people. I can taste the bitterness of my hatred. But I know that before I can free myself and not let them destroy my life, I have to forgive your parents and my mother."

Sophie's tears spilled over onto her cheeks. "Whatever loathing I felt toward you has evaporated, but I have no idea what lies ahead of us. We are strangers to each other. I need to heal myself first so I plan to continue in therapy, and I'd like for the two of us to meet with our pastor."

"I'll do anything for you. Are you going to talk to Addie? Your mother?"

Cold fear inched down the back of her neck. *What would I say to my mother without wanting to strangle her? What if she didn't believe me? How can I explain the anger I felt toward Addie? The way I treated her? Those years of turmoil that filled the space between the two of us has become a permanent fixture.* Control. That's what she needed: to be able to control how it would all end.

FORTY-EIGHT

Mary popped in and speaking over the blaring radio asked Addie if she needed any help unpacking. Nodding, Addie continued lip-syncing the lyrics to John Lennon's song, "Starting Over," as she unfolded a couple of shirts.

"How was the drive back home with Mags?"

"Fine." Addie opened a few of her dresser drawers and tossed in some wadded-up underwear.

"How is she doing?"

"Fine."

"Wow! This weather is ridiculous." Bolts of lightning flashed through the blinds as rain pounded the windows. "The forecast says this will last 'til Thursday."

"Yeah, it is."

"Addie. I can't take it. What's up with you?"

Shoving her suitcase aside, Addie slumped down on the bed. "I'm so fucked up. I blew it with Mark, I'm nervous about my next audition, and I miss my dog." Addie started to tug at the hairs from her eyebrows.

"Stop that!"

"And what's driving me crazy is that Sophie doesn't know I know or that Babcia knows. I have no idea how I'm supposed to act when I'm with either of them. This is fucked up, Mary! We have to stop with the secrets, and now I'm holding on to a supersized one." As that comment entered the airspace, Addie was haunted about the secret she was keeping from Mark. But that was over anyway.

"Not to worry. Mother wants to talk to us, but it has to be on her terms. The good news is that she's is in therapy with the psychiatrist who treated her in the hospital."

"Well, therapy hasn't done me a helluva lot of good. But then again, I was like an angry bouncing ball bobbing from one to the other. Never landing anywhere." Addie's forehead creased as if she dredged up the last letters of crossword puzzle.

Mary shared the conversation she had with their grandmother on the drive home from Cincinnati. Addie was silent for the longest time while the F word zipped in and out of her head. Would her grandmother forgive her for being such a bitch? Pondering the love and kindness her babcia showered her with over the years, Addie was ashamed of using their thread as a way to hurt the old lady.

In between tapping on the *STOP* sign, Addie started chewing on her nails.

"Who is it?"

"Me. Your prodigal granddaughter." Addie was startled to see her babcia flat on her back, doing what appeared to be leg lifts.

"I Ok. I exercise. Good for old people. I did three. Help me up."

Grinning, Addie clasped her grandmother's bony shoulder, then swung her bird like legs over the side of the bed. A loud grunt zipped out from the old lady.

It was difficult for Addie to see the furrows and wrinkles that covered Babcia's face as well as the skin gathered in folds drooping from her neck. When she was younger, Addie thought those rivulets of flesh were secret hiding places and would ogle them waiting for hidden treasure to tumble out.

"I'm sorry. And it's not bullshit. Family *is* everything—"

"Ya ... everything and nothing ... depend on forgiveness." Patting her granddaughter's tear-streaked cheek, she said, "I love you no matter what, you my paczki."

"You do! Don't you?"

"Paczki, get up! Turn in circle three times fast." She twirled her crooked index finger. "Go!"

Addie toppled onto the bed when she stopped.

"You dizzy? Good. What you sorry for fly away. Bye-bye. Now, let's have brandy and hug." And they did. Irina explained that Addie's great-grandmother taught her to do this spin any time someone she loved needed to be forgiven.

"It's how you shake *wino* off!"

That was one Polish word Addie was quite familiar with ... guilt. If she were to turn circles for the guilt she felt about her mother, Mark, Winston, and that ugly side of herself, she'd spin to her death, like the ballerina in *The Red Shoes.*

Relieved that things were back to normal with her babcia, Addie still moped about and spent a lot of time in her room, snoozing under her pierzyna or staring at TV.

No word from Mark about Winston. In her mind, the two were one. *Can I love a dog and a man the same? Do I truly love Mark? I can't imagine life without my Winston. Well, then why the fuck did I leave him?* These thoughts buzzed in her head as if a brood of cicadas landed there.

She was surprised that the voices of her therapists were alive and well, living happily ever after in her head. Their insights would pop up at interesting times, and today she heard from the latest one she had sacked.

If you let yourself love Sophie, you'd have to forgive her and then, yourself. Not because she's your mother and you're her daughter. That's the easy kind— it's the "supposed to" kind. The other kind is much more challenging. That forgiveness is a choice that flows from the heart. It will free both of you to find peace within yourselves and with each other.

Peace? What does that really mean? Dropping the barrier that kept her safe was intimidating. But safe from what? Sophie was her mother. Whenever she imagined tearing it down, Addie felt as though she was in a free fall descending into a bottomless pit.

FORTY-NINE

After spending the day in bed, she chewed the last of her gum as a way to appease her belly—the grumbles of which startled Winston. She tiptoed down the stairs, inspecting the house to see if anyone was home. Creeping like an impatient cat into the kitchen where, to her delight, she found herself alone, she smelled freshly baked paczkis drizzled with icing beckoning her.

Before Addie could determine which flavors they were, Sophie walked in.

Addie froze, and her mother's comment about Babcia rumbled in her head. *Your grandmother is not who you girls believe she is ...*

Whenever she pictured Sophie's scrawled writing detailing the abuse, Addie tried to erase it, as she did with her babcia's admission of failing to protect her own daughter. But they both had bruised hearts. Imagining the suffering the two of them endured during their lives sparked a surge of compassion within her. Addie puzzled over how forgiveness or compassion can exist without a belief in the innate goodness of each person. For an instant she was back in Sister Bibi's religion class, but without warning, a glimmer of her mother being abused by the grandfather she never knew along with his wife who did nothing to stop it, jabbed her. What goodness could these people possibly possess? And then, according to her grandmother, everyone has a bruised heart.

Fuck! I think too much!

"Have you had lunch?"

Addie tried to speak but a pitiful rasp was all that popped out. Guilt bubbled through her veins and brought countless shreds of regret right to the center of her heart.

How can I ever let my mother be a mother to me? I don't deserve one iota of kindness from her.

"Uh, no. But I'll have a paczki. Thanks."

The hum of the refrigerator silenced the awkwardness between them.

"You should have lunch first." Taking mayo, pickles, slices of ham, and swiss cheese from the fridge, Sophie placed them along with a loaf of rye bread, in front of her daughter.

"Uh ..." Searching for a way to ease the tension, Addie found the answer to her dilemma on the plate before her. "What are the paczkis filled with?"

"Apricot, but I did fill a few with strawberry jam. I'll get you a glass of milk."

Her mother's voice carried a soft, loving cadence, filling her with more remorse than she could tolerate. She shouldn't have lingered so long. "No. No. I ... I ... ah ,..."

"I understand. Go do what you have to do." Sophie's voice seemed out of place this time as much as the smile she spread across her face.

Addie beelined up to her room.

Fireworks had been so integral in her relationship with Sophie, she was at a loss about how she should behave because the last years between the two of them were so abnormal. How could she skip over that?

Then she heard the question another of her psychiatrists posed as she was venting about Sophie: "What would happen if you let yourself love her?"

If I let myself love her, I'll want to stick her in my pocket and never let her go.

FIFTY

For the past few weeks, there were days Sophie remained in the darkness of her bedroom not wanting to even take a shower. And then there were times she was able to step into her life as she did with Addie in the kitchen. Waves ... that's how Dr. Meizner described the process of her recovery. The crests were short-lived but they gave her glimmers of hope.

Sitting in the dimness of the living room, Sophie felt as though she was underwater, struggling to breathe. On awakening she had the energy to abandon the comfort of her bed but then after her shower, she chastised herself for doing so.

"Mary, is that you?" Sophie straightened up and pushed the loose strands of her hair away from her eyes.

"Yes, it's me." Since the secret was laid bare, Mary couldn't predict which of Sophie's moods would greet her. Some of their interactions were surprisingly normal like the time she mustered up the self-confidence to announce her engagement to Jeff. Although Sophie didn't say too much, she smiled and hugged her daughter asking if they could marry at St. Stanislas and have the reception at the house.

"Come sit." Sophie moved the Good Housekeeping magazine that was beside her and placed it on the coffee table.

The drawn curtains and the shadowiness of the room made Mary hesitate before joining her mother on the sofa. Without asking permission, Mary leaned over and turned on a lamp that was nestled between a few paperback books and framed pictures of the family.

Sophie brought her hands to her eyes and sighed.

Determined to break the thorny uneasiness that plagued their conversations on days like this, Mary grappled with her discomfort until she noticed a spider on the floor.

"Eww, we don't have bugs in the house," Mary muttered. When she rose to squash it, Sophie held her back.

"Oh ... let it live. It's harmless," Sophie commented.

The two of them were mesmerized by its threadlike legs as it crawled through the fibers of the carpet.

"Do you remember the time I read *Charlotte's Web* to you and Addie?"

"I do! Addie wouldn't let you out of her sight for days after you read about Charlotte dying, and I was mad at Fern for forgetting about Wilbur. And you wiped Addie's tears, explaining that Charlotte's baby spiders would pass on her love to the devoted piglet." The cover of the book with that little girl in her red dress and tousled hair pulled back in a pony tail hugging Wilbur momentarily popped out of that memory.

"And I explained that Fern had to grow up and that meant leaving Wilbur." A photo of her girls dripping wet, splashing in the park pool, captured Sophie's attention as it rested on the TV.

"We all have to leave and grow up, don't we?" Sophie closed her eyes.

Mary was toying with possible ways to perk up her mother's spirits.

"Well, good news! I talked with Jeff, and he agrees about having our wedding at St. Stanislaus and having our reception here afterwards as long as it isn't too much work." She went on gushing about a wedding dress that she saw in Bride's Magazine—assuring Sophie it was nothing as pompous as Princess Diana's.

Sophie clamped down on her daughter's bouncing leg.

Sneaking a peek at her mother, Mary was disheartened that Sophie's face could barely muster a smile as if she was telling her about a day at work. Fooling herself into thinking normal conversations would lure her mother out of her despair, Mary recognized with some trepidation that unless she was able to step more fully into her mother's pain and not be fearful of it, they would never have an authentic relationship.

"How are you doing, Mom?" Startled at the word she hadn't verbalized since she was a child, Mary pinched her lips together and then opened them to form an O as she pronounced the letters, M, O, M. *That's what normal daughters call their mothers.*

"The world has no color for me today." The words hung in mid-air.

"How do you feel toward Dad's parents, the man who abused you and his wife who never stopped it?" Leaning forward, Mary noted the fingernail marks on her mother's forearms. Those crescents of red jolted Mary into a more profound realization of how agonizing these questions were. "This is too painful, isn't it?"

"Yes. I'm troubled about how to deal with your grandmother. I'm not sure how that will work out."

And then Mary shared Babcia's story and what she tried to do, along with Mrs. Gurin's lies about the doctor.

"So, your grandmother knows?"

"Please don't be mad, but yes and Addie, too."

"I went through this, years ago, Mary. If family is everything, where was she while I was being abused? She should have known."

"You and Addie are ridiculous. What does that mean? 'A mother should know.' That's a blanket statement that doesn't consider individual circumstances. Babcia was an immigrant in a country where her husband died, leaving her alone with their child—with no family. Her command of the language was sketchy. Can't you see her as a young woman? She trusted Dad's mother. She couldn't comprehend how an adult man would want to have sex with a child ... let alone her child."

Sophie rearranged herself on the couch, angling away from Mary.

It confused her why her mother wouldn't soften toward Babcia since she was a mother herself.

"Babcia sobbed something in Polish on our way back from Cincinnati. She wailed so desolately I thought she was dying. I repeated it as best I could to dad and asked him what it meant."

The dead air wedged itself between them until Sophie murmured, "Well?"

"It means, 'I am a failure as a mother.'"

Sophie retreated behind her bedroom door.

Mary threw her head back as she watched that spider creep up the wall. It struck her that she ruminated on what her mother did to her. Her eyes blinked slowly as she realized that she had never considered what suffering her mother endured for having left them. And it wasn't Sophie, the mother, who left them, it was Sophie, the child.

Sophie kicked off her shoes. She squirmed when the word "failure" fell from her lips. These past years she'd hated her mother for failing to protect her ... and now, she would have to live with that failure: the depression, the anxiety, her inability to trust people, her lost innocence.

And because of it, she, herself, didn't deserve the name, Mother. Her girls would be affected by it for the rest of their lives, as well. As she pondered how the evil actions of one man could ripple out and damage so many people, Sophie imagined the violent deeds she wanted to inflict upon him. If he were alive, she would derive a great deal of pleasure to see him dangling by his purple balls in front of St. Stanislaus as Sunday Mass let out.

Irina's legacy as a mother impacted hers ... that thread.

Sophie was hell-bent on learning to cope with the abuse and not be a victim to it. God, it was difficult. She kept repeating over and over that she would never let it define her. In a recent session, Sophie asked Dr. Meizner if she would ever have a normal life.

"A controversial diagnosis has recently been identified known as Post Traumatic Stress Disorder, referred to as PTSD. I believe with therapy and hard work, you will have a normal life, but in the beginning, as you heal, it will be interrupted by episodes of PTSD. As we continue to work together, Sophie, these incidences are likely to occur farther apart. There will be triggers, but your coping strategies will strengthen as you consistently use them.

"I want you to think about what the abuse *gave to* you ... yes, you have developed resiliencies as a result of those experiences, Sophie— the resilience to live in spite of it. That resilience is your legacy to your daughters."

It offered her hope.

Mary's question about the man who abused me: I despise him. But looming over that is this more contemptuous bitterness I feel toward my own mother. Why? He deserves my rage. I'm angry at her, but much more than I am with him. *Why? Because mothers are supposed to know. Mothers are supposed to protect their children.*

The word "failure" morphed into the word "forgiveness." Yes, she failed as a mother as well. She didn't protect Addie from her cruel outbursts or Mary from her need to control her life. Clearly not the same as sexual abuse; but abuse just the same. As a mother, shouldn't she have been able to transcend her emotions?

The thread, the thread is about forgiveness. The kind of forgiveness that let's go ... of any resentments or judgments. If my girls could remember the ways that I loved them and cared for them, they would be able to see that, although I'm imperfect, I loved them with my whole heart.

Before she could accept forgiveness from her girls, Sophie knew she needed to forgive her own mother, and that was a most daunting task and all because Irina was a Mother.

FIFTY-ONE

As Mary entered the kitchen, she caught her sister wolfing down a peanut butter and jelly sandwich and sat across from her.

"Can you tolerate wearing a maid-of-honor dress and a tad of makeup that day?"

"What! Hell yes!" With grape jam sliding down to her chin, Addie puckered up for a smooch, but not before Mary handed her a napkin, gesturing where a purple smear lodged itself.

"When?"

"Not sure yet, but soon. Since Jeff was married before, he isn't interested in any big celebration."

"What about Soph—Mother? Hard habit to break."

"Well, she's good with it, except she wants us to marry at St. Stanislaus and have the reception here." Mary started the dishwasher as Addie was pondering the changes in her mother. Their last contact was filled with edgy chatter, but it seemed Sophie was trying to connect with her.

What a time to plan a wedding with this crap going on.

Heading up to their rooms, Mary said, "Mother is having a difficult time. I did let her know that I gave both of you a copy of her notes, so be ready. I also told her how I felt about Babcia's failure to protect her. It doesn't relieve the suffering she's endured, but at least she was able to remain present with me the whole time."

When Mary opened her bedroom door, she heard murmuring at the shrine.

"Babcia. How did you make it up here?"

"It take long time. I take one stair, catch my breath, then another. Never before I do this, without asking, but I had to." Her chest heaved in an effort to slow her breath down. "I ask for forgiveness. I make novena. I come for seven days, Ok?"

"Of course! But all those stairs—"

"My penance."

Mary snuffed the flame in the votive candle with her two fingers and wanted to bring a bit of joy to her Babcia. "I'm engaged to be married!"

"I so happy!"

Addie charged over to her room and danced back with a box covered in newspaper comic strips, her traditional wrapping paper.

"The Shalimar I gave you!" Taking the bottle out and spritzing the perfume on her neck and wrists, Mary released pleasurable rumblings as if she was on the cusp of an orgasm.

"Ach, that stink." Several explosive sneezes from Babcia jiggled the shawl from her shoulders.

"I agree! I was saving it for the right occasion." Addie snickered.

"Hey! You might be great-babcia ... great-grandmother! How do you say that in Polish?" Addie had a mischievous smirk on her face.

"Pra-Babcia ... pra great," Irina replied, letting another sneeze out.

"Stop it! No babies for a while, ladies!" Mary stuck her tongue out.

"Let's celebrate with brandy and hug!" Irina winked with both eyes.

Marriage. Addie had flirted with the idea of being married, but since she was such a head case, her fantasies never lasted longer than a rumble of thunder. Wavering back and forth between "maybe" and "not a chance," Mark came to mind. Lying on her bed with her arms tucked behind her head, she entertained being Mrs. Mark Lansing, which was extinguished quicker than blowing out a candle.

She recognized she was a nut job and ruminated over what would have to happen in order for her to join the world of "normal people." Knowing her mother's secret didn't unfuck her, which was what she spent years obsessing about. Both Mark and Mags lectured her about her habit of blaming other people for her misery and encouraged her to stop defining herself by what other people have done to her, because it was that anger that fueled her victimhood.

She might not have listened to what she didn't want to hear in therapy, but the two people she loved penetrated her line of defense. And maybe those therapists had planted the seeds she refused to accept. She wasn't ready then, but she was now.

Mary knocked on Addie's door the next morning. No response. She poked her head into an empty room and saw a tattered sheet of paper taped to Addie's headboard. *Going to Cincinnati*, signed with a squiggle.

FIFTY-TWO

Cincinnati

Addie was surprised that it took four hours to return to her old haunt, but then why not since her speedometer remained fixed at 85 MPH. While packing, she debated whether or not to call Mark but then decided against it. What if she had to suffer another rejection again? Better she took control of the situation.

As she cruised into Chester's parking lot, she saw his car and shut the engine off, coasted to the other side of the building and slid down until her throat crashed into the steering wheel. She laughed. *I'm here now. What am I doing? See this through, Adelajada! It's time to be bossy pants with yourself.*

The whirring of the drink blender and the hum of conversations met her as she sauntered in. The bartender was fawning over two young women who were lapping up his attention in the hopes of getting a date. Resembling Robert Redford, he acted as though he could charm the panties off any female. With the exception of him, Chester's was pretty much the same until smatterings of smoke and a blend of bourbon and scotch aromas breezed past her nose. Her sprays of flowers were nowhere in sight.

"Well, hellll-o! What may I get for you, young lady?"

Addie morphed into Irma. "How do you know I'm a lady? Snort. I'll have a Chardonnay. Snort."

Without warning, a hand began climbing its way up her spine. Grinning, she couldn't believe her luck. But when she spun around and was welcomed by the chef with his crooked nicotine-stained teeth and breath that matched, Addie glanced over his shoulder, and was disappointed Mark wasn't anywhere to be seen. As the chef yacked about how the place wasn't the same without her, he abruptly paused. "Hey! Mark. Guess who's here?"

As Addie swiveled in her bar stool, Mark clamped down on her shoulders and delivered a wet and unyielding kiss, his late afternoon stubble chafing her skin. "I'm glad you're here, I've missed you," Mark admitted. "C'mon." He led her to his office and as the door closed, their passion led to a clumsy grappling with shirts, pants, buttons, and belts followed by a nose-dive to the floor.

"This time, imagine you are drugged and or that you're paralyzed. I'm in control, and I intend to do sinful things until you beg me to stop!" Kissing his chin and moving down his neck, she was startled when without warning Mark flipped her onto her back and entered her whispering, "I've waited for this too long. You can be in control next time."

"You are an amazing lover now that you let go of that self-preservation thing!" As she declared this, she began moaning. Her body synchronized to the swaying of his. After an hour of pleasure and laughter, huffing and puffing, Mark rolled onto the floor next to Addie and let out a whoop of pleasure.

"How's Winston? I can't wait to see him." Buttoning or zipping themselves up, Addie planted wet kisses on Mark's neck, hoping the truck driver fiasco had faded from his memory bank. "And what happened to the flowers? They added pizazz to the bar."

"That dog of ours is great. I bring him into work and spoil him with leftover steaks. As for the flowers, they reminded me of you and FYI, I didn't hire another female bartender, for obvious reasons."

"Didn't think you'd be able to control yourself, huh?" Addie smacked Mark's rear as he was bending over to tie his shoelaces. "What an ass!" she declared, with a grin.

"You've dubbed me an ass several times before, but not in a complimentary way!"

Mark's phone rang when Addie suggested they have the chef rustle up a few steaks. She draped herself in that same faded vinyl armchair, ran her finger over a few spidery cracks, and studied Mark as he chattered. The fragrance of his cologne triggered a strange desire within her. It had sexual undertones, but it pulsated with a softer, warmer sensation that flooded her with a surge of contentment. Mark mattered to her. She loved him and was tired of pretending otherwise.

Without warning, like an unexpected crack of lightening, that greasy truckdriver pawing her breasts appeared before her. Her throat tightened, leaving a hot, prickly sweat rising up to her face. *Mark deserves to know the truth. But what if he dumps me? Doing something so reckless all because I was jealous!* The biggest life lesson she learned in the last several months was how dangerous secrets are to any relationship. *Secrets breed shame. Lies are secrets.*

Standing up, she opened the office door and began pacing in and out. She despised herself for the sleazy thing she did, but hurting Mark would be worse, more painful.

Dark thoughts swarmed into her mind like a horde of angry drones. The fury she had leveled at Joe and Scott and the havoc she wreaked to their homes flittered before her. *Who does that?* Was it possible for her to control those crazy reactions from Mark if he pissed her off? Why these questions now right when she thought she had things figured out?

If love was capable of forgiveness, why was she filled with such uncertainty? *Maybe not everything is forgivable. Surely my dad could never forgive his parents. But that's not the same. If Mark loved me, he would be able to. My family is working hard on forgiveness.* Her stomach thrashed about as strands of memories from that night in the truck bobbed before her. *Decent girls aren't supposed to act that way. Mary would never do that. Mags either. It isn't right for him not to know me inside out. I have to tell him the truth.*

She rushed down to the lounge where she staggered into a blue haze of smoke hovering about. The place was overflowing with fashionably dressed people along with a few overserved guests joining Peggy Lee as she crooned, "Is That All There Is?" Shoving her way to the bar, she ordered a drink when an off-key singer pinched her ass.

"Hey, let me buy you a drink, hon. What'll it be?"

That voice grated her ears like a knife scraping a plate. Hot, clammy bodies were crowding against her.

I can't breathe. My head, my head. I'm going to faint. Oh my God. She was certain her heart would rip right through her chest and crash into someone's head. The room began to close in on her.

Colliding into a group of men as she barreled out of there, she bit her hand to stop from screaming and made her way to the parking lot. A railroad tie that served as landscaping ornamentation outside the restaurant offered her a place to rest where she fought for breath. She shook so violently it felt as though her insides would splinter into jagged pieces.

"Addie!" Mark's voice was edgy.

As soon as he caught her in his peripheral vision, he stormed over. "Why did you leave in such a huff?"

She teetered back and forth on the cold bricks.

"And what are those? What the hell happened in the last fifteen minutes?" He examined the bite marks, shaking his head.

Her voice was locked in her throat.

"Addie. What's wrong? Are you Ok?"

"Hey! Aren't you the bitch that propositioned me and then destroyed my windshield?" A gruff voice bellowed from a secluded area as this hulk of a guy wobbled toward them.

Mark blocked the intruder's path.

Addie pulled herself together and leaped up terrified when she realized the parking lot was ominously empty.

"Hey, buddy. How about if you go on in and tell the bartender Mark bought you a drink?"

"Not until I choke the shit out of that bitch!" he slurred, shoving Mark aside.

"I'm the guy you settled with. I paid for the damages; don't you remember?"

"I hope that's not your girlfriend, buddy. I never met a prick teaser quite like her before. My dick has never been the same since she ..." The trucker bolted toward Addie and wrested a wad of her hair. She lurched forward and kicked him in the groin. In the midst of his groans, Addie raised her leg to repeat the action.

"Addie, stop! Go get Steve." As Mark wheeled around, a balled fist collided with his chin, snapping his head back.

Trying to gain more traction, Addie ran farther back, sprang toward her adversary and attempted to kick him again when Mark shoved her backwards onto a nearby car.

"Fuck, Mark! Why did you stop me!" Addie thundered.

"Did you hear me? Go get Steve!" he yelled, as he ducked from an oncoming fist. The trucker swayed and collapsed from the power of Mark's wallop. Sprawled out on the asphalt, he lay motionless.

Mark bent down and checked his pulse.

"Is he alive?"

Ignoring her, he thrust his car keys at her face. "Lock the doors and wait for me. Under no circumstances are you to go near that guy. Do you hear me?" Mark bounded into the restaurant.

As Addie brooded in the car, she leered at what resembled a dead beached whale dressed in a Bengals sweatshirt.

"Are you Ok?? Should I call the police?"

A middle-aged man, tapped on the window.

"No. The manager is getting help. But, thank you."

She flicked the radio on full blast to hear Rick Springfield singing "Don't Talk to Strangers."

"Too late," she barked.

It wasn't long before Mark unlocked the door, shutting Springfield off. "Steve is getting an ambulance."

"Does he come here often?"

"No. Must be your lucky night."

"Where are we going?"

"My place."

While at a stoplight, Mark scrutinized Addie with eyes that were cold and hard. Of all times to come here. Peering out at the traffic, she saw a tiny insect no bigger than a pinhead climbing up the window. As it crawled to the top, it disappeared into the crevice. Addie wanted to do the same. Her secret was a secret no more. *I needed to be the one to tell him.*

When Addie dragged herself into the condo, Winston vaulted over an ottoman and knocked her the ground slobbering over her face. Cuddling her four-legged buddy, she wasn't able to experience the usual joy of his sloppy kisses.

"At least someone likes me."

"Go to bed. This was an exhausting night."

With her beloved pet at her heels, she stripped off her clothing, and flopped onto the plush king mattress, with the dog burrowing against her. Sleep came swiftly.

Sun light brushed her face. The warmth of the sheets that shrouded her naked body seduced her to remain in bed until Winston's exuberant tail thumped against her shoulder.

A long, low moan slipped from her lips. What she hoped would be a respite from the emotional turmoil in Chicago landed her in a more considerable mess.

"Did Mark sleep here last night?" she asked the empty side of the bed knowing full well he didn't.

Knocking a few times, Mark appeared carrying a cup of coffee with a leash loosely draped over his neck. As if on cue, Winston galloped to the back door, sliding on the wood floor, wagging his tail, waiting for Mark.

Addie reached for the steaming cup and was surprised that the indentations she inflicted upon herself resembled a row of bloodied tombstones. "This might be trouble since I haven't had a rabies shot. If I start foaming at the mouth, shoot me. At least you'll have Winston. *Woof!* *Woof!*" The last "woof" barked unenthusiastically when she realized Mark wasn't laughing.

Mark clipped Winston to the leash as he strode out the door.

Why did that ass have to come back there? God was punishing her. The person she loved had witnessed her other side, the dark side, as well as hearing about it from that creep. She was certain that Mark would not let this rest. These thoughts whizzed inside her like a spider frenziedly spinning webs without a place to anchor the threads.

Well, fuck him! Why am I so worked up? I love him, that's why!

Addie glanced at the clock on the nightstand and was startled to see a framed photo of herself on that motorcycle in front of that rickety General

Store in Rabbit Hash. Her heart drummed against her rib cage as she entertained the idea that Mark loved her.

With nails clicking on the hardwood floor, Winston barreled into the bedroom and, as he was about to soar onto the bed, Mark commanded, "*No!*" Bewildered, the dog peeked at Addie, and then at Mark, who repeated his order more firmly. Without hesitating, the invader skulked to his basket in the living room.

Standing with hands on his hips, Mark leaned into the doorframe. "Last night was a disaster in many ways."

Addie inhaled a lungful of smoke, formed an O with her lips, and exhaled perfectly shaped smoke rings that floated one after another as if they were in a silent marching band. "How about a contest?" She asked, hoping to erase the crease in his forehead.

"Get dressed."

She scanned the room for an exit. But she was trapped. No matter how determined she was to vanish, leaping from a third-floor window was not a viable option. Addie continued to ruminate about the unfairness of the events of last night, just as she was trying to straighten herself out.

"Prick teaser" reverberated in her head with such vengeance that she knew the letters PT bled through and tattooed itself on her forehead. At least Hester Prynne had to deal with a single letter for her sins. Mark wasn't the kind of guy who would take well to his girlfriend being a two-lettered woman.

Seeing herself as a sordid, cheap slut invited her red blotches to sprout more prolifically in their usual location as well as creep up into new territory. Though she accepted that she was a head case, "slut" was a label that churned her stomach into a pre-vomit mode.

The day she left Mark's office, that panic attack was identical to the anxiety she experienced when she learned about Sophie. Although these spells were no stranger to her, this felt as though a thousand firecrackers were flying in bits under her skin.

When she thought back to last night, she remembered that he was on the phone when memories of her escapade with that truck driver descended upon her like a poof of black magic. It went to hell from that point on. Or was it when she admitted to herself how much Mark mattered to her? Once again, she wasn't able to unravel the mishmash of her feelings.

Coffee and a few pastries were on a nearby table. Mark was thrumming his fingers on his cup, which felt like drumbeats in her ears. His face was splotched with grubby stubble and winter gray circles rested under his eyes. When she felt Winston's fur nuzzling against her skin, her shame skipped a beat knowing that at least she had one sympathizer.

"Hi." Scoping out the pastries, she chose a donut glazed with gooey icing, then regretted it since her fingers stuck together. Winston whiffed the sweetness and before his tongue leapt out, she tossed him a morsel. Licking her fingers and munching her breakfast, she kept stalling.

"Time's a wastin' here. Why would that guy call you a 'prick teaser?' And exactly what did you do to his dick?"

A veil of shame descended slowly until she constricted every vulnerable zone in her being.

"Addie? I have to go to work soon."

Spasms contracted in her chest as she tried to breathe. Since her heart was on perpetual overdrive, she expected to die a premature death and hoped that time was right this minute. However, if she died, her shame would keep strangling her beyond the grave.

"Oh fuck." Once she began speaking, her words sped out uncontrollably and crashed into one another. "I don't know what you need to know. I drove here without calling you first. I don't know why I did that. You have a life, and the last time I saw you, we sort of left it wide open, but I missed you. I've never let myself care about anyone the same way. I haven't and I'm not sure what to make of this ... us.

"And then you answered your phone. That truck thing played before me and it felt as if I had been thrown back in time. Next thing I became wedged in between clumps of people down in the bar, and I freaked out. It was awful. And if that wasn't enough ... that jerk surfaced." She wanted to transport herself somewhere, anywhere, but she kept talking. "I stormed out of your office," she took a breath. "I was disgusted with myself. And then, there I was, face-to-face with him and the man I love."

"What did you actually do with him? Did you proposition him? Did you intentionally tease him?"

"Well, y-yes sort of. I was pissed off, so I picked up that guy. Well, jealous, too. How would I know Dee was your brother's wife? And when I saw the two of you together I—"

"Wait. Wait. That's who you were jealous of? It would have been a lot easier if you simply asked me who Dee was."

The stillness was like a suffocating blanket drowning out unspoken words.

"You told me he made it all up. It was a lie. Tell me he was lying. Tell me you didn't do any of that," Mark insisted.

"No. He didn't lie." She could see the storm in Mark's weary eyes. It was over. Wiping her eyes in preparation for the waterfall, she went on in a flat voice. "I made it pretty clear that if he bought me a drink then, well, I'd meet up with him with the intention of having sex, but then ..." Addie's tongue was so dry it was getting in the way of her words.

"You hooked him into buying you a drink to have sex with him? Because you were jealous of Dee? You intended to have sex with that guy because you were jealous?" He took a hard swallow. Stroking the back of his neck, Mark glared at Addie's flushed face.

"I respected you so much. I couldn't believe that you'd do something so dangerous and stupid, and now I find out you hustled him for a drink? And all because you were jealous of my sister-in-law? I don't want to imagine all that happened in that cab. When you were gone, I missed you and realized I was in love with you ... until this."

Addie took a swig of coffee and felt the cold liquid slide down her throat. *Forgiveness does have its limits. But if he was in love with me, why wouldn't he give me another chance?*

She bit down on her tongue but was unable to control her fury. "Well, fuck you! Who needs you? And Winston comes back with me!" After she blurted out a string of obscenities, she knew from the expression on his face that they hit their mark. Immediate regret.

Mark flattened his fingers against his forehead and let out a long breath. "That's what I mean, Addie. Love for me isn't all or nothing like it is for you. If I love you, I love all of you, no matter what you do. But love does have its limits. You crossed those limits that night. How could I ever trust you? Since we haven't been together for a while, I forgot the internal chaos that I tolerated when we were together. Life with you is predictably unpredictable." Rising to his feet, Mark squatted on an ottoman farthest from her. "Your volatility and lack of self-control scare me, not to mention your poor judgment. I can't deal with that. I'm sorry." Mark slumped back against the wall, staring at the ceiling.

Breathing heavily, Addie reminded him. "I warned you quite a few times that I was fucked up."

"Oh, for chrissakes, Addie ... stop hiding behind that fucked up stuff. Own up to your actions. Do you have any idea how your anger affects other people? And by the way, I don't think you're stable enough to take care of yourself much less a dog. He needs to stay here."

Another "fuck you" socked him in the face. At that point, Addie threw caution to the gods. "Are you crazy? I saved his life."

When she stormed out of Mark's condo with him, Winston paused and scampered back to Mark whimpering.

"Winston!"

As their dog raced toward Addie, he swiveled his head back and forth between his two owners. She whistled for him to follow her, but his whimpers were coated with such anguish that Addie caved and suggested they work out a visitation schedule since Chicago was a five-hour drive from Cincinnati. Well, four in Addie's case. It was as if their pet sniffed out their decision. After dancing circles around the two of them, he loped to the car, waiting for Addie to open the door.

No matter how hard she tried to fix herself, whenever she experienced the pain of rejection—like a magic trick—that ugly part of herself arrived on the scene to rescue her.

FIFTY-THREE

On the drive back to Chicago, Addie sped, weaving in and out of traffic, cutting cars off and flipping drivers visual obscenities. Car horns blared. Drivers rolled their windows down, firing profanities at her.

Whimpers from the back seat broke into her anger. When she saw Winston cowering, Addie slowed down and swerved toward the shoulder of the road, giving no signal or indication of what she was about to do ... more screeching tires and blaring horns. Winston was shaking with such fear, he peed.

Addie apologized and to atone for her sins, she stopped the car, opened the door, and decided to let Winston's nose sniff around the bottom of the embankment. The terrain was slick from morning dew, so as she followed him, she slipped, dropped the leash, and tried to brace herself as she toppled over—gravel cut into her legs and knees as the underbrush snagged her clothing. She collided into a large tree leaving her breathless.

Dizzy, bloodied, and nauseous, with dirt and twigs trapped in her hair, she gripped the rough bark of the tree which kept her from plunging farther into the ravine.

Angling herself so she could see where her dog was, she saw nothing other than dead foliage brushing against clusters of daisy weeds, clover, and masses of trees crouched together. *Oh my God! Please! Please let me find him.* She made every effort to stand using a broken tree branch, but her ankle buckled. As fear overpowered her, she wailed, "Winston! Winston!"

She stumbled, twisting her ankle, letting out a painful cry. Massaging her foot, an image of Winston with blood spouting from his shaggy fur, dying on the side of the road, jumped out at her. With stones and twigs digging into her hands and knees, she crawled back nearer the highway; but all she could hear was the sizzling of tires on the asphalt above.

Wriggling alongside a tree, Mark's words echoed in her head: "Think about how your actions affect others."

He's right. This anger is destroying me and the people I love. I am a selfish fuck. When am I going to learn? Addie sank back on the hillside and closed her eyes in defeat, and as she wept, a warm tongue dried her tears.

FIFTY-FOUR

Chicago

It was beginning to get dark as Addie arrived at the house. Her thoughts skipped forward then backward as if they were playing hopscotch—Mark was out of her life, and she had her mother yet to deal with. She wanted to be on the Enterprise and have Scotty beam her to a mysterious planet with inhabitants who are interesting robots. Winston began whimpering his urgent need for food and a place to pee.

"Sorry, buddy."

She let him loose in the yard where he found a suitable place to relieve himself. Not sure what Sophie's reaction would be to the new family member, Addie verified her original decision that if her mother wouldn't agree, she would find a new home for the two of them.

She was struck by an unfamiliar stillness that slipped out as she opened the front door. Then she heard her *STOP* sign shudder, and out came Mary with Babcia. Winston tore loose and bounded for Mary who shielded her grandmother from being knocked over. Since the old lady's apron was soiled with remnants of the *bigos* she was preparing for dinner, the dog dawdled near her the longest.

"I'm glad he's here! How did your trip go?" Mary asked.

"Fine. Our newest family member is starving—so is the old one."

"Hey! Where in the world did you get so banged up? What's with the limp?" In spite of Addie's protestations, Mary helped her to the sofa.

"I tripped and slid down an embankment. No big deal." Addie examined her leg to see the damage for herself.

"I go get ice," Babcia declared with her new friend traipsing close behind.

"I'm fine. Where's Sophie? I mean mother."

"She's in her bedroom, but I was hoping you and I could catch up first."

"We can, but she needs to know about Winston. It is her house."

Addie stopped short before the closed door, thinking back on the last time she'd been in this room—the day she opened fire on her family's armored façade. Her heart was on overdrive again, but compared to other times, it was a slow, irregular thumping.

"It's me, Addie, may I come in?"

"Of course."

Sophie rested in the love seat with a quilt surrounding her. Addie was drawn to Sophie's wedding picture on her dad's bureau. A beam of light from the room's window illuminated Sophie's face.

Without the label of "Mother" or "Sophie," Addie was able to see her as a woman and able to appreciate how beautiful she was. Her skin glowed like polished moonstone ... her mother's eyelashes were thick, dabbed with the perfect amount of mascara, and her hair, the color of burnt cinnamon, was drawn back into a low bun with an ivory lace mantilla draped on her head. The ornate altar at St. Stanislaus served as a magical backdrop to her slender figure, which was covered in a satin gown with beads and crystals that encrusted the scoop neckline and sleeves.

"You can sit down here, if you wish." Sophie broke the spell of Addie's musings as she pointed to the cushion next to her. "Addie! What in the world happened to you?"

Situating herself in the farthest corner of the sofa, Addie said, "I fell. Babcia's getting an ice pack for my ankle. Nothing to worry about. I'm here because I need to ask you a question ..." Addie caught herself. "Uh, not *that* question."

"From what I gather, you have the answer to *that* question." Sophie surveyed her daughter's face.

"Ahhh. Well, yes, but I'm not here for that."

"But I am, Addie. It's time, don't you agree?"

She peered at this woman sitting next to her. The voice was too soft to be Sophie's.

So, it must be her mother's.

Is it time? Addie wasn't sure. In spite of the fact that the secret had been exposed, listening to her mother speak about it made her squirm in her seat. It would make it more real for Addie and lay bare the anguish that bore through her for being the daughter she was. She doubted that she was strong enough to handle that.

Sophie cradled an envelope with Addie's name written on it. Hoping her mother wouldn't ask her to read aloud whatever was in there, Addie braced herself. She was the instigator who stripped the secret from her mother's past. Maybe secrets were best left tucked in boxes in dark closets. Maybe her mother needed those secrets to protect herself from returning to the pool of suffering that would otherwise drown her.

Addie wasn't a big Shakespeare fan, but there was a quote from *Macbeth* that clung to her memory since she was a junior in high school.

> *Give sorrow words:*
> *The grief that does not speak,*
> *Whispers in*
> *The over-wrought heart*
> *And bids it break.*

"Addie." Sophie spoke quietly. "This is for you. I hope you read through it and do whatever you wish with it. I wrote your letter this morning. Your sister helped me recognize quite a few things I was blind to."

Addie grasped her mother's suffering as if it were a featherless chick fallen from its nest. A dark and heavy silence insinuated itself upon them. But it didn't need to be filled. Addie felt that thread ... Babcia's thread.

"May I ask you a favor?"

Addie nodded.

"Do you remember the day I came home, and you wouldn't let me hug you until you were good and ready?"

"Yes."

"Well, I'll wait again, however long it takes."

How could Addie explain that the thought of being affectionate with her own mother filled her with anxiety? She was terrified of being loved by her because she didn't deserve it, and she was fearful of being a bitchy daughter again. But then, how would a hug make her mother feel? The words *selfish* and *fragile* knocked about in her head. Mulling over her visit in Cincinnati, she smiled as she taunted herself, *Fragile, maybe. Selfish, definitely, but working on it ... again.*

"Am I hearing a dog?" Addie's mother cocked her head toward the barking.

"Ah ... yes ... I came in to ask if you'd agree to let him stay. His name is Winston. He won't be any trouble. I promise."

"Winston, huh? Of course. Remember that pathetic stray you adopted? I didn't have the heart to take the poor critter to the pound. I was beside myself. I didn't want to disappoint you, but we already had another of your refugee dogs." Sophie shook her head and chuckled.

"I remember. Who were our neighbors then? The Miller's? I was elated they volunteered to take him in. I could still play with him!" Startled to see Sophie grin, Addie couldn't recall the last time she saw those crinkly laugh lines peek out from the corners of her mother's winter gray eyes. This moment stretched long and lovely, reminding Addie of their thread—in spite of everything, it was still there.

"That's right. I was so relieved I didn't have to break your little heart."

Their eyes met. Addie scooted closer to her mother and tenderly placed her hand on Sophie's knee until Winston's whimpers just outside the door demanded Addie's attention.

"Go on, honey. Remember, no pressure about that hug."

Wandering in the past with her mother felt like noticing a rainbow for the first time. Although their joyful memories abruptly ended years ago when Sophie left, Addie hoped the two of them would be able to make-up for lost time.

FIFTY-FIVE

The usual hum of bar talk and clumps of bodies at Murphy's entertained Addie to no end: it was earthy and chaotic compared to the ambience and clientele at Chester's. There were no regrets leaving Cincinnati, but Addie did miss the action from behind the bar, bantering with the regulars and, of course, being with Mark.

She was surprised that Mary was late for this get-together with her husband-to-be. Sipping her wine, Addie's attention strayed to her mother's letter, which she hadn't read yet. For several days now she went through the same ritual: she placed it on her dresser, gingerly picked it up as though it contained an explosive and then hurled it across the room. Her emotions about her mother were like soap bubbles ready to pop at any moment. That envelope begged her to toughen up.

Addie's mental wrangling was interrupted by her sister's voice.

"Hey! Sorry we're late, but this guy is never on time!"

Mary razzed Jeff about his tardiness until Addie interrupted, giving her future brother-in-law a smooch on the cheek. After taking their orders for drinks, Jeff made his way through to the bar.

The two of them chatted about the wedding but, as Mary was insisting that Addie would have to wear make-up and tame her hair into a French twist, Addie interrupted.

"Mary, I see you so happy with Jeff. I get so angry at the way I treated Mark. His last words to me have become a sort of mental chewing gum. 'You need to take responsibility for your actions.' I'm trying hard to fix what's wrong with me, but that fiery temper of mine is outrageously uncooperative." She slanted her head back to keep the tears from streaming down her face.

"Adelajda! What's wrong with you is that you think something's wrong with you. You'll keep acting the fool and be angry as long as you believe that. Start behaving as if *nothing is* wrong with you ... my God."

"But I *am* selfish, Mary."

"Well ..." Mary's raised an eyebrow.

"Mags says I'm too fragile on the inside and that's not normal."

"We're all fragile on the inside. So, get over it."

"But it's hard to change, Mary. I'm trying."

"What happened to your idol, Mr. Churchill?"

Addie chuckled and pumped her fist in the air. "I'll never give up! Or is it 'I'll never give in!' Whatever."

"Now, that's the sister I know!"

Jeff strutted up with their drink order, grasping a few dollar bills in between his fingers.

Addie heard a "Hey!" from behind her. She shriveled inside when she heard Mary introduce Mags and Tom to Jeff.

Mags thrust her face in front of Addie's and mouthed the word "please." Addie fought against her usual "fuck you" reaction to Tom, the creep who deserted his pregnant girlfriend. The voice of the old Addie insisted that she maintain her nasty demeanor toward Tom, but this new version of herself, breathed the word "forgiveness" in her ear. *My chance to fix me.*

"Hey, Addie. It's been a long time." Tom rattled the ice in his drink.

"Yes. It has."

"I screwed up and I'm sorry. I'm seeing a therapist, and we will as a couple, too. What I did was awful, but I will make it up to Mags. I've loved you as a friend and hope we can be friends again.

It took every shred of will power to curb her impulse to unleash her fury. A chill slid down Addie's back as if a cold drink was resting against it.

Catching Mags standing on her tiptoes gazing at her, Addie knew this was the time to start practicing forgiveness.

"For Mags," she offered, clinking glasses with Tom.

Mr. Churchill won.

FIFTY-SIX

Addie and her four-legged roommate took their daily constitutional in the neighborhood regardless of the weather. It was difficult to be with Winston without Mark popping up in her head, particularly when she hadn't heard from him. Was Winston important to him? Except for the fact that she didn't want to share time with him, it bothered her.

She landed another job as the voice for a tub of butter that resembled Irma's tone but it was decibels higher. The debut commercial was a success and lead to another kids' show ... *Tubs of Fun*. Addie celebrated with a shopping spree.

Then there was the letter. She promised herself this was the day she needed to read it. *I'll break down. Can I handle my mother's forgiveness?* In between her never-ending mind babble, she did her laundry, slapped a slice of ham between rye bread slathered in mayo, and soon after, whistled for Winston to join her for a jog to the park.

As soon as they were in sight of the house, Winston picked up speed and dragged Addie through the front door. Her lips puckered as the sharp scent of lemons accosted her which meant Sophie was baking one of her favorites ... lemon pound cake.

"Addie? Is that you?"

"Yes. How soon will the cake be ready?" Once again, she was filled with a desire to take her mother into her arms, but Addie's feet remained locked in place. *Do other daughters feel like this? Do they think about it, or do they just do it? Yeah, but other daughters aren't consumed with shame.*

Sophie wagged a spatula coated with cream cheese frosting before Addie and dabbed a smidgen on her nose.

Addie took her mother's offering and gave the spoon a hearty lick, passing it back to her. Sophie's tongue slurped at what was left.

Smiles flittered across their faces as if they had met for the first time and were eager to discover more about each other.

It's time to stop being such a coward and read that letter.

On the verge of revealing what she was about to do, the words jammed in Addie's throat.

Winston soared onto the bed, rolled onto his back, and wiggled to get a good rub. Sticking his legs straight up, he let out a pleasurable rumble. Addie peered at Sophie's envelope propped against the gold and black enameled coffer that her grandmother had given her years ago.

"Hey, do you think I can deal with what's in here?"

Struggling to loosen his legs from the pierzyna, Winston hopped off and circled to where Addie was sitting Indian style, planting himself in front of her.

"I don't know how I'm going to react, so will you stay with me?"

He barked twice and snuggled against her leg.

"Here goes." Ripping it open, she unfolded the pages, surprised at the length of the letter.

Dearest Addie,

The word you've used frequently to describe what I did when you and your sister were children is 'abandonment.' I understand why you felt that way because, in fact, I did abandon the two of you. I had no choice. I fell apart when the trauma ripped through my consciousness. They're called flashbacks ... night terrors ... and they continue to haunt me today although infrequently since I've been in therapy. The hospital helped me at first, but I refused to receive more treatment. It was too painful.

I'm sorry I made your grandmother and your father swear to keep why I left a secret. I didn't want you girls to ever know such evil existed in the world. Later on, I was consumed with shame. Shame for what someone else did to me. Shame for being unable to stop what was happening. I believed something was wrong with me. Why else would someone do what he did to me? Why else wouldn't anyone help me? Over time, I hated your grandmother, who didn't protect me, your dad who I thought knew, his father, and his mother ... secret keepers. And then there was you.

When you were a tot, you were so much like me ...loving, spirited, stubborn, and clever. And through no fault of yours, that shopping trip opened up that horrible time in my life.

Before I left, you and I were close. I'm not sure you remember that, but I do. You were my baby.

After I came back, you were so mean toward me, and it kept getting worse. Bear with me. My intention is not to criticize you, but to help you understand my actions and reactions, many of which I sincerely regret.

The way you treated me was a reminder that I wasn't a good mother and that kept reminding me how flawed I was ... how much of a failure I was.

I hated you because you had the courage to be outrageous and speak out, and all I could do was keep secrets. What I've come to realize is the hate I felt toward you was what I felt toward myself. Hatred for my cowardice.

Your sister was my favorite. I saw her as weak and the person who would keep me from facing my internal chaos. Having her agree with me and do whatever I asked, made me feel safe: That I wasn't alone.

The times I withdrew or stared vacantly into space were the times I needed to shut down because I wasn't able to handle what was happening inside of me. I felt so weak. I ask your forgiveness not only for the void between us but also for the abuse I unleashed on you. I pray we can draw nearer to one another. I've asked Mary for forgiveness and pray she and I can be close with our differences intact.

Knowing you as I do, I believed a letter was an effective way to communicate this. That way, you can read it and reread it if necessary. The spoken word can fade with time.

I'm back in therapy, and I'm beginning to shed the belief that the rapes and brutal sexual acts I endured were my fault, which means my self-loathing can no longer be a barrier in my relationships. After all, I was just a child.

Love,
Your mother/a.k.a. Sophie

Addie held her mother's forgiveness close to her heart. The lump in her chest crept up into her throat making it difficult for her to breathe. Squeezing her eyes shut, she braced herself, but her anticipated emotional collapse didn't materialize. Even though it felt as though a rug had been yanked out from under her fear, leaving her battered, she felt safe.

Her mother's recognition of their similarities ... "you were like me ... *loving, spirited, stubborn, and clever"* made her weep. And here she thought her own mother didn't love her—worse yet, hated who she was. During those years, it felt as though she was on this untethered boat drifting alone in angry waters.

My mother saw parts of herself in me! Knowing this, grounds me in a way I can't explain.

*I now know I'm loveable not because we're alike necessarily but because she was able to **see** me ... Addie, Adelajda. I always thought that I didn't matter.*

I guess that's what any daughter wants from her mother. To be recognized as a person, to be seen, and I need to give the same to her.

FIFTY-SEVEN

Addie's thoughts were in constant motion, trying to decide how to respond to her mother's innermost feelings. With pen to paper, a few words came to mind, but they never touched the page. Once again, her emotions loitered inside of her creating more doubt about what to do. Maybe it would be better if she talked to her instead of writing, but her mother was suffering with enough of her own pain right now.

The clock reminded her that if she didn't get moving, Babcia would be annoyed with her tardiness. This was a big day and a first-time ladies' luncheon for the Gurin women. How weird since they lived in the same house.

The jangling of her phone startled her as she was about to leave.

"Hello!" Addie sang into the receiver.

"Addie, how are you? It's me, Mark."

For months she imagined having this conversation with him. She scrabbled over the top of her dresser for the script she painstakingly composed. Tossing pictures and books aside, she couldn't find it. *Shit!*

"Addie? Hello?" Mark's voice was terse as if he was in a rush.

"Oh, sorry. Winston's pestering me to go out." *Why did I say that?*

"Oh, I won't keep you long. I'll be in Chicago next weekend. Where can we meet?"

Blinking, Addie couldn't keep up with the turmoil swirling in her head. Life without her dog would be devastating, but a deal was a deal. Sitting on her bed, she fidgeted with Winston's collar.

"Oh, wow. Has it been that long? Well, ah, my sister's getting married, and the next few weekends are filled with that. I'm happy to drive to Cincinnati and drop him off at your place." *Why did I say that? Shut up.*

"Oh. No. I have a friend in Chicago that I visit once in a while. Will you be free the weekend of the twenty-eighth?"

"Sure. Where does this friend live?" Once again, Addie wanted to smack herself. *Don't be so eager.* And, without missing a beat, interjected, "Just curious cause I'd be able to suggest a mutually convenient meeting place."

"How about I give you a ring that week, and we can figure it out then?"

"Sure." After their good-byes, Addie slammed the receiver down. Why didn't he tell her where this friend lived? *It must be a woman. He's seeing a woman here in town.* After she reminded herself how her jealousy screwed her over the last time, she wanted to choke the shit out of it. She hated herself for blowing it with Mark. She loved him ... and missed him terribly. Winston hopped up on the bed landing right next to her.

"You're what's keeping us together," she confided, as she patted his paw.

Addie knew this hand-off with Mark was a chance for her to impress him with her transformation. Maybe he'd realize what a catch she was.

FIFTY-EIGHT

Wearing a dark gray suit, a multi-colored beige blouse, and what she referred to as her "old lady shoes," Irina was drum rolling her fingers on her lap. The large coral cameo pin and matching earrings her mother passed-down gave Irina a regal aura about her. Instead of her signature hairnet, she wore a small pea green hat, which covered her grizzled white curls.

"Adelajda, we be late! We shop for wedding dress. Your matka and Marysia wait for us."

"Wowie! Lady!" Addie let out a wolf whistle, which fired up her four-legged friend, causing him to run in circles, colliding into Irina. Addie nabbed him by his collar and reprimanded him.

"He happy I look so good! Uh ... Adelajda. Your matka and I say nothing about... you know. We don't look at each other. How will lunch go?"

Mary and Addie knew this would be a stressful day since their mother had yet to discuss the abuse with Irina and dodged any opportunity to do so. The wedding was just a few weeks away and Addie insisted that they not let the secret continue to control their lives. Promising them she would deal with Irina after the wedding, Sophie agreed that this was Mary's special time and nothing should get in the way.

"You sit next to me and remember, this is a very happy day for your Marysia. Everything will be fine."

Since Mary scheduled appointments well into the afternoon at Field's, Carson's, and Steven's, she planned an early lunch. When Addie and her grandmother arrived, Mary and Sophie were seated, skimming the menu. Tension hovered above them and remained in spite of the artificial greetings they doled out except for Irina. The old lady smiled so broadly at her daughter and granddaughter that her dentures clattered.

"Where's Katie?" Addie was eager to meet Jeff's daughter.

"She's down with the flu. Sounded terrible. She could hardly talk without coughing."

Their server, dressed in a non-descript black uniform, introduced herself as Joyce announcing in a flat voice a list of beverages the restaurant offered.

Scanning the tabletop, Irina frowned at the tall glasses of iced tea sitting before Mary and Sophie. Knowing her grandmother's penchant for brandy, Addie was prepared to order for her, especially since alcohol would hopefully loosen the awkwardness among them.

"Well, Joyce! We are celebrating, aren't we ladies? This is a big day!" At first, Addie's voice wavered, but as she studied their faces, it increased in volume as if she was a cheerleader trying to rally the losing team. "This is a first luncheon for the four of us, Joyce. My sister's getting married so we're going to be shopping for her wedding dress! This will be fun, fun, fun, won't it, Mary? We should get a bottle of wine, dontcha think?"

"Ya. That be good. Wine for Sunday mass. Brandy for me."

Once the drinks were ordered, Mary fiddled with her napkin, Sophie squirmed in her chair as if she were sitting on spikes, while Addie observed them in disbelief because this wasn't how it was supposed to be.

"Sophie." Irina spoke haltingly as her eyes darted from Mary to Addie in need of their support. "We come here to shop your wedding dress. Remember?"

"Is that right?" Addie was thrilled. *This is normal!*

The night before she and Mary gabbed about how this day would go and wished for the same thing ... normal. They imagined that other mothers and daughters who meet up would jabber about their jobs, world events, share gossip about relatives and friends, and complain about their weight as they ordered fattening entrees, justifying their sinfulness by splitting the desserts.

But a stiff silence strangled Addie's optimism.

"Mother ..." Two scarlet blotches bloomed on Addie's cheeks. Saying that word where so many ears could hear it, she felt like a thief taking what didn't belong to her. Uncoiling her fingers, Addie straightened up and continued. "How does it feel to shop for a wedding dress with Mary?"

"Ya." The memory of Sophie's big day dampened Irina's earlier caution. "Remember Frank say for you to wear his matka's dress, and he wear his papa's fancy suit ..."

Noticing her mother's colorless eyes, Addie began yammering about her latest episode at the agency. Mary let out a nervous cough and then tipped her wine glass in her mother's direction.

What the hell did Mary want her to do? Her usual response to her mother's estrangements was to yell or leave; but this time she yearned to breathe in her mother's pain, take it away, and comfort her.

"Babcia! Why would you bring those people up?" Addie snapped.

"What? What I do?" Irina's chin quivered as she saw red stains popping up over Sophie's neck. "Marysia, I need bathroom."

Moving next to her mother, Addie became alarmed when Sophie stared ahead. "Mother, I'm here. You're here. You're not alone, and I promise nothing bad will happen to you. I love you. Don't go back to the past. We're here for lunch, and I'm sure you want this to be a wonderful day for both you and Mary." Addie kissed her cheek and waited, sliding a stray curl behind Sophie's ear.

Nothing.

Racing thoughts about what to say or do next silenced Addie until a rush of words poured out from a mysterious place in her heart.

"In your letter, you said that we were alike. That made me feel so good knowing that you thought there were parts of you in me. I'm sorry it took me so long to appreciate you. Dig down inside and find your spunk. Where do you think I got mine from? It's there. Whatever you weren't able to do as a child, you can do now."

Sophie began trembling while squeezing Addie's hand. As the pressure increased, pinpricks of goosebumps sprang up on Addie's arms. In that moment, she realized that it was the thread that held her together while she read the letter. And although strands of sorrow and regret stood in its shadows, she knew they could transcend the pain of the past.

"Thank you ... for making me stay with you." A tear drop made a circle on Sophie's blouse.

"I love you, Mom. Not just because you're my mom. I love you for who you are on the inside."

Turning to face her daughter, Sophie's eyes were wide with disbelief. "Oh my."

"You can hug me now, but I want you to wrap your arms around me as if I was a child again."

Sophie squeezed her so tightly, Addie felt as though she was trying to atone for all the cuddles and caresses that were squandered all these years. Using their napkins to muffle their grief, neither would let go until Addie uttered under her breath, "Would you like to powder your nose?"

"Well, you know me better than I thought."

As Addie watched her mother leave, she became dizzy and disoriented, so much so she had to grasp the table to steady herself. Within a few minutes, she began laughing as she rested her forehead on the linen cloth. *I guess I entered a forbidden and foreign zone with her and I have to adjust to this feeling!*

"Where is Sophie? I do wrong again? Marysia say to talk never about wedding. So sorry. I not want to upset her. I try to make happy talk. Remember time we were happy."

Patting her babcia's hand, Addie apologized for her angry outburst earlier and reassured both Mary and her that although Sophie recovered from her withdrawal, they still needed to be sensitive to her instability.

When Sophie sat down, the four of them straightened up and grasped their menus. Mary was holding hers upside down while Addie, hiding behind hers, was uncertain as to what should happen next.

Waving at Joyce as she was dashing by, Addie caught her attention. "It's time for lunch, ladies. We'll have four signature chicken pot pie lunches with house salads, dressing on the side."

Mary began thrumming her fingers on the table. Irina kept her face buried in her hanky and Sophie poured herself more wine.

Brief, unimportant statements were punctuated by not so brief silences. From nearby lunch ladies who were sharing plates of food, Addie heard laughter and the buzz of what she assumed was gossip about people they loved as well as those they didn't. Gazing at her sister and grandmother, who were rearranging the silverware and glasses, Addie knew that before they could be 'normal,' they needed to break open those secrets that held them hostage because of one fucking sick guy.

"Forget what I said before! Let's stop pretending," Addie demanded. "We should be having fun! Why do I feel as if we're watching a roadside car accident? We've been affected by that secret, a painful secret. But how can we ever have normal times together?" Wrapping her arm around Sophie's, Addie whispered, "Hang in there, mom."

Nodding her head, Sophie grasped Addie's clammy hand.

"I want this day to be a happy memory for all of us. I want it to feel joyous and exciting. Is that possible?" Crouched over the table, Addie thought they resembled orphans watching the other waifs dashing into the arms of their new families, while they were left behind.

"Hey, let's stop hiding the abuse and bring it into the light of day. Other families have bad things happen, but, as I learned in a therapy session, some have the balls to deal with their problems head on. Mom, we've been trying to protect you from your pain and our own, but what we're doing is making it worse.

"Is that Polish 'family is everything' empty talk?"

Irina sniffled. "No, they not. We here. We feel but we don't speak ... that's how it been. It hard. Women hard to each other ... Matkas and daughters so much so. My Sophie, I so sorry."

"It's time." Mary scooted closer to the table.

Irina picked at a flaw on the tablecloth.

"Ok, Babcia, let's get down to it. Did you have any idea she was being abused?" Mary whispered as though she was in church.

"Mom, if you have to leave, we'll stay with you for however long it takes."

Addie and Mary peered at their grandmother and nodded in support.

"Sophie. This so hard." Irina said in a tight voice. Each word sounded as if it would break open into tears. "I love you. Can you forgive me? I not know. You come to me and I not sure until I ask Helen to take you to doctor. I work and she say you Ok. I hate at myself I not take you. But I scared. Your papa dead. We had nothing. Work more important. I scared we be on street. I fail you." The tears came, the ugly ones that scrunched Irina's face into what looked like a withered apple.

Addie felt the vibration of her mother's trembling hands.

Sophie's voice circled around them like a whoosh of cold wind that eventually blew itself out. "I can't let the abuse define me or our relationship. I try to remember our thread ... to remember the sacrifices you made for me and the other ways you loved me; however, I have to heal from what you didn't do."

Irina shuddered as she tried to breathe.

"Mother, remember the time we talked about forgiveness?" Mary asked.

"I do. That I would live my life as a victim if I couldn't forgive my own mother. If I couldn't forgive myself."

Irina and her daughter locked eyes in a shared understanding.

Sophie inhaled deeply. "It's time to burn that envelope."

PART V

Addie

FIFTY-NINE

For weeks, her body felt too heavy to hold up. Since the wedding and, in its aftermath, Addie's mood continued to slide farther into the pits. There were times she was able to wriggle through these black clouds that darkened her days by being active. Her usual sure-fire remedy, roller skating, wasn't enough to motivate her. What disheartened her was that regardless of how much time she spent with Winston, her spirits remained in the toilet. *How could I be so stupid?* Addie invited herself to another of her pity parties.

Rambling in her room, she tried to disappear from herself. Since her closet was a mess, she started to rummage through the piles of clothes scattered on the floor. After straightening a wrinkled skirt, the word "stupid" preyed upon her with a vengeance. As a way to escape her admonitions, she refocused her attention to her shoe boxes, which were in complete disarray. Her bartender footgear from Chester's dangled out at her. She yanked them off the shelf and threw them into her waste basket, which toppled over.

"Well, Mr. Churchill, this time I give up *and* give in."

As she lay on her bed, staring at the ceiling, she played with her faithful companion's ear. It was time to tell someone what she didn't want to hear. *There it is,* she mused. *Another secret.* She was beginning to appreciate her mother and what she did to protect herself. Weeping silent tears that splashed over her cheeks, she rolled over to her side and kissed Winston's paws. His tail wagged the towel off his back. Since she had lathered and rinsed him, he smelled like the fragrant lavender dog soap she bought the other day. His breath, however, was another matter.

Addie grumped at her phone's interruption, even if it could be Mags.

"Hey, it's me. How about if you meet me at Murph's for a quick beer? I have to pick up a few things downtown."

"I'm gonna hang out at home today."

"It's either sinuses that's plugged you up or you've been crying. What's up?"

If Addie told Mags, she'd have to believe what was happening, and right now, she'd rather pretend nothing had changed.

"Sinuses."

"C'mon. I know the difference between sinuses and tear snots."

"Well, you're wrong this time. How's Tom?"

"Ok. I get the point. Addie, what can I do to help?"

"Not a thing. Not a thing. But thanks. I'll talk to you later."

Flipping from side to side, then sitting up, and then crumpling into her pillow, she let out a groan. Winston snorted, objecting to all the fuss. Procrastination made her sink further into her desire to disappear. She dragged herself out of bed and decided to get as far from the world as possible.

Addie rooted out her grandmother's bottle of brandy and, along with her buddy, hauled herself down into the bowels of the house. She shuffled toward the cedar closet, and entombed herself and her bottle under a few musky comforters. For a few minutes, the odor reminded her of being in the fourth grade when she was in charge of sharpening the pencils which she hated doing. What she loved best was scattering the shavings on Mags' head.

A whine outside the closed door alerted her that she wasn't alone.

"Sorry, buddy." Addie limped out and stamped her leg to wake it up.

"What will I do?" she stroked her dearest companion's fur while he draped his tongue over the side of his mouth.

With a low rumble, he placed a paw on the edge of the cushion.

"Well, you will soon have a playmate."

No way would she ever be the bride at a gunshot wedding. And then, when she entertained the notion of being a sole parent, the heat of fear burning in her belly began to creep up to her face. How could she take care of a baby? She'd probably end up maiming it with her temper. Gulping a swig of brandy, she coughed.

Being trapped in a situation that didn't have any positive solution, Addie wanted to scream but didn't have the energy to let it out. *I'm too smart for this to have happened. I never missed a single fucking birth control pill. The doctor was so cavalier about it. 'It doesn't happen often, but it can happen.'*

Never in her life did hopelessness have such a grip on her. She needed a distraction. "Just one ... It can't hurt."

Reaching for a smoke, she fumbled over the coffee table in search of matches and when she found none, she figured her dad would have a lighter on his desk. Hauling herself over there, she plopped into his chair, scrunched her feet up and swiveled in circles until she felt woozy. Yet to find any matches, she began hunting through his piles of papers, coming up empty-handed. More determined to smoke, she rummaged through drawers until a spark of silver concealed under boxes of paper clips and bags of rubber bands, captured her attention.

Digging through the mess, she touched the buried object and was shocked at what was before her. *What is Dad doing with a gun?* She shivered at the thought that he must have been depressed about his own father ... pedophile ... and then his mother ... a mother who was his accomplice. The cold steel felt like ice as the gun rested in the palm of her hand. Of course, he'd been upset but it never occurred to her that he would want to take his own life.

Clenching the weapon, she closed her eyes and held it to her head. Living inside herself was wearing her down.

"Oh my God! Addie!" Frank's voice was cracking with fear. "Put that gun down!"

Winston began yowling.

Startled, Addie let go of the gun.

Frank fell on his knees before her. "My God! Addie! What are you doing? Do you have any idea how much we love you? Addie, were you—"

"Didn't mean to scare you. I don't know. Not really. I was imagining how anyone could pull the trigger. I've been depressed but, no, not that. But you? Buying a gun is pretty serious."

"It was a few weeks after I found out about my parents and how my fear betrayed your mother and God knows who else. Another tragedy for our family to deal with was something I couldn't let happen. And remember, my mother took her own life. I've been meeting with Father Ted who's given me a better perspective on the whole situation. Your mother and I are working on rebuilding our relationship. How about telling me what's going on with you?"

Addie hesitated. It would be incredibly awkward telling him she was having sex, to say nothing of a baby. Since her dad was religious, she suspected his ideas about how that sort of stuff worked now was pretty outdated.

Propping her elbows on her knees, she dropped her head into her hands and briefed him on Mark and their current status. "I'm in trouble, Dad." A surge of embarrassment shaded her face. "Uh, uh, I'm pregnant with his baby," she confessed with her voice as soft as falling snow.

"A baby? You're pregnant?" He sank back into the cushion. "I didn't know you were dating someone til this very moment!"

"Oh, Dad. Please don't lecture me about premarital sex."

"Give me a few minutes here. I suspect you're too old for that sermon, and apparently, it's too late for any father-daughter talk. And I wouldn't do that anyway. Have you been to a doctor? Does the father know?"

"Yes on the doctor front but not yet on the father front. We're meeting next week."

"Do you love him?"

"Yes, I do."

"Is he the kind of man who will do the honorable thing?"

"Yes, he is, but I don't want a marriage based on guilt and obligation."

"Addie, you know I love you. I'm sure it's no surprise to you that I don't approve of premarital relations, but that's of no consequence at this point. Abortion is not happening. Does your mother know?"

"Not yet. I plan to tell Mary the next time I see her. Dad, will you tell Mom? I've disappointed her so much I can't bear to see her reaction."

"I'd rather you did it. But, come here." Frank snuggled her close to him for the longest time and then kissed the top of her head. "Don't worry. We'll figure this out."

Family is everything.

The *STOP* sign vibrated as she tapped on the S. In a raspy voice, Irina invited her to come in. Wearing her flowered flannel robe, her grandmother was clasping her rosary sitting back in her recliner. It was unusual for her to be dressed in nightclothes in the middle of the day.

"You Ok?"

Before Addie came too close to feeling her grandmother's forehead, Irina said, "No fever. Lazy day today. Come sit. Tell me how are you."

The color spread across Addie's face like a wildfire. "Babcia ... was it hard raising my mom by yourself?"

"Ya. Much better to have *mąż*. Better for your matka to have papa. Maybe then ..."

In no way did Addie want to stir up any pain from her grandmother's past.

"I have to tell you something, but this is hard for me to do."

"You forever tell me your trouble."

Facing the window, Addie took a breath.

"You're going to be Pra-Babcia."

"What? Marysia have baby so soon?"

"Ahhh, no. Me." Addie patted her belly.

"You?"

"Yes. Me."

"Adelajda, what wrong with you girls? Birth control easy to get, no?"

"It's not sperm-proof. What should I do? The father broke up with me, so he has no idea." Addie perched herself on the edge of the bed.

Irina wobbled toward Addie, and settled down next to her.

"Your *jaja* forever dream of America and say we go. I say no I stay home. I scared. After I tell my papa, I more scared and say maybe no good idea to come to US ... too far. Jaja say he go without me. Oh. I get so mad. I keep secret I had sex with neighbor boy, Jan. I lucky. No baby. But in old country, if you do sex you must marry, and Jan want me to marry him.

"I say Ok to hurt your *jaja* and make him jealous. But I feel no good inside. I tell my papa, and he tell me to follow my heart. So, here I am." Irina's attention shifted to the aged photo of the two of them on her nightstand, when they first docked in the United States.

"Ya ... your *jaja*." She pointed to the picture. "He nice-looker guy, no?" Irina stepped into that memory.

"Adelajda, if pill not work, other ways to stop baby with calendar ... next time do both," Irina advised. "You love this guy? He love you?"

"Me, yes; he, no."

"Ach. He stupid. He know?"

"Not yet, but I'm not sure I want to tell him. Remember what you used to say about love? 'Don't push river, it flow on its own.'"

"Well, sometime river needs shove. Adelajda, I do your *matka* myself but you lucky you have us. Not to worry. *Rodzina nie jest czymś ważnym. Jest wszystkim.*"

"I do love him, but I don't want a child to be the reason for marriage."

"Adelajda. Remember I tell you to spin three times and *wino* fly off? Well, if you have trouble like this, you spin five times. C'mon ... spin."

A grin sailed across Addie's face.

"You dizzy? Ya? Good. Bye bye confusion. Now, let's have brandy and hug."

Addie thought her babcia's spinning rituals were old country hocus pocus, but this time was different.

When her head stopped spinning, the photo of her grandparents stuck in the darkness of her closed eyes. She knew what she needed to do.

She consumed two pints of ice cream, three glazed donuts and a cherry popsicle waiting for Mark to pick up the phone. Disgusted with herself for a variety of reasons, she decided this was a time to give in.

"Addie? Hey, I'm sorry for not getting back to you on Winston. How are you?"

Pregnant and guess what? You're the daddy! "Fine. How are you?"

"Fine. Hey Steve, would you seat those people at table 22?"

"How are things at Chester's?"

"Ok. Ah, I'll be on the near Northside, Saturday. Where should we meet that would be convenient for you?"

"It will be easiest if you come to my sister's place. She's at 492 Golden which is near where you'll be. How about two o'clock?"

"Sure. See you then." His voice had a frosty restlessness to it as if he dreaded hearing her voice.

That was it. Addie hoped he would accept her offer to have a drink, but suspected he would refuse, and leave with Winston at his side. Either way, it was going to be awkward.

With a swath of guilt for casting off her faith, Addie defaulted to Babcia's novena praying that Mark would want to marry her no matter how, what, when or where. And not because of the baby, but because he loved her.

Once again, she wasn't able to be a normal woman making a joyful announcement to a husband who loved her. *I'm so weird. Shut up! No more self-pity! But how do I tell him? After hearing his voice, I'm not so sure.*

Many scenarios prevailed upon her: *Did you notice I'm not smoking? Too oblique. I have a surprise for you! We are going to have a baby. Too direct. I am going to have a baby. Too vague. He'll ask who the father is. What if he begs me to get back together before I tell him? Ha! Unlikely.* Or was it?

Pounding her fists on her pierzyna, she let out a scream that mimicked the piercing shrieks of the shower lady being stabbed in *Psycho.* Winston hid under the bed.

Unable to sleep the night before her meeting with Mark, Addie was awake long before the sun welcomed in a new day. Her movements were quick and frantic as she showered and messed with her hair while Winston served as her fashion consultant.

She needed her daily injection of caffeine as well as something to tame her churning stomach. Surprised that she heard dishes and silverware clattering near the sink, she called out, "Mom?"

"Addie, why are you up at this hour?"

Since the lunch at Field's, the fears that kept them distant evaporated. Once Mary began her new life, there was more room for Addie and her mother to have a private joke or to have a conversation about ordinary things: a movie, her job, her mother's retirement. Addie was certain that what changed between them was that F word: forgiveness.

"Has Dad mentioned anything to you?"

"Hmmm. He has."

Addie's coffee cup missed the saucer.

"How come you're not upset? You're not mad?"

"Maybe several years ago I might have been. Not now. No judgements anymore, honey. They take way too much energy and make people feel bad; and that negativity doesn't do much for me, either. C'mon. Sit down." Picking up the plate of pastries, Sophie inspected the nicks to see which were stuffed with Addie's favorite filling and pointed to the middle paczki. "Strawberry. Here. It's yours."

"Thanks."

"And he explained why you wanted him to tell me. Addie, you're not a disappointment to me. Whatever happened between us happened because of sick people, and we reacted out of ignorance. But that isn't the case any longer." Sophie stepped back, held Addie's face in her hands, kissed her on her forehead, and pulled her close. They swayed and squeezed each other tightly.

"Now back to business. I assume you've been to a doctor."

"Yes. I was on birth control. I'm pissed that this happened. Why me? Why am I being punished? How can I take care of a baby I don't want!"

"Addie, while I was being abused and, even afterwards, I begged God to stop it and give me peace. But I realize now that I was praying for the wrong thing. My prayers now ask for courage ... the courage to accept what happened to me, not to take it away. I ask now for the courage to deal with it ... to accept it! And besides, I refuse to waste my precious life in a perpetual cycle of blame. Fuck that!" Sophie pinched Addie's cheek.

Addie sat back and set her half-eaten paczki down.

"You do get yourself into some doozies. I would like to meet him. What's his name?"

Briefing her mother on Mark, how they met, and their tumultuous relationship, Addie experienced the bliss that deepens that connection between mothers and daughters because there is no fear of judgement or rejection. The truck driver incident was left hidden. After all, a daughter doesn't have to tell her mother everything.

"We'll come up with options once Mark knows. His decision will affect what we'll do."

"Why should I tell him?"

"It's the right thing to do."

The conversation whiplashed as Sophie placed her finger under Addie's chin. "What do you bring to a relationship?"

Addie became quiet. "Why do you ask?"

Sophie shrugged. "I understand that you plan on stopping in at Mary's later. This will be a big day for you. Your dad and I will support you in any way we can. So, let us know what you need." Sophie lifted Addie's hands to her lips and gently kissed them.

Winston darted up behind her and became tangled in her feet. He let loose a deafening squeal.

"Are you Ok? Did I hurt you?" Regaining her equilibrium, she gripped his collar and checked to see if he was injured. When his tail swooshed against her legs, she was relieved.

Holding her buddy's face close to her own, she confided in him. "I never considered how you or Mark would feel about being separated. I was more focused on how I'd feel. Same way with my mother and my dad. It was all about me."

And now, this pregnancy—her major concern focused on what Mark would do and not how this would affect his life.

I'm so damn selfish. I bring nothing to a relationship. All at once, she understood what Mary tried to tell her that day at Murphy's. As long as she believed that she was flawed, she had the perfect reason not to have to change, as though it was outside of her control.

Plopping next to Winston, who was knotted up in the sheets on her bed, she laughed. *The time and money I doled out to those psychiatrists was a waste when my mom knew the right question to ask all along.*

SIXTY

The Gold Coast was a fabulous historic district that Chicago's elite identified as home. It was filled with a potpourri of sprawling mansions, shoulder-to-shoulder row houses, and high-rises that appeared as if they brushed against the sky.

Several months before they married, Mary and Jeff had purchased a dilapidated row house in the neighborhood with the intention of rehabbing it. Addie and Mary were incredulous as to how a Polish girl from Jefferson Park ended up hob-knobbing with the rich and famous.

Addie was the first guest to see their new home, and it was on the same day that Mark was to collect Winston.

Dragging Addie to the middle of a tree-lined street with an array of luxury cars parked on either side, Winston was on hot pursuit of a squirrel.

"Winston! Please stop!"

A car horn blared. Addie sprang up and deposited herself in front of her tormentor. The driver kept motioning for her to get out of the way. Wrapping the leash around her wrist, she was on the verge of waving her digital obscenity, when she yanked her arm down.

"I'm sorry, so sorry." For weeks now, Addie spent hours perusing the self-help section of books on anger management at Barnes & Noble and bought several. This was her test! It took every shred of willpower to keep her hand imprisoned under her armpit. The driver flung an expletive at her as his car screeched by.

"Hmm," she mumbled to her companion, "Some people can't control their tempers!"

Winston agreed with her with a howl that pierced her ears longer than usual. She bent down and scooped him up breathing in traces of his lavender doggie shampoo. Mark would be quite impressed—Winston's ash gray teeth sparkled. Picking strands of grass from his paw, she knew the next few months without him would send her into a pit of the doldrums.

While she was packing his doggie paraphernalia in the garage, her grandmother stuck her head out the door. "Paczki, what you doing?"

Addie didn't want to tell her grandmother about the visitation schedule until he was well on his way to Cincinnati but, unable to lie, she explained the situation and suggested that Babcia say goodbye to their beloved pet.

"Why you do that? There's Bible story. Two women fight for baby, so judge say to cut baby in half ... real mother say no and give up baby. Judge know who real mother is. Love is sacrifish."

"Sacrifice. Sac-ri-fice. Are you saying I should give Winston up?" Addie was shocked at her suggestion.

"Tell story to boyfriend ... it say lot about him when he hear it."

Sacrifice. That's what I must remember about being in a relationship.

The skies darkened and the thunderclap over the lake confirmed the weather report she'd heard earlier in the day. Addie was known to abuse umbrellas, so the one she carried with her had a spoke jutting out of it. With gray clouds scudding above, she was glad she brought it along. A wet flat head was never an attractive hairstyle for her.

The numbers on the address plaques were miniscule and difficult to make out, so Addie had to creep up quite a few entrance ways before she found Mary's house. With her mouth wide open, she craned her neck up as she scanned the 4 stories of windows dressed with flower boxes spilling over with violet and pink pansies. The front door swung open, and her sister glided onto the portico waving a flute of champagne. "Welcome!"

Running up the winding stairwell with Winston at her feet, Addie high fived Mary with such enthusiasm that the champagne spilled, giving the dog the treat of his life.

"Oh my God, Mary! Sorry about the booze, but wow, oh wow! Invite me in!" Addie declared while sashaying her hips as she coasted into the foyer.

"Whoa! Winston, you lie down here. Mary, we could do with a bowl of water."

Addie made her way in and sunk into the sumptuous texture of the emerald green and ivory Oriental rug that overlaid the glossy hardwood floor. With the exception of a few items, the furniture harkened back to the Victorian era and was oversized; but in spite of that, the room radiated a coziness. Crystal containers of jasmine potpourri were scattered on various tables. Walnut bookshelves grazed the sixteen-foot ceiling and were filled with leather-covered tomes showing off their gold lettered spines in perfect rows. A library ladder with wheels rested against a corner.

"Give me a few minutes before we go on a tour."

"Of course! Sit!" Mary pointed to a creamy white leather sectional scattered with pouf pillows. Surprised by the depth of the cushions, Addie giggled as she spilled a few drops of her champagne while she settled in.

While Mary was talking about one of her student's, Addie began biting her chipped nail.

"Stop that! Here take one." Mary pointed to a tray of appetizers sitting on a latticed doily that appeared to be stolen from the cover of *Bon Appetit!*

"These are too beautiful to eat!" Addie didn't have the heart to refuse as much as her stomach churned at the smell. So, she nabbed a bacon-wrapped shrimp and placed it on a plate.

"Mary." Addie began shredding a cocktail napkin.

Mary settled herself and grabbed the ragged paper. "Do you remember how I was supposed to keep mother's secret from you but didn't?"

"It's amazing how some family secrets can be kept and others, not so much. How did you find out?"

"Dad. Don't be mad!"

"I'm not. Well, I'm glad he did but I should have told you myself."

"Hey. Not to worry. Down to business. From a selfish standpoint, I'm excited to be an aunt!"

"Hold on. What if he wants to give it up for adoption? I'm tormented about whether or not to tell him. He's the kind of guy who would do the right thing to give the baby a name and maybe make a respectable woman out of me. And that's not a good enough reason."

"As I recall, dear sister, you were the poster child for doing what people are *supposed* to do. That banner of 'supposed to do's' is now waving in your face. You have to tell him. It's what is right."

"Damn it! I'm scared."

"You'll do what you're supposed to do. What time is Mark due?" Mary tapped her fingers on her champagne flute.

"In a few minutes."

"Well, I'll be in the study. Lesson plans to do. Jeff won't be home till late. If you need your big sister, holler. I love you." Mary blew her a kiss and waved a tube of lipstick at her.

"*No! Au naturel!*"

Addie explored the room, checking out the unusual decorative items displayed in various places ... a brass scale of justice with a carved gavel nearby. In her peripheral vision, she saw Winston in the foyer, lying on his back with his legs twitching as he snored. Babcia's Bible story about sacrifice haunted her.

The doorbell rang. Winston leapt up and squealed.

When she peered out the beveled glass window, she saw three of Mark standing on the other side. She blinked several times trying to focus on the real one. *I can do this. I can do this. I am normal. Blessed Mother, don't let me down.* Winston wouldn't let her open the door fully before he squeezed himself outside and pounced on Mark. Laughing, he squatted down, gathered the dog into his arms, and massaged his back. Winston released a low rumble of pleasure.

"How's my boy?"

"Hi Mark. Welcome to Chicago." Watching the two of them wrestle, she longed to join in on the love fest.

"Hi, Addie." With the help of the door knob, Mark slowly straightened up. "Sprained my back hauling a few cases of wine to the basement."

"I hope you didn't break any bottles. Precious stuff!" Their laughter was in direct contradiction to their puckered foreheads.

New creases surfaced on his usually wrinkle-free face. Were those laugh lines? Or worry lines? Addie decided they were the latter. Maybe he was as bothered by their separation as she was. Wishful thinking. Wearing navy khakis, a leafy green golf shirt and camel loafers, Mark reminded her how gorgeous he was.

"You look great, Addie."

That came across as a patronizing compliment. Earlier in the day, she had considered jazzing herself up as she did for the wedding, with the French twist coiffure and face paint. She had borrowed an outfit from Mary, teal blue slacks and a pink striped long sleeve blouse.

"What was I thinking?" she'd muttered to herself. Twirling before a mirror, she admitted, "I'm a hybrid, a cross between Princess Diana with a black coif that looks as if I ironed it to my head and Mary with big boobs."

So, she ripped the pins from her head, wiped the make-up off, and threw on jeans, a *Flashdance* off-the-shoulder oversized shirt, moccasins, and a few bangle bracelets: her normal fashion wear.

A bark from Winston disrupted her recollection of her pre-Mark jitters.

"Thanks. How about coming in for a drink? My sister, Mary, you remember her, made a few apps." Addie signaled for him to step into the living room.

"I do remember her and your grandmother. How are they?"

"Fine."

"Beautiful place." Mark's eyes flittered about but never rested on her. "I can't stay long."

"Of course. Have a seat, this couch is comfy. Reminds me of yours."

Sitting on the edge of the cushion, Mark toyed with the band on his watch.

"What can I get you? I have—"

"Ahhh, wine?" He tented his fingers.

"Still red?" Addie scanned the room for a wine rack until Mark pointed his finger above her head.

He attempted to stand up. "This is too much bother, Addie."

"*No!* I mean, no, not at all. How are you? How are things at Chester's?" she inquired as she pried out a bottle of red and was relieved to see the wine opener on a nearby tray. She poured the ruby liquid about halfway into a balloon shaped glass and was grateful that the wine scarcely rippled as she offered it to Mark.

"Thank you. Good. We're busy. You? How's Irma doing?"

"Fine! *Snort, snort.*" Addie could judge his mood if he snorted back and he didn't disappoint her today. "But I'm now a voice for a kids' cartoon, *Tubs of Fun.*" Using her butter voice that floated from the bottom of her tonsils, she sang the chorus to the show's opening jingle.

> *Give me your hand*
> *And your heart*
> *And follow my story*
> *From the start.*
> *You'll be happier*
> *If you do*
> *And this tub of butter*
> *Will be too!*

No response.

He smiled to the absence of sound between them.

Maybe this was the time. She needed to soften the blow but wasn't sure what the right words were. *Do it!* She commanded herself. As she was about to stand up, Mark interrupted with a voice that sounded as chilly as a Chinook wind.

"Addie, as tough as this is for me, it's better if Winston isn't shuttled between us, and since you saved him, you're his rightful owner. And, another thing, ahh, I am seeing someone and—"

"What?" Addie's eyebrows crashed into one another, pleating her forehead; the bit of hope she clung to disintegrated. When she heard him admit that there was someone else, the heat of her anger began creeping up her neck.

Breathe! I can be normal. I can. What to do now? What I'm supposed to do? Babcia help me.

Without warning, she twirled five times.

"Ah, what are you doing?"

"Mark, we're going to have a baby."

"Who's having a baby?" He choked on the words trying to control his voice.

"You and me." She wanted to crawl inside his head. "I'm so sorry. So sorry, now that you're, ah, involved with someone but—I wish you weren't.

I do love you, but I realize I'm to blame for what happened between us. I took to heart what you told me the last time I saw you."

Those spins caused a rearrangement within her. It wasn't the dizziness, but an off-centered sensation that pitched right side up. Worries about her future dissolved. Babcia's statue on the makeshift altar delivered her miracle.

Sliding back against the cushions, Mark flushed red. "Oh, no!"

"Mark, don't worry. You don't have to marry me. I'm Catholic, so abortion is not an option. I've explored adoption—"

With shoulders bowed, Mark rasped. "Uh, Addie. Isn't that a decision you and I should discuss?"

"Well, of course but I can't have an abortion." Tom's letter to Mags kept poking at Addie since the day she made her first OB appointment. Who ever dreamed Tom would suggest such a thing let alone pay for it?

"Of course not. Please let me get used to this bit of news." Mark paced back and forth in front of the bookshelves.

Addie snatched an appetizer she didn't want but stuffed it in anyway. *Please give me another chance.* But this wasn't about her anymore.

"May I have a drink? I see a bottle of bourbon over there."

"Sure. Help yourself."

"Hmm. Whistle Pig. Interesting choice."

Pouring himself a full glass, he finished off a hearty gulp and then situated himself into a shiny satin settee.

"Addie. Please sit down."

She bit her tongue.

"I remember that you are a fan of old movies. Not certain a 1969 flick is old enough, but are you familiar with *The Sterile Cuckoo?* Liza Minelli?"

Her patience was thin. *What is he babbling about? What do you want to do?*

"Bear with me, here. This is far too complicated of a situation for a quick response. Ok? This zany girl named Pookie comes into this guy's life and turns it upside down. She gets him to open his heart to her. He does. Then she leaves. End of story."

"Help me here. The end of our story happened because you ended it."

"Well, it's not a perfect rendition of us, but that episode with that truck driver crossed over the line."

"Rather than rehashing the past, we have a more important issue to deal with." Addie patted her tummy.

"Oh Addie, I don't have a girlfriend. I lied so you'd go on your merry way."

"What? Why in God's name would you do that?"

"I didn't want to have to see you anymore. I can't live with you, and I can't live without you." Mark gulped another slug of bourbon. "I can't forgive you for what you did. It was so reckless. But now with our baby ..."

"Hold on. What does our baby have to do with that?" Addie's voice had a thin sharp edge to it. "Let me ask you this, Mark, if any of your brothers or sisters betrayed your trust, would you forgive them?"

Mark made his way to the bottle of bourbon and placed his glass next to it.

"Well, what's your answer?" Addie was inches behind him.

Mark admitted, "Well, of course. They're family."

"Hmmm. Interesting. One of my many therapists explained that there are two kinds of forgiveness. The first kind is the 'supposed to' kind of forgiveness, and I'm not interested in that one because I'm pregnant.

"The other type of forgiveness is a decision that comes from here." She jabbed her finger into his chest. "That's what I learned from my family, and it was quite a journey. Genuine forgiveness is painful and difficult to do—it's a letting go. It's about compassion which brings peace to both the forgiver and the forgiven."

Mark took a step toward her as she stepped back.

"I'm sorry that I hurt you. I do love you, Mark. I am working on myself. We'll figure out what's best for this child as well as for ourselves. Go back to Cincinnati and take time to decide. Which will it be for us?"

"How will you know which of the two I can do?" he asked.

"*Sawubona.* Remember? Since I've gotten out of my own way, I'll be able to see you ... the real you."

Mark grinned. "Fair enough. In the meantime, I will send you a weekly check for whatever you might need for yourself or for our baby." Mark glanced at the tiny bump protruding from her tummy and asked, "So, how much time will you give me?"

"That's not up to me."

As she watched Mark sprint down the stairs, Addie beamed. She reveled in this new version of herself. Although she was scared and uncertain about her future, she was filled with a new found confidence to accept all of the contradictions that make her who she is: fragile and strong. And to think it all started with her mother.

EPILOGUE

Whenever I searched for a support group for my patients who had been sexually abused, I came up with less than a handful. Since abused individuals blame themselves for what happened to them, shame prevents them from talking about it to anyone which only deepens their emotional isolation. Mothers are the main target of their anger for not protecting them while mothers feel the shame of having failed their daughters: a complex dynamic supported by the cultural expectations of motherhood. So who's going to seek support for any of that? Thus, The Secret Keepers are born.

According to the CDC, about 1 in 4 girls and 1 in 13 boys experience childhood sexual abuse. Ninety-one percent of the perpetrators are someone known and trusted by the child or the child's family member—most disturbing.

Most mothers and daughters have the most intriguing of relationships fraught with mercurial emotions: love, anger, resentment, and frustration. I chose to write about a most difficult situation that affected the Gurin family because I wanted readers to reflect on how they can transcend whatever challenges they are faced with personally as well as with their own families.

Therapy and the support of family are the portals through which abused individuals can lead meaningful lives and shed the shame of their victimization. It is not easy and requires a tremendous amount of hard work. By learning to manage the symptoms through meditation, yoga, exercise, compassion, and some spiritual practice, they become empowered to discover their resiliencies and inherent goodness.

They are no longer invisible or without a voice. They can look in the mirror and sincerely say, *"Sawubona...I see you...you are important to me and I value you.*

If you or anyone you know has been abused in any way, I encourage you to utilize the resources listed below.

Child Welfare Information Gateway

Organizations that have information on adult survivors of child abuse. If you are aware of any others, please contact Child Welfare Information Gateway at OrganizationUpdates@childwelfare.gov. Inclusion on this list is for information purposes and does not constitute an endorsement by Child Welfare Information Gateway or the Children's Bureau.

Adult Survivors of Child Abuse

PO Box 281535
The Morris Center
San Francisco, California 94128
Phone: (415) 928-4576
Email: info@ascasupport.org
http://www.ascasupport.org/

Adult Survivors of Child Abuse (ASCA) supports and assists survivors of child abuse to move on with their lives. In addition, ASCA was created with the intention of guaranteeing that all survivors of childhood abuse, regardless of their financial situation, have access to a program focused on recovery from childhood abuse, including physical, sexual, and/or emotional abuse or neglect.

Child Welfare Information Gateway

Children's Bureau/ACYF
330 C Street, S.W
Washington, District of Columbia 20201
Toll-Free: (800) 394-3366
Email: info@childwelfare.gov
https://www.childwelfare.gov/

Child Welfare Information Gateway connects professionals and the general public to information and resources targeted to the safety, permanency, and well-being of children and families.

A service of the Children's Bureau, Administration for Children and Families, U.S. Department of Health and Human Services, Child Welfare Information Gateway provides access to programs, research, laws and policies, training resources, statistics, and much more.

Childhelp

6730 N. Scottsdale Rd
Suite 150
Scottsdale, Arizona 85253
Phone: (480) 922-8212
Toll-Free: (800) 4AC-HILD
TDD: (800) 2AC-HILD
Fax: (480) 922-7061
https://www.childhelp.org/

Childhelp is dedicated to helping victims of child abuse and neglect. Childhelp's approach focuses on prevention, intervention and treatment. The Childhelp National Child Abuse Hotline, 1-800-4-A-CHILD, operates 24 hours a day, seven days a week, and receives calls from throughout the United States, Canada, the U.S. Virgin Islands, Puerto Rico and Guam. Childhelp's programs and services also include residential treatment services; children's advocacy centers; therapeutic foster care;

group homes; child abuse prevention, education and training; and the National Day of Hope, part of National Child Abuse Prevention Month every April.

MaleSurvivor

Po Box 276
Long Valley, New Jersey 07853
https://malesurvivor.org/index.php?fbclid=IwAR3DyHc--TQrgjqXI5czy
ZTGjGHIdlW13I3nkkDUB576VCZk0Cv9dAVstys
http://www.malesurvivor.org/contact-us/

A goal of MaleSurvivor is to overcome the sexual victimization of boys and men by helping professionals and others to better understand and treat adult male survivors of childhood sexual abuse.

National Sexual Violence Resource Center

2101 N Front Street
Governor's Plaza North, Building #2
Harrisburg, Pennsylvania 17110
Phone: (717) 909-0710
Toll-Free: (877) 739-3895
Fax: (717) 909-0714
https://www.nsvrc.org/

General Scope: The National Sexual Violence Resource Center (NSVRC) is funded through a cooperative agreement from the Centers for Disease Control and Prevention's Division of Violence Prevention. The organization collects information and resources to assist those working to prevent sexual violence and to improve resources, outreach, and response strategies. The Center provides access to resources on reporting and recovery planning, serving child victims of sex trafficking, and addressing issues for specific populations vulnerable to sex trafficking, including children in foster care, missing and exploited children, adolescent boys, and Native women.

Rape, Abuse & Incest National Network

2000 L Street NW
Suite 406
Washington, District of Columbia 20036
Phone: (202) 544-3064
Toll-Free: (800) 656-HOPE
Fax: (202) 544-3556
Email: info@rainn.org
http://www.rainn.org/(opens in new window)

The Rape, Abuse & Incest National Network (RAINN) is an anti-sexual assault organization. RAINN operates the National Sexual Assault Hotline (**1.800.656.HOPE**), which provides victims of sexual assault with free, confidential services around the clock, and it carries out programs to prevent sexual assault and to help victims.

Sidran Institute

7220 Muncaster Mills Road
Suite 376
Derwood, Maryland 20855
Phone: (410) 825-8888
Fax: (410) 825-8888
Email: sidran@sidran.org
http://www.sidran.org/(opens in new window)

The Sidran Institute, a leader in traumatic stress education and advocacy, is a nationally focused nonprofit organization devoted to helping people who have experienced traumatic life events. The Institute promotes improved understanding of the early recognition and treatment of trauma-related stress in children, the long-term effects of trauma on adults, and strategies that lead to the greatest success in self-help recovery for trauma survivors. The Sidran Institute also advocates clinical practices considered successful in aiding trauma victims and the development of public policy initiatives that are responsive to the needs of adult and child survivors of traumatic events.

Stop It Now!

351 Pleasant Street
Suite B319
Northampton, Massachusetts 01060
Phone: (413) 587-3500
Toll-Free: (888) 773-8368
Email: info@stopitnow.org

Stop It Now! prevents the sexual abuse of children by mobilizing adults, families and communities to take action before a child is harmed. Stop It Now! provides support, information and resources for adults to take responsibility for creating safer communities.

Visit the Online Help Center at StopItNow.org for guidance and resources to prevent child sexual abuse.

The Blue Ribbon Project

PO Box 4412
Annapolis, Maryland 21403
Phone: (800) 757-8120
https://blueribbonproject.org/
http://theblueribbon.org/about/contact-us.html

The Blue Ribbon Project is a non-profit, online and community resource for both child abuse victims and adult survivors. It also offers several outreach programs, such as "Backpacks of Love" which provides backpacks of essentials to kids on the night they enter foster care.

Printed in the United States
by Baker & Taylor Publisher Services